KENNETH BURKE

AND THE DRAMA OF

HUMAN RELATIONS

BY

WILLIAM H. RUECKERT

University of Minnesota Press
MINNEAPOLIS

PUBLISHED IN GREAT BRITAIN, INDIA, AND PAKISTAN BY THE OXFORD UNIVERSITY PRESS, LONDON, BOMBAY, AND KARACHI, AND IN CANADA BY THOMAS ALLEN, LTD., TORONTO

THANKS are due the following persons and organizations for permission to reprint quotations from copyrighted materials. To Kenneth Burke, for his collection of stories *The White Oxen*, Albert & Charles Boni, 1924; from his novel *Towards a Better Life*, Harcourt, Brace and Company, Inc., 1932; and from a manuscript version of "Poetics, Dramatistically Considered." To Burke and Hermes Publications for *Counter-Statement*, 2nd ed., Hermes Publications, 1953, © 1953 by Kenneth Burke; *Permanence and Change*, 2nd rev. ed., Hermes Publications, 1954, © 1954 by Kenneth Burke; *Attitudes toward History*, 1st ed., Editorial Publications, Inc., 1937, and 2nd ed. rev., Hermes Publications, 1959, © 1959 by Hermes Publications; and *Book of Moments*, Hermes Publications, 1955, © 1955 by Kenneth Burke. To Prentice-Hall, Inc., for *A Rhetoric of Motives*, Prentice-Hall, Inc., 1950, © 1950 by Prentice-Hall, Inc. To the National Society for the Study of Education, for Burke's "Linguistic Approach to Problems of Education," in *Modern Philosophies and Education*, 54th Yearbook, Part I, of the Society, © 1955 by the Secretary of the Society. To the Conference on Science, Philosophy and Religion, for Burke's "Freedom and Authority in the Realm of the Poetic Imagination" and "Fact, Inference, and Proof in the Analysis of Literary Symbolism" in *Freedom and Authority in Our Time* and *Symbols and Values: An Initial Study*, © 1953 and 1954 by the Conference on Science, Philosophy and Religion. To the Hudson Review, Inc., for Burke's "Othello: An Essay to Illustrate a Method" and "Symbol and Association," vols. IV and IX of the *Hudson Review*, © 1951 and 1956 by the Hudson Review, Inc. To Kenyon College and Burke, for Burke's "Three Definitions" and "On Catharsis, or Resolution," volumes XIII and XXI of *The Kenyon Review*, © 1951 and 1959 by Kenyon College. To the Chicago Review, for Burke's "The Language of Poetry 'Dramatistically' Considered," vols. VIII and IX of the *Chicago Review*, © 1954 and 1955 by the Chicago Review. To the Speech Association of America, for Burke's "A Dramatistic View of the Origins of Language" and "Postscripts on the Negative," volumes XXXVIII and XXXIX of the *Quarterly Journal of Speech*, © 1952 and 1953 by the Speech Association of America. To Alfred A. Knopf, Inc. and Edward Arnold (Publishers) Ltd., for E. M. Forster's *Howards End*, Vintage Books, 1958, © 1921 by E. M. Forster. To Oxford University Press, Inc., for G. M. Hopkin's "God's Grandeur" from *Poems of Gerard Manley Hopkins*, 3rd ed., Oxford University Press, 1948, © 1948 by Oxford University Press, Inc. The quotations from Kenneth Burke's *The Rhetoric of Religion*, Beacon Press, 1961, are reprinted by permission of the Beacon Press, © 1961 by Kenneth Burke.

Thanks are due American university presses for making the following material readily available under their "fair use" resolution: Burke's "Policy Made Personal: Whitman's Verse and Prose-Salient Traits" in *Leaves of Grass One Hundred Years After*, Stanford University Press, © 1955 by the Board of Trustees of the Leland Stanford Junior University; Burke's "Rhetoric – Old and New," vol. V of *The Journal of General Education*, © 1951 by the University of Chicago Press; and Burke's *The Philosophy of Literary Form*, Louisiana State University Press, © 1941 by Louisiana State University Press.

FOR BETTY

"To hell with Brand; at least, *we* have been purified."

PREFACE

FOR MANY PEOPLE Burke exists in fragments, as the originator of a few stunning ideas and the writer of sporadically brilliant applied criticism. And yet his power comes from, and his real achievement consists in the monolithic dramatistic system he has developed. Everything since the early forties has been written from within that system, and is either an application or an extension of it. Even the material written before that date is all best understood as moving in the direction of dramatism. Now that dramatism has been presented adequately both in theory and practice so that it can — as it must — be taken as *the* perspective from which Burke as a whole may be analyzed, at least two kinds of basic studies can be undertaken. Both depend upon the fact that dramatism is the culmination of a long intellectual and spiritual development, and constitutes a point beyond which Burke has no desire — he certainly has the necessary vitality — to go.

The first kind is a more or less chronological, developmental study which presents as organic the development through stages to the final synthesis; like the development itself, such a study culminates in the presentation and application of the system. The second kind begins where the first one ends; its organization would come from the structure of the system itself and it would be complete when the system had been adequately presented and applied or illustrated. Since dramatism includes — in the sense that it incorporates into a larger framework — most of Burke's important early ideas and methods, the significant material from the pre-dramatistic works could be covered in the appropriate place *while* the system was presented and applied. A wonderful kind of simultaneity and coherence would be achieved in this way, for the beginning and middle works could be seen, not as *culminating* in dramatism, but in *terms* of dramatism. Though each approach has distinct advantages, it is the first which I have used in this study because it is better suited to my purposes. My interest has always been in Burke's literary theory and critical practice, and it was about this that I wished to write. But it soon became apparent to me that by 1935 (*Permanence and Change*) Burke's primary interests had shifted from literary to social criticism, and by 1945 (*A Grammar of Motives*) from social criticism to linguistic analysis as a way of confronting the world. To write of Burke's literary theory and critical practice it became necessary to master the larger system of which it was but a part. At this point, another fact became apparent, and it was this which finally determined the approach used here. I realized that Burke's whole development is characterized by the gradual expansion of a literary theory and method into the larger dramatistic system and methodology, the very name of which derives from a literary type.

Around this central perception the whole book is organized. Chapters I, III, and V deal with Burke's literary theory and practice at various stages of development; Chapters II and IV with the expansions into "Poetic Realism" and "Dramatism." In general, I have followed the chronological order of publication, though to stress various stages in the development, I have occasionally broken this chronology. Chapter I covers a ten-year period (1921–1931) and deals primarily with the aesthetic of *Counter-Statement*. Chapter II covers another ten-year period and deals primarily with "Poetic Realism," the central tenet of which is the theory of symbolic action presented at the end of that chapter. In Chapter III, I have broken the chronology in order to present a systematic exposition of the analysis of poetry as symbolic action. The whole complex logic (or grammar) of

Preface

substance developed and applied in *A Grammar of Motives* is implicit in the theory of symbolic action and the method developed to apply it; this logic is presented in the first part of Chapter III, along with certain other basic assumptions drawn from all of Burke which are also implicit in the theory and method. Again, without regard to chronology, I have gathered together in the second section of Chapter III the six-part critical method which Burke uses to apply the theory of symbolic action.

Chronologically, Chapter IV begins where Chapter II ends and presents, briefly, the development of "Poetic Realism" into dramatism. Thereafter, the chapter follows neither chronology nor development, but primarily the logic of the dramatistic system itself. I have, however, tried to suggest at what point in time — about 1950 — and with which of the basic concepts of dramatism — the definition of man as the symbol-using animal, the theories of hierarchy and the negative — dramatism becomes Burke's final and coherent way of viewing man and the universe. Chapter V covers the same period as Chapter IV, but is devoted entirely to the literary theory and critical method developed within the context of the dramatistic system. A peculiar relation exists between literature and the rest of the system, for dramatism derives its name from a literary type and takes tragedy as the representative anecdote for the drama of human relations. The relation is peculiar because, though dramatism is essentially a systematic view of human relations rather than a theory of literature, Burke proceeds "on the assumption that the 'perfect case' for analytic purposes is a definitive literary text" (MPE,274–275). Hence, though the dramatistic theory of literature does not constitute the whole system, it is crucial to it; and though the system and method can be used to analyze any text, a major work of literature constitutes the "ideal" text. The book ends with an exposition and application of Burke's theory of tragedy and catharsis. In this theory, the development traced throughout the book is properly concluded, for in what he says of tragedy Burke achieves a masterful synthesis of his literary, social, ethical, rhetorical, and linguistic theories. Tragedy is the representative anecdote for dramatism itself.

Throughout the book, I have tried to apply and illustrate Burke's ideas and critical methods with as many concrete examples as possible. Sometimes these applications and examples are Burke's; sometimes they are mine; and sometimes they are a combination. Wherever the specific illustration is from Burke and I have merely tried to condense it, there is always an allusion to the specific source in Burke; where the applications and examples are entirely mine, there is usually no specific reference to a source in Burke; and where I have taken an illustration from Burke and amplified rather than condensed it, I have usually indicated both the source and the nature of the amplification. In Chapter III,ii, for example, the Cummings, *Othello*, and Keats examples are from Burke; the Wordsworth, Flaubert, and Meredith examples are my own; and the Matthew Arnold example is partly Burke's and partly mine because I have not only amplified what Burke said of *Sohrab and Rustum* in *A Rhetoric of Motives* but added many things which he never said. In Chapter III,iii, where there is a single extended example which is again partly Burke's and partly mine, I have done exactly what I did with *Sohrab and Rustum* — attempted to make explicit and systematic what is often only implicit and suggestive in Burke. I have summarized and amplified what Burke says about Coleridge in *The Philosophy of Literary Form* and, using his own ideas and critical methods, added to this as a means of filling out the analysis of *The Rime of the Ancient Mariner*. Finally, wherever I have written my own Burke analyses — as in the *Howards End* piece at the end of Chapter V,i — I have aimed always at the same thing: the exposition and illustration of Burke's ideas and critical methods first, and then the demonstration that they can be used by others to produce illuminating results.

A person incurs many debts in writing a book. I would especially like to thank the Research Board of the University of Illinois for a Faculty Fellowship which enabled me to get a substantial portion of the book written during the summer of 1959 and for extraordinary generosity in financing three typings of the manuscript; the Agnes Scott College Library for the kind loan of books and journals during all of one summer; and Mrs. William Simmons for twice typing the manuscript. I would like publicly to thank Professor Norman E.

Preface

Nelson, of the University of Michigan, who directed me to and through Burke for the first time; my colleague Sherman Paul, whose dedication to the profession included two readings of the manuscript more thorough and helpful than any colleague has a right to hope for; Professor Glauco Cambon, of Rutgers University, whose meticulous reading of the manuscript for the Press saved me from more errors than I like to think about; and Miss Marcia Strout, of the Press, who is an exemplary (patient, exact, and exacting) editor. Finally, I would like to thank Kenneth Burke for all the unpublished material he so readily made available to me, and for other acts too numerous and generous to specify.

KEY TO
ABBREVIATIONS

All documentation of quotations and points from Burke appears in the text in parentheses, usually at the end of the sentence. Where a number of points or quotations from the same source appear in the same paragraph, only the last reference is documented. To keep the documentation as unobtrusive as possible, I have used the following abbreviations for books by Burke and for journals and books in which there are essays by Burke. The full citations are to be found in the Bibliography, I

ATH — *Attitudes toward History*, first edition
BOM — *Book of Moments*
ChiR — *Chicago Review*
CS — *Counter-Statement*, second edition
EIC — *Essays in Criticism*
FAT — *Freedom and Authority in Our Time*
HopR — *Hopkins Review*
HR — *Hudson Review*
JGE — *Journal of General Education*
KR — *Kenyon Review*
LOG — *Leaves of Grass One Hundred Years After*
MPE — *Modern Philosophies and Education*
PC — *Permanence and Change*, second edition
PLF — *The Philosophy of Literary Form*, first edition
Poetics — Unpublished version of *A Symbolic of Motives*

QJS — *Quarterly Journal of Speech*
RM — *A Rhetoric of Motives*
RR — *The Rhetoric of Religion*
SAV — *Symbols and Values: An Initial Study*
SeR — *Sewanee Review*
SoR — *Southern Review*
SPCL — *Spiritual Problems in Contemporary
    Literature*
TABL — *Towards a Better Life*
WO — *The White Oxen*

TABLE OF CONTENTS

Key to Abbreviations   xiii

Introduction: Toward the Partial Purification of Burke   3

I   Both/And: The Aesthetic of *Counter-Statement*   8

II   Towards a Better Life through Symbolic Action   34

III   The Analysis of Poetry as Symbolic Action   64
i The Assumptions, 64. *ii* The Method, 83. *iii* The Application, 111.

IV   Dramatism: Language as the Ultimate Reduction   128
i The Drama, 128. *ii* The Interlocked Moments, 134. *iii* Logologic, 153.

V   The Dramatistic Theory of Literature   163
i Imitation and Indexing, 163. *ii* Poetry and Beyond, 191. *iii* Tragedy as the Representative Anecdote, 208.

Bibliography   229
Works by Kenneth Burke, 229. Works about Kenneth Burke, 237. Related Material, 243.

Index   246

KENNETH BURKE
and the Drama of Human Relations

INTRODUCTION
TOWARD THE PARTIAL
PURIFICATION OF
BURKE

MY APPROACH to Burke is so purely intrinsic that some readers may suppose the book to have been written in a historical and theoretical vacuum. And my treatment of him is so devoted to his literary theory and critical practice and so severely limited to a particular presentation of them that it also may be cause for wonder. I have not, for example, done justice to dramatism as a coherent system, but have included only as much on it as I thought necessary for an understanding of Burke's literary theory and critical method; and I have made only passing references to Burke's stories, poems, and novel — all of which are interesting in themselves and worthy of serious and extended analysis. Only occasionally have I related the works to the man, and only now and then have I attempted to relate the man and his works to the literary and cultural life of the times. I have not discussed Burke as a music critic or the possible effect of this activity on his literary theory and critical practice; and I have not discussed Burke as a reviewer — by my own count, he has written at least a hundred reviews — or the importance, which is considerable, of the books he reviewed to his own thought and development. Burke's influence and reputation, both of which are, as one recent commentator has put it, "massive," have not been dealt with, nor has the problem of influences on Burke. And I have nowhere

[3]

systematically evaluated Burke's literary theory, critical method, and applied criticism — though an evaluation (my own deep commitment to Burke) is implicit in the approach and treatment.

There is, to be sure, a certain safety in an approach so purely intrinsic as the one I have used; and every limitation, as Burke is fond of pointing out, is a negation of some kind. But, as Burke has also pointed out, negations are a means of achieving positives, and I like to think that it is less a matter of safety and more a matter of achieving a positive goal that accounts for all of the things which were systematically — rather than arbitrarily — eliminated from this book. Certainly my own resources are such that I could have handled some of them, more or less adequately, and come closer to writing the ideal book on Burke which everyone wants someone to write. But some of them I could not do at all and some I could only have done in a fundamentally dishonest way that would have produced an effect of knowledge where no real knowledge exists. Though I have attempted to familiarize myself with the writers who influenced Burke most profoundly, my knowledge of most of them is not of the kind one goes into print with, and though I know something of the literary and cultural life of the twenties and thirties, my knowledge is of the kind that is most often used to decorate a text. Accurate and useful historical and theoretical placement — best represented to my mind by such books as Meyer Abram's *The Mirror and the Lamp* — must be the work of minds attuned like critical seismographs to detect the slightest theoretical tremors, and programmed, as it were, to place each one in the long line of abstractions which make up the history of literary criticism. Finally, curious as it may seem, I could not write an adequate life of Burke; my own interest in biography and what Burke calls the agent-act ratio came so late that all my knowledge of Burke's life is of the bits and pieces variety — odd, unrelated facts picked up here and there and useless save as the basis for idle speculation.

Ultimately, all the negations were deliberately imposed in order that the limited positive goal — the partial purification of Burke — might be achieved. Many of Burke's apologists (see the bibliography, Part II) suffer, in varying degrees of intensity, from Burke-sickness, a disease which produces hysterical enthusiasm and loss of perspective. And many of Burke's adversaries suffer from Burke-nausea, a state which produces hysterical anger and a corresponding loss of perspective. In between, there is a small group of ideal critics who have attempted to purify Burke: they have in common a perspective of distance which has enabled them to avoid both Burke-sickness and Burke-nausea. Each of these critics has purified some part of Burke; each has been willing to cut through the stylistic and terminological underbrush that began taking over Burke's ideas and methods in the late thirties in order to rid Burke of his own foibles and quandaries. All have recognized this underbrush for what it is — an irritation, a distraction, the rank growth of a fecund mind — and have been able to hack through it — which is all one *can* do — to Burke's ideas and methods.

When one has purified Burke to the extent of being able to apprehend the ideas and methods and, finally, the whole coherent system, one discovers a systematic view of man and the drama of human relations, and a methodology for its application, of great power, beauty, and persuasiveness. However, I have not attempted to purify all of Burke, but have undertaken a limited endeavor toward the purification of Burke's literary theory and critical practice. Since a unique relation now exists between the literary theory and the rest of the dramatistic system — Burke is the only writer I know of who has ever developed an inclusive system out of a theory of literature — it was necessary to over-purify the whole in order to present a coherent exposition of the part. Burke's mind is such that he is almost incapable of resisting the temptation of the many side roads which he comes on in all his intellectual journeys; a corresponding temptation is set up for anyone who writes about Burke, for he moves forward by multiple side excursions. Purification is not only a matter of hacking through the stylistic and terminological underbrush, but of finding and then mapping the main route.

I have attempted to chart that route — organically to recapitulate Burke's development. The route leads, finally, to the dramatistic pyramid Burke has been building for himself out of literary and other materials accumulated in a lifetime of prodigious work. The temptation after one gets there (in Chapter IV) is to explore not only the great central chamber (the core of dramatism) but all the other chambers and corridors in the honeycombed structure. But I have only walked — rather quickly — through the central chamber and then into the poetic chamber for a long stay and then once — rather quickly — around the whole. I suppose this is being partial with a vengeance. But, again, it is not so much a question of safety — though it is certainly easy to get lost or distracted in that pyramid — as it is of limiting the tour.

The last thing Burke has ever aimed at is safety; he has speculated boldly, often wildly, but brilliantly from the very beginning and has usually managed to pack his better essays with enough material for a book and each book with enough material for three or four more. He is a dazzling performer, a virtuoso of ideas and a master of methodological prestidigitation. But he combines these with a Germanic thoroughness that is frequently demoralizing and a patience for detail that is often tedious. To treat such a man safely is to deny him his virtues. It is only from real hurricanes that one should flee to safety. If one can find a man who has let loose a torrent of ideas the thing to do is not to flee but to face the torrent, stand still and wait. Vituperation — fist-shaking at the clouds — does not do any good, for this "peaceful" verbal storm is going to run its course. A quick retreat to an entrenched position — dogmatic nay-saying in the shelters — doesn't do much good either. And to run into print while still possessed by the dazzling power of the verbal storm and — to combine the metaphors — before one has figured out the methodological tricks, is to caricature the master, to make an unintentional clown out of a man who, though he does, as one critic put it, have something of the circus rider about him, is no mere performer.

If one is not to deny Burke his virtues — which are great — one must wait and watch, resisting the three common temptations and, by a deliberate act of will, withholding judgment until the sanity of distance can be combined with the power of commitment. I waited and watched a long time before setting down what I saw, long enough, in fact, to have succumbed to all three temptations in varying degrees of intensity and to have purged myself (I hope) of their

Toward the Partial Purification of Burke

disastrous effects. I have set down some of the things I saw from what I take to be a relatively sane distance. Greater distance is certainly possible, perhaps even desirable, and, if one were writing that ideal book on Burke, absolutely necessary. It was never my intention to write that book, and it was never my intention to judge — in the sense of a systematic evaluation — Burke. My object was to purify without sitting in judgment, and the distance I aimed at was like the mythical ideal of so many modern writers of prose-fiction: anonymity of point of view and objectivity of presentation. But, as in the work of Katherine Anne Porter, who nearly achieved the ideal, one of the anonymous voices soon begins speaking in the moral dialect of the author and the whole selection and arrangement of detail — the purification — is experienced as the work of the willful moral imagination. As Burke has so often pointed out, purification without judgment at the human level is impossible; for me to claim that I have not judged Burke would be as absurd and dishonest as writing a book about something one did not believe in.

I have selected and arranged, pruned and shaped, deliberately, in order to create a clear limited view. In this respect, the purification has been radical; and this, I take it, is the main point and the last step in the argument for my own defense. I have committed myself — at some length — to Burke; the real intention of this radical purification is to present the object of that commitment with as few distractions as possible — including my own obstructive, intrusive self. I regard Burke as one of the great men of our time, but it was never my intention to present the force of this commitment, for that would have resulted only in a long and probably hysterical polemical essay, a kind of verbal echo chamber for my own voice. It was certain qualities of Burke's greatness which I wished to present, and it is toward this positive goal that the whole purification is meant to move.

· I ·

BOTH / AND: THE
AESTHETIC OF
COUNTER-STATEMENT

KENNETH BURKE belongs to a generation of artists and writers troubled by a division of loyalties as to the nature and function of art; his achievement consists, in part, of his ability to develop a theory which unites the divided artistic allegiances of his time. This is the real significance of *Counter-Statement*, the second of Burke's ten books and his first book of literary criticism. Burke began his career as a poet (used here, and throughout, in the inclusive sense) with the publication, in 1924, of *The White Oxen and Other Stories*. Had he continued in the direction indicated by that book, he probably would have created a fictional universe in which to embody his vision and satisfy the compulsive need for synthesis which he has had from the very beginning. But after *The White Oxen*, Burke did not publish another story until 1957; and in 1932 he published a novel, appropriately entitled *Towards a Better Life*, which announced the termination of his career as a poet. Near the end of the novel, John Neal, the representative of Burke's poetic self, whose principal difficulty consists of his inability to obey the imperative contained in the pun on his name, says: "*Resurgam! resurgam!* I shall rise again! Hail, all hail! Here is a promise: *resurgam!* (TABL,217.) It is not as poet but as critic that Burke fulfilled the promise made by John Neal and moved in the direction suggested by the title of the novel. Because

[8]

of some profound inner necessity Burke silenced himself as poet; but he did not silence poetry, for in the aesthetic system begun in *Counter-Statement* he acts as its oracle with a passion and eloquence he never achieved as a poet.

Poetry is the real point of departure and *Counter-Statement* the first significant book so far as an understanding of the dramatistic system which Burke subsequently built is concerned. Written during the twenties and published in 1931, *Counter-Statement* is a collection of essays which in part systematizes the theory of pure art Burke practiced and defended in *The White Oxen*. Of the stories in that book, Burke says, "I see these stories as a gradual shifting of stress away from the realistically convincing and true to life; while there is a corresponding increase of stress upon the more rhetorical properties of letters. It is a great privilege to do this in an age when rhetoric is so universally despised." (WO,author's note.) The progression in the book is toward symbolic and fantastic stories which are primarily vehicles for achieving a variety of stylistic and formal effects. Toward the end of the collection, the stories approach the condition of music; as far as prose fiction is concerned, the progression is toward silence, toward the exploitation of words as non-cognitive counters. In *Counter-Statement*, Burke cites a passage from Flaubert which accurately describes this silent prose-fiction:

What seems beautiful to me, what I should most like to do, would be a book about nothing, a book without any exterior tie, but sustained by the internal force of its style . . . a book which would have almost no subject, or at least in which the subject would be almost invisible, if that is possible. The most beautiful works are those with the least matter. (CS,6.)

It is evident in the Author's Note and in the Preface to *Towards a Better Life* that Burke-as-poet thought of himself as a counter-agent; and the essays in *Counter-Statement* devoted to the explanation and defense of pure art constitute one of the variations upon the theme of the book as a whole.

One might say that Burke countered his own counter-statements, for out of the interior dialogue between Burke-the-poet and Burke-the-critic came the realization that poetry is after all about something and that it causes effects other than the aesthetic charge ("exaltation at the correctness of the procedure") which so excited Flaubert and Burke's contemporaries. *Counter-Statement* is actually a kind of dialogue, with the three speakers apparently contradicting each other. One of the speakers defends pure art by arguing that the end of poetry is eloquence and exaltation; the second speaker defends art as revelation by arguing that the end of poetry is wisdom; and the third speaker defends art as catharsis by arguing that the end of poetry is purgation. The dialogue is resolved by transcending the contradictions; all three attitudes can be accepted if one adopts an attitude of critical openness which permits many angles of vision. Growth is an expansion: to the end of intellectual and spiritual growth, openness is all. As William Knickerbocker pointed out in a penetrating essay-review of *The Philosophy of Literary Form*, many contemporary critics — he cites Ransom — are characterized by the "wam" (maw spelled backwards; the closing mouth) whereas Burke is characterized by the "maw" (the wide-open mouth). What emerges as one of the central ideas of *Counter-Statement* is the attitude of critical openness, the both/and doctrine which enabled Burke, in his own phrase, to "ripen without rotting."

In the preface to the second edition of *Counter-Statement* (1952), Burke points out that the "book begins on the word 'Perhaps' and ends on the word 'norm.'" It fills him, he says, with "unqualified delight" to realize that the "over-all trend" of the book "is *through* Perhaps *towards* the norm." "Add," he says, "the theory of form that is developed in these pages . . . and I believe you have, in these three moments, the gist of this book, and maybe also of the books by me that grew out of it." (CS,xi.) There is a certain danger in accepting at face value ex post facto statements by an author on his own development; some authors make sure that they are correct by altering the original texts to fit the later statements. This, however, is not Burke's practice; and his ex post facto comments, though incomplete, are reasonably accurate. Two other major "moments" must be added to the three he gives if one is to get at the "gist" of *Counter-Statement* and properly understand the first stage in the long development which culminated in dramatism. These moments are "catharsis" and "grace." When amplified and properly related to each other, the five pivotal moments make up the aesthetic of *Counter-Statement*.

In an essay on the poetic process where he is attempting to explain how effects are produced by the re-individuation of "norms" in specific subject matter, Burke makes a distinction between metaphysical and psychological universals which is central to all of his subsequent thinking on literary as well as other matters. "So eager," he says,

were the nominalists to disavow Plato in detail, that they failed to discover the justice of his doctrines in essence. For we need but take his universals out of heaven and situate them in the human mind (a process begun by Kant), making them not metaphysical, but psychological. Instead of divine forms, we now have "conditions of appeal." There need not be a "divine contrast" in heaven for me to appreciate a contrast; but there *must be* in my mind the sense of contrast. The researches of anthropologists indicate that man has "progressed" in cultural cycles which repeat themselves in essence (in form) despite the limitless variety of specific details to embody such essences, or forms. Speech, material traits (for instance, tools), art, mythology, religion, social systems, property, government, and war — these are the nine "potentials" which man continually re-individuates into specific cultural channels, and which anthropologists call the "universal pattern." And when we speak of psychological universals, we mean simply that just as there is inborn in the germ-plasm of a dog the potentiality of barking, so there is inborn in the germ-plasm of man the potentiality of speech, art, mythology, and so on. And while these potentialities are continually changing their external aspects, their "individuations," they do not change in essence. (CS,48.)

Actually, to call the universals psychological in origin is somewhat misleading until one realizes that Burke is simply offering a naturalistic explanation of the perceived universals of psycho-physical experience. The explanation turns upon biological and neurological norms, certain "potentials" inborn in the "germ-plasm" of man, which are inherited from nature as every man's portion when he comes into the world. The interaction between agent and scene (man and environment) actualizes the potentials to produce experience (CS,150). Though experience is almost endlessly diversified due to variations in both agent and scene, any agent in any scene will "naturally" experience some of the recurrent emotions such as fear, love, tenderness, delight, and anger; and some of the fundamental universal attitudes such as "belief, cynicism, skepticism, expansiveness, reclusion," and the like (CS,107). In short,

the various kinds of moods, feelings, emotions, perceptions, sensations, and attitudes discussed in the manuals of psychology and exemplified in works of art . . . [are] universal experiences. Mockery, despair, grimness, *sang-froid*, wonder, lamentation, melancholy, hatred, hopefulness, bashfulness, relief, boredom, dislike . . . we call them universal because all men, under certain conditions, and when not in mental or physical collapse, are capable of experiencing them. (CS,149.)

Aside from these "universal experiences" and again because of the biological and neurological norms, there are also "patterns of experience which seem to arise out of any system of living" (CS,171). Finally, there are what Burke calls "innate forms of the mind" (CS,46), certain universal forms of experience which are, again, "inherent in the very germ-plasm of man" (CS,46). Some of these forms are "crescendo, contrast, comparison, balance, repetition, disclosure, reversal, contraction, expansion, magnification, [and] series" (CS,46).

As Burke explains in *Counter-Statement*, the universals of psychophysical experience are made up of such things as universal situations, recurrent emotions, fundamental attitudes, typical actions, patterns of experience, and "forms of the mind." Taken together, these make up what Burke variously calls "psychological universals," "universal essences," and "constants of humanity" (CS,107). Burke's point is that all human experience is reducible to these universals and finally *analyzable* in terms of them. Consider, for example, the common human situation in which an agent loses something. For purposes of this schematized analysis, neither what is lost nor the manner of the loss is important, for given a human agent in a "loss situation" the agent is sure to experience some of the recurrent emotions, assume some of the fundamental attitudes, perform one of the typical actions, undergo some pattern of experience, and experience some of the innate forms of the mind. The loss, for example, may result in any of the following emotions: grief, elation, anger, or fear; the emotion may in turn lead to any of the following attitudes: resignation, despair, cynicism, or aggressiveness. And the attitude may lead to some action, such as suicide, alcoholism, or promiscuity. The progression from situation to emotion to attitude to action is a pattern of experience. Loss–grief–despair–suicide; loss–grief–despair–alcoholism; and loss–elation–promiscuity – all are patterns of experience. Finally, the whole pattern, or any part of it, will necessarily follow the "innate forms of the mind." If, for example, a wife bore her husband a son which he had always wanted and she died suddenly, the loss would follow a period of elation and would be a violent *reversal* and *contrast*; there would have been a *crescendo* and *decrescendo* of elation followed by a *crescendo* and *decrescendo* of grief; there would have been a *repetition* of the *crescendo–decrescendo* pattern, and a kind of *balance* between the elation and grief; the elation would have been an *expansion*, the grief a *contraction*; both elation and grief would have been *magnifications*; as the man came to knowledge of the inevitability, or the finality of the loss, or of the fact that not all was lost, there would be a *disclosure* of some kind; and finally, the whole pattern would be a *series*.

Though ten thousand people underwent the pattern of experience just described and though its specific details were all radically different, the general content, the pattern, and the forms of the experience would be similar, if not identical. This is so, Burke says, because of the biological and neurological norms which determine the forms of experience. All norms are reducible to two kinds of forms, a feat made possible by the pun on the word form. In English, form means both essence and structure, logical formula and spatial or temporal form. Of the norms discussed above, recurrent emotions and fundamental attitudes are essences and reducible to logical formulae; but patterns of experience and the "innate forms of the mind" are structures and must be discussed in terms of progressive form. Because of the pun, Burke is able to merge in the term form both logical and temporal, essence and narrative, static and rectilinear, equational and progressive – a merger which is central to the aesthetic of *Counter-Statement* and to Burke's work as a whole.

Burke and the Drama of Human Relations

These norms are the basic materials of art and provide the link between the poet and his audience. This is the other reason why Burke calls them "conditions of appeal"; the forms and formulae are the conditions, and they appeal because all men share them, if not always as actualizations then at least as potentials. In the most general sense, the poet communicates by exploiting the norms; he does this by re-embodying or individuating them in specific images and subject matter, drawn, as they must be, from "the chance details of his own life and vision" (CS,46). Since the forms and formulae are the basic materials of art, to write anything at all, a poet must, above and beyond his own experience, have intuitive or acquired knowledge of the psychological universals.

The poet, though similar to other men, is somehow different and acquires this necessary knowledge *because* of his nature and the nature of his purpose. There is, Burke explains,

. . . much to indicate that the artist is, of all men, equipped to confront an issue. The very conventions of art often provide him with a method for freely admitting experiences and situations which the practical man must conceal . . . [for] intensity of fear or pain will generally produce in most people a kind of "stereotypy," a mental and physical numbing which leaves the individual almost without memory of the painful or terrifying event . . . [whereas] great artists have shown capacity to keep themselves receptive at precisely such moments. They may bear the full brunt of an experience without psychological evasions, because their attitude enables them to feel partially as opportunity what others must feel solely as a menace. (CS,75–76.)

Because of his greater receptivity, the poet is able to become an expert, a specialist, in certain patterns of experience. Then the poet's "skill in articulation is expended upon the schematizing of his subject," and in this process there is another difference between the poet's ways and those of others:

the schematizing is done not by abstraction, as in science, but by idealization, by presenting in a "pure" or consistent manner some situation which, as it appears among the contingencies of real life, is less effectively co-ordinated: the idealization is the elimination of irrelevancies. (CS,154.)

Both / And: The Aesthetic of *Counter-Statement*

Because the poet is distinguished from other men by being more sensitive, perceptive, and receptive, he is capable of experiencing more intensively and can acquire superior knowledge of the forms and formulae which are the basic materials of art. Burke believes that a superior knowledge of the forms and formulae implies a deeper knowledge of the self — the self and society, the self and history, and the self and "eternity"— and that because of his profound knowledge, the poet is able to mediate between the particular and the universal, the temporal and the eternal, the self and society.

The poet's superior knowledge of the forms and formulae may be said to constitute his revelations; in making a poem the poet ritualizes his revelations in symbolic processes (CS,168–169). "We may imagine [for example] the poet to suffer under a feeling of inferiority, to suffer sullenly and mutely until, being an artist, he spontaneously generates a symbol to externalize this suffering" (CS,56). Although in this instance the original impulse may have been self-expression or self-revelation, as soon as the poet begins to ritualize his revelation a second impulse arises as problems unique to the techniques of ritualization make themselves felt. A poem is not just an outpouring of words; it is a highly stylized revelation and involves the poet in problems of technique. The poet starts with his "emotion [revelation, form or formulae], he translates this emotion into a mechanism for arousing emotion in others, and thus his interest in his own emotion transcends into his interest in the treatment" (CS,55). Thus, there are three impulses or motives in the creation of a poem: revelation (self-expression and illumination); ritualization (stylization, technique); and rhetoric (persuasion, the producing of effects) (CS,210). According to the aesthetic of *Counter-Statement*, every poem is simultaneously revelation, ritual, and rhetoric, and may be analyzed as any one or as all three.

Whether poetry is considered as revelation, ritual, or rhetoric, the basic creative process is the same. Burke believes, with Maud Bodkin, that the psyche of the artist, like that of the dreamer, spontaneously generates images which individuate or re-embody the various psychological universals. If, for example, a person is suffering from some kind of physical depression, a corresponding psychic depression is called forth which, in the dream,

> in turn translates itself into the invention of details which will more or less adequately symbolize this depression. If the sleeper has had some set of experiences strongly marked by the feeling of depression, his mind may summon details from this experience to symbolize his depression. If he fears financial ruin, his depression may very reasonably seize upon the cluster of facts associated with this fear in which to individuate itself. (CS,49–50.)

Like the dreamer, the poet spontaneously generates images and symbols to externalize and embody his revelation; but unlike the dreamer, the poet is also interested in communicating his revelation. At the moment the desire to communicate becomes a conscious motive, dreaming passes into creating. Dreams, Burke says, are wholly subjective and obey no principle of selection but the underlying pattern; poems expand by the conscious ramifying of the symbol and hence have the symbol as a principle of selection (CS,73,157). The poet first spontaneously and then deliberately converts his own experiential patterns into the symbols which are the verbal parallels of those patterns of experience. The symbols are the means of communication; they embody the poet's pattern and evoke a similar one in the reader. As examples of such symbols, Burke cites Emma Bovary, Don Quixote, and Childe Harold. The "ramified symbol" or completed work of art in which a major symbol such as Emma Bovary figures is an extended definition of the symbol itself. *Madame Bovary*, for example, is "an elaborate definition of a new word in our vocabulary" (CS,153).

A ramified symbol does more than evoke a similar pattern of experience in the reader, for once ramified the symbol functions as the poet's "interpretation of a situation" and may be treated as a formula which provides one with "a terminology of thoughts, actions, emotions, [and] attitudes for codifying a pattern of experience." The symbol-as-formula gives "simplicity and order to an otherwise unclarified complexity" (CS,154). As such, it often functions as "a diagnosis (simplification) of our partially conscious, partially unconscious situation" and in this way provides us with the "illumination" which is the chief function of art as revelation (CS,58). Art as revelation can lead to "increase of perception and sensitivity through increase of terminology . . . [for] a character or a situation in fiction is as much a term as any definition in a scientific nomenclature." In this sense, literature is "an equipment, like any vocabulary, for handling the complexities of living." (CS,182–183.)

The "symbols" Burke lists to illustrate his points — Childe Harold, Manfred, Madame Bovary, Hamlet — and the ramified symbols (works) in which they appear are indeed verbal parallels to patterns of experience, and as such, are interpretations of life (CS,176–177). One could adopt as equipment for living (as people have) the attitude of protest which characterizes Byron, or the naive idealism of Shelley, or the hopefulness of Browning, or the satirical attitude of Swift, or the "primness" of Jane Austen (CS,151); or one could accept as definitions of romanticism both *Don Quixote* and *Madame Bovary*, and noting the disastrous consequences which the submission to wild romantic impulses produces, apply the lessons of these two books as a corrective in one's own living; or one could treat these books simply as formulae, learning from them without applying them. As revelation, the "ramified symbol" will affect a person and be useful to him depending upon his own character and situation in life.

More specifically, *Madame Bovary* is clearly "the interpretation of a situation." It deals with one of the consequences which the boredom natural to all living may produce in a particular romantically inclined person in a situation common to life as a whole. A person familiar with this kind of situation might read the novel and say, "yes, this is exactly what it is like"; a person disinclined to accept romanticism as a vital force in life might read the novel and then admit the power of romanticism as he made connections between the material of the novel and life as he saw it around him; a person in a situation potentially similar to Emma Bovary's might read the novel and, shocked to an awareness of possible consequences, avoid an "actualization"; a person bored and yearning for the same things Emma wants might, by vicarious experience, avoid the actual experience and thus be eased in his own situation. It is with such things in

[17]

mind that Burke speaks of art as revelation as "the interpretation of a situation," as helping one to accept a situation, as "the corrective of a situation," as the "exerciser of 'submerged' experience," and as "an 'emancipator' " from a situation (CS,154–156). In these ways the superior "revelations" of superior men can function as a vital social force; the artist's private vision becomes public illumination for all men who will have it; art becomes useful by bringing depth knowledge of the "norms" to bear upon the problems of living.

Just as the poet's knowledge of the "norms" can be brought to bear upon the problems of living, so can they be used in the creation of purely artistic effects. To study poetry as revelation is to concentrate on the content of the work, though at many points such a discussion must deal with technique, for the "ramification of the symbol" is part of the method of art. To study poetry as ritual is to concentrate on the technique of the work, though at many points such a discussion must deal with content, for there must be something which is given form. To concentrate on the technique of art is to focus on the ways in which a poet manipulates his material in order to produce the desired effect. The materials of art are "psychological universals" which Burke defines as "conditions of appeal" because, being universal, they are shared by poet and audience as part of the psychology of both. The artist really gets his effects by "manipulating" the "psychology of the audience" (CS,31). He does this by re-individuating the psychological universals in symbols and then ramifying the symbols in a work of art in such a way that the audience is aroused and then gratified by the progression of the work and thus experiences "exaltation at the correctness of the procedure" (CS,37). "Exaltation" is produced by "eloquence," which is "the result of that desire in the artist to make a work perfect by adapting it in every minute detail to the racial appetites" (CS,41). "Eloquence," itself, is

. . . a frequency [and intensity] of Symbolic and formal effects. One work is more eloquent than another if it contains Symbolic and formal charges in greater profusion [and intensity]. That work would be most eloquent in which each line had some image or statement relying strongly upon our experience outside the work of art, and in which each image or statement had a pronounced formal saliency. (CS,165.)

Both / And: The Aesthetic of *Counter-Statement*

"Eloquence" depends upon the intrinsic power of the symbol and the formal excellence of the work in which it is ramified by the poet, that "manipulator of blood, brains, heart, and bowels" (CS,36).

The symbol is a Janus device. Besides serving as an interpretation of a situation, it acts as a vehicle for creating artistic effects, as a technical form (CS,156). Like the experiential patterns which they embody, symbols can be either simple or complex, and, depending upon certain contingent matters, to varying degrees powerful. And symbols may be "ramified" in a simple or complex manner, and with varying degrees of power. Obviously, there are many variables at work here. All experiential patterns are potentially complex beyond imagining. Consider the pattern of acquisition and loss: one may acquire a dollar, a book, a dog, a ribbon, a self, a way of life, a wife — and then lose any of them. Some people, depending upon their psycho-physical equipment, might experience all the above variants of the pattern as simplicities. If they were sensitive, perceptive, and very receptive, they would experience the pattern as profoundly complex, and they might present it in such a work as Faulkner's *Absalom, Absalom!* or Shakespeare's *Othello*, the one dealing with the acquisition and loss of a whole way of life, the other with the acquisition and loss of a wife. In both of these works, a complex and powerful pattern is re-individuated in a complex and powerful symbol, which is ramified in a complex and powerful way. The same pattern, of course, could be re-individuated in a simple symbol, and the symbol ramified in a simple and less powerful way.

Such a pattern, however, is "categorically" a powerful condition of appeal, though certain variables control the degree of its power when it is re-individuated in a specific work at a particular point in history, and certain variables control the lasting power of any work. Some symbols and works — Arthur Miller's *The Crucible*, Ibsen's *Ghosts*, and Shaw's *Mrs. Warren's Profession* — receive a powerful charge from the historical situation in which they are written or from their relevance to an immediate problem. *The Crucible* and *Ghosts* have transcended their historical situations and survived because each has that timeless symbolic charge peculiar to great works of art; but *Mrs. Warren's Profession* seems to have lost most of its symbolic charge and retains only the formal one. So topical was the play, and so topical were the images in which Shaw re-embodied the pattern, that the universal is obscured by the topical and the content of the symbol no longer seems interesting or relevant. In Burke's terms, the play was too much an "occasional" one. The same objection can be raised against some of Dryden's and Pope's satires, though it could hardly be made against *Gulliver's Travels*.

It should be clear that certain patterns — sometimes called "motives" by Burke — as well as certain symbols will appeal powerfully to most people at most times. One of these is the quest and its variants: all kinds of hunts to satisfy such basic biological needs as food, shelter, and sex; all kinds of ritualistic hunts, such as the sexual and big-game hunts which serve as forms of initiation into manhood; any kind of search for adventure; all voyages of geographical exploration and discovery; all pilgrimages; all kinds of quests for such things as knowledge, God, power, love, perfection, and vocation; and the master quest itself, the internal voyage of exploration and discovery, the search for the self which seems to figure as a basic motive in any kind of quest. The quest pattern, with the search for the self as the basic motive, has been re-individuated with great complexity and power in such works as *The Odyssey, Oedipus Rex, The Divine Comedy, The Aeneid,* Chrétien's *Percival, The Quest of the Holy Grail, The Faerie Queene, Venus and Adonis, Faust, The American, The Adventures of Huckleberry Finn, Heart of Darkness, Le Grand Meaulnes, Light in August,* and *The Bear.* Though the pattern has a universal rather than a historical or individual charge because its occurrence and appeal are continuous in human history, the power and complexity of the work in which this pattern is exploited depends primarily upon the depth knowledge and artistic ability of the poet. To exploit this pattern rather than some other is to begin with a certain advantage; but the pattern itself guarantees nothing beyond a condition which has the potential to appeal powerfully to most people.

The poet first decides upon the pattern of experience, the "conditions" he will work with. Then he generates a master-symbol — Emma Bovary, Don Quixote, Othello, The Waste Land — in which to re-individuate the pattern. Finally he works out the ramifications of the master-symbol in one or more of the three literary modes (lyric, narrative, dramatic) by supplying such corollary details as are necessary, and arranging these details into a coherent work of art by giving them form. All forms are psychological universals which in turn are "conditions of appeal" in that "they exercise the formal potentialities of the reader," "the potentiality for being interested by certain processes or arrangements . . . of subject-matter as produce [such responses in the reader as] crescendo, contrast, comparison, balance, repetition, disclosure, reversal, contraction, expansion, magnification, series, and so on" (CS,142,46). In so far as form is concerned, any particular work of art can be discussed as "an individuation of formal principles [for] each work re-embodies the formal principles in different subject-matter" (CS,143).

According to Burke, there are four kinds of form in terms of which the technique and formal appeal of any work can be exhaustively analyzed — progressive, repetitive, conventional, and minor — all having to do with the "creation of an appetite in the mind of the auditor, and the adequate satisfying of that appetite" (CS,124,31). "A work has form," Burke says, "in so far as one part of it leads a reader to anticipate another part, to be gratified by the sequence" (CS,124). In the most general sense, progressive form has to do with the appropriateness of "what follows what" in a given work. Though in his later books he was to be more thorough in differentiating between different kinds of progressive form, in *Counter-Statement* Burke groups all of them under two headings: syllogistic and qualitative. The syllogistic includes the two principal kinds of "rectilinear" progression, plot and pattern of experience, because they frequently resemble a "perfectly conducted argument" or a predictable cause and effect chain reaction. As such, they are characterized by a kind of relentless inevitability. The plots of *Oedipus Rex* and *Ghosts* are perfect examples of syllogistic narratives; and Oedipus' tragic rhythm is a perfect example of a syllogistic pattern of experience. Many plots — even some highly inventive and original ones — and all patterns of experience are syllogistic because they are, to greater or lesser degrees, characterized by the "predictable" forward

[21]

movement that is the counterpart in art of well conducted deductive and inductive arguments. After the fact, of course, all good plots are inevitable, even in such a loose and rambling work as Byron's *Don Juan*, for what appears as chance in the course of the work's unfolding becomes fate by the end of the work and the whole plot, as well as the pattern of experience, is seen in retrospect as a completed chain. Burke has both kinds of inevitability — before and after the fact — in mind when he speaks of the syllogistic form of a work.

The second kind of progressive form is qualitative. Burke says that it comes about when "the presence of one quality prepares us for the introduction of another" in the sense that the reader is "put into a state of mind which another state of mind can appropriately follow" (CS,125). Qualitative progressions are seldom predictable and are almost always recognized as appropriate only after the fact. The poetry of T. S. Eliot and Hart Crane, for example, depends to a large extent upon brilliant and unexpected qualitative progressions for many of its effects and meanings. A single perfect example of qualitative form is found in Keats's "Ode to a Nightingale" in the jarring but wonderfully appropriate progression from "faery lands forlorn" to "Forlorn! the very word is like a bell / To toll me back from thee to my sole self." Another example is the gravediggers' scene in *Hamlet* — and most other "comic" scenes in Shakespeare's tragedies — where the actual event has been prepared for by a previous event in the plot and is thus part of the syllogistic progression but where the tone of the scene is unexpected and is recognized as an appropriate qualitative progression only after the fact.

In addition to progressive form, Burke discusses three other kinds, two of which are more or less self-explanatory. The first is repetitive form, "the consistent maintaining of a principle under new guises. . . . [the] restatement of the same thing in different ways" (CS,125). A succession of images, each of them regiving the same lyric mood; a character repeating his identity, his "number," under changing situations; the sustaining of an attitude, as in satire; the rhythmic regularity of blank verse; the rhyme scheme of *terza rima* — these are all aspects of repetitive form. By a varying number of details, the reader is led to feel more or less consciously the principle underlying them — he then requires that this principle be observed in the giving of further details. (CS,125.)

The second is conventional form. Though the term is clear by itself, two points which Burke makes about it need to be mentioned. One is the simple fact that conventional form involves the "appeal of form *as form*," and the other is that the element of "categorical expectancy" is always present when one approaches a conventional form. As a result of this "categorical expectancy" there is a simple but important difference between progressive and repetitive form, where "the anticipations and gratifications . . . arise *during the process* of reading," and conventional form, where the expectations are usually "*anterior to* the reading" (CS,126–127).

Finally, there are the "minor or incidental forms"—"metaphor, paradox, disclosure, reversal, contraction, expansion, bathos, apostrophe, series, [and] chiasmus" (CS,127). Actually, these are best understood as "simple" forms which, though distinct in themselves and analyzable as such, serve in completed works as parts of the three complex types of form. One can enjoy any of these minor forms for its own sake, but a paradox, for example, "by carrying an argument one step forward, may have its use as progressive form; and by its continuation of a certain theme may have its use as repetitive form" (CS,127). Similarly, in the syllogistic progression of *Oedipus Rex*, there is a series of disclosures, each one moving the plot forward one step; the final disclosure is a reversal which brings the plot to a close; and the whole plot up to the reversal has been paradoxical for Oedipus.

The four kinds of form are necessarily interrelated and act, not in isolation, but more often simultaneously to produce multiple effects. "A closing scene," for example,

may be syllogistic in that its particular events mark the dramatic conclusion of the dramatic premises; qualitative in that it exemplifies some mood made desirable by the preceding matter; repetitive in that the characters once again proclaim their identity; conventional in that it has about it something categorically terminal, as a farewell or death; and minor or incidental in that it contains a speech displaying a structural rise, development, and fall independently of its context (CS,128).

[23]

Burke and the Drama of Human Relations

Of such a closing scene (Othello's speech beginning "Soft you, a word or two before you go," and ending "Seized by the throat the uncircumcised dog and smote him thus"), Burke says:

this suicide is the logical outcome of his predicament (syllogistic progression); it fits the general mood of gloomy forebodings which has fallen upon us (qualitative progression); the speech has about it the impetuosity and picturesqueness we have learned to associate with Othello (repetitive form), it is very decidedly a conclusion (conventional form), and in its development it is a tiny plot in itself (minor form) (CS,128).

Burke's point is that "though the five aspects of form can merge into one another, or can be present in varying degrees, no other terms should be required in an analysis of formal functionings" (CS,129). Any work, down to its smallest detail, can be analyzed for its formal appeal in terms of the four kinds of form. Basically rhetorical, such an analysis tells one both what and how effects are produced, and ultimately permits one to determine the "formal charge" or "formal saliency" of a given work. And this, coupled with the "symbolic charge," is equal to the degree of "eloquence" in the work itself.

The purpose of art as ritual is to produce exaltation; the quality and intensity of the exaltation ideally are in direct proportion to the degree of "eloquence" inhering in the work itself. Exaltation is essentially a matter of the creation and gratification of needs, and the work is "eloquent" or "correct" in so far as the needs created in the audience are adequately gratified by the artist. Exaltation is thus a terminal experience which is to be sought and enjoyed for its own sake, by both artist and audience (CS,36,37). The particular quality and value of this terminal artistic experience is clarified by Burke in the following discussion of the differences between art and life:

. . . once one is taught to seek in art such experiences as one gets in life itself, it is a foregone conclusion that one must discover how trivial are artistic experiences as compared with "real living." A mere headache is more "authentic" than a great tragedy; the most dismal love affair is more worth experiencing in actual life than the noblest one in a poem. When the appeal . . . of art as experience is stressed, art seems futile indeed. Experience is less the *aim* of art than the *subject* of art; art [as ritual] is not *experience*, but *something added* to experience. (CS,76–77.)

[24]

Both / And: The Aesthetic of *Counter-Statement*

Art as ritual is the "conversion, or transcendence of . . . [experience] into eloquence, and [is] . . . thus a factor added to life" (CS,41). The factor added is eloquence, which produces in the auditor a state which might be called "aesthetic exaltation," and results from experiencing a beautifully executed work of art having a maximum symbolic and formal charge. Examples of such works are *King Lear, The Odyssey, Oedipus Rex, The Divine Comedy*, and *War and Peace*, where the artist, having depth knowledge of certain patterns of experience and equipped with consummate technical skill, does indeed manipulate one's racial appetites — the "blood, brains, heart, and bowels"— in such a way as to involve one profoundly in the work, creating needs which are proper to one's experience of that work, and gratifying those needs in such a way as to produce the terminal joy which one derives from a work of art.

Though the purpose of art as ritual is "aesthetic exaltation," and, ideally, is an end in itself, it does not take very much thought to discover that what Burke calls "exaltation" is very close to catharsis, and that "exaltation" can also be described as an aesthetic, emotional catharsis which may be much more than just the gratification of the needs created by the work itself. Art as ritual very easily becomes art as rhetoric, with the ritual as homeopathic magic, the artist as medicine man, and the exaltation as the purgation or catharsis of extra-literary individual and social tensions. Rhetoric, according to Burke, is persuasion to change by means of identification. Now if, as Burke argues, "form . . . is an arousing and fulfillment of desires," then a work of art can be considered as something which induces tensions in the audience and then resolves them; and the greater the work of art the greater the induced tensions and ensuing resolution. Imagine, for example, that a person comes to the work of art taut with the tensions natural to life and peculiar to living in any highly organized social order; he comes to the work with "needs" that may have nothing to do with those created by the artist in the work itself. In the course of his involvement with the work, however, his tensions become identified with and gradually absorbed by those induced in him by the artist. The resolution of the work effects a resolution of his own tensions, so that he leaves the work a "changed man," having somehow been purged and restored to "normal" by the cathartic exaltation produced in him. So considered, the form (structure) of the work becomes a magical formula for effecting a catharsis in the auditor, and one's experience of the work becomes a purgative journey, sometimes as abstract and generalized as the one just described and sometimes very specific and individual.

The more abstract and generalized purgative journey is perhaps best illustrated by one's experience of a musical composition, such as a symphony. Since music, though obviously not meaningless, arouses and gratifies desire by non-cognitive means, one's involvement tends to be less localized and more purely formal; one's feelings are manipulated almost in the abstract by the formal harmonies of the piece; and as the theme is gradually complicated and then resolved, so is one involved and aroused, then resolved and appeased, ending the journey in a state of rest. If one came to the work in a state of tension, or went to it because one was in such a state, the resolution of the work may indeed become the resolution of extra-musical tensions, no matter what their nature is. Where the work is more specific, as in literature, the purgative journey may in turn be more specific, more localized. Where, for example, the work deals with sin, guilt, expiation, and redemption, and where the auditor himself suffers from tensions caused by these things, the symbolic transference and merger is usually much more immediate, direct, and powerful. Again, the resolution of the work would produce a catharsis in the auditor which purged him, perhaps only temporarily, of various extra-literary tensions.

Many works function as a kind of abstract rhetoric of catharsis; many function as a kind of universal rhetoric of catharsis; and some function as a historical and individual rhetoric of catharsis. A work may deal with a problem that is unique to, or especially prominent in a given historical period, localizing the terms of the cathartic journey in a way that is especially relevant and powerful at a given time: examples of this would be Arthur Miller's *The Crucible* and *Death of a Salesman*; Maxwell Anderson's *Winterset*, and Clifford Odets' *Golden Boy*. These works deal with historical (and sometimes universal) problems which make up part of the fabric of our lives; and they may, by purging tensions caused by these very problems, better enable us to live with, cope with, or adjust to them. Finally, a work may deal with a problem which involves certain individuals in a very private way and thus may become a highly individual or personal rhetoric of catharsis. One of Katherine Anne Porter's stories (*He*) is about a couple who have an idiot child whom they must finally incarcerate for his and their own good. The problem itself is a terrible one, touching upon the deepest kinds of human loyalties and complexities of sorrow and guilt. For anyone with first-hand experience of such a situation, the cathartic charge of the story would be powerful and probably effective in a way that it could not be for others, even though the story could function as a rhetoric of catharsis for anyone capable of imaginatively experiencing the problem.

Any work, then, may function as a rhetoric of rebirth for anyone in any of the following ways: abstract, universal, historical, and individual. The way it functions will naturally depend upon the nature of the work, the historical period, and the individual. However it functions, the same kind of mysterious process occurs: through exploiting the psychological universals, the poet effects an identification between the auditor and the work; once identified with the work, the auditor becomes involved to the point where an internal movement corresponding to the forward movement (progressive form) of the work begins; the internal movement continues to the point where the auditor is persuaded that the work's resolution is his own; at this point, a cathartic change in the auditor takes place; when he is released from and by the work, the auditor is changed to the extent that he has both dissipated some of his tensions during the purgative journey and symbolically transferred others to the work itself; finally, the end result is that the auditor is persuaded to an improved psychophysical state in the sense that his experience of the work has been unburdening.

Aside from the cathartic function, there is at least one other very important function which poetry as rhetoric performs. According to Burke, every poem represents the author's "adjustment to a situation"; every poem, in other words, is a piece of personal rhetoric for the author which better equips *him* for life, makes him feel more

[27]

"at home in social tensions" (CS,xi), in what Burke has variously called the "jungles of society" (CS,viii), the "chaos of modern life" (CS,35), and the "wilderness, not of nature, but of social forces" (CS,105). Every poem, therefore, becomes a "formula" which the auditor can adopt for his own use in attempting to adjust to various situations, to make himself at home in the "chaos of modern life." Thus, poems can function both as magical forms (structures) for effecting a catharsis and as formulae (statements) for defining situations (problems) and indicating modes of adjustment (solutions). Collectively, poems can be treated as a manual for sane moral conduct.

In a sense, all poems are occasional, representing the poet's particular mode of adjustment to a particular cluster of conditions. Every poem is a personal statement made in some historical context about a problem that is always personal and may be historical and universal. If the poem is about a completely private and non-recurrent situation, it is worthless as a formula for others; if it is both personal and historical, it becomes valuable to others in the same personal and historical situation; if it is personal, historical and universal, it becomes valuable as a formula for all who wish and are able to use it. Actually, there probably is no completely private and non-recurrent cluster of conditions, though a poet surely could individuate it in so private and opaque a manner that no one else could understand it. In fact, some of Burke's stories in *The White Oxen* seem private to the point of incomprehensibility; but as Burke's later explanations of them make clear, it is the individuation rather than the cluster of conditions — the problem — that is private and makes the stories opaque. Man and the nature of "brute reality" being what they are, the individuation of any cluster of conditions, no matter how private, can be reduced, if one but has the key, to the personal, historical, or universal cluster of conditions which must have given rise to the work. A classic example of this is Hart Crane's poem "At Melville's Tomb" which Crane explained in a letter to Harriet Monroe. In fact, Crane's poems in general illustrate Burke's point very clearly. The letters and the two biographies make it evident that all of Crane's poems functioned for him as personal, historical, and universal rhetoric. *Voyages*, heterosexual love poems written in praise of a homosexual love affair, represents a particular mode of adjustment to a cluster of personal conditions. *The Bridge* represents a particular mode of adjustment to a cluster of historical conditions; it is an attempt to convert the disintegrative forces of modern industrialism and mechanization, what Crane himself calls the Babylon of modern life, into a synthesizing and integrative force, by seeing them as a bridge into the Whitmanesque American future. All of Crane's poems represent a particular mode of adjustment to a cluster of universal conditions: they are an attempt to build a self, to integrate the self, and to make it at home in the social wilderness. Consider the last two years of Crane's life, when he was able to write only one or two poems because of the rapid disintegration of his poetic self, a process intensified by his alcoholism and homosexuality. When he could no longer counteract this disintegrative process by the rhetoric of rebirth offered him through poetry, he gradually ceased to exist as a poet and became instead a destitute alcoholic homosexual; at that point, without a self he considered worth preserving, he literally ceased to exist by leaping from the end of a ship at sea.

Now it seems unquestionable that Crane's works, or anyone else's, for that matter, could be made to serve a personal, historical, or universal rhetorical function for anyone who wished to so use them. One has only to find the problems which they solved, determine the nature of the solution, and then reapply it in one's own life. For example, in an essay on Mann and Gide in *Counter-Statement*, Burke very carefully examines their work, isolating, comparing and contrasting the fundamental attitudes of both authors toward life in general. Then he applies these attitudes to the contemporary scene:

Irony, novelty, experimentalism, vacillation, the cult of conflict — are not these men trying to make us at home in indecision, are they not trying to humanize the state of doubt? A philosopher has recently written of this new wilderness we now face, a wilderness not of nature, but of social forces. Perhaps there is an evasion, a shirking of responsibility, in becoming certain too quickly, particularly when our certainties involve reversions to an ideology which has the deceptive allurement of tradition. . . . Need people be in haste to rebel against the state of doubt, when doubt has not yet permeated the organs of our body, the processes of our metabolism, the desire for food and companionship, the gratification with sun and water? . . . Since the body is dogmatic, a generator of belief, society might well be benefited by the corrective of a disintegrating art, which converts each simplicity into a complexity, which ruins the possibility of ready hierarchies, which concerns itself with the problematical, the experimental, and thus by implication works corrosively upon those expansionistic certainties preparing the way for our social cataclysms. An art may be of value purely through preventing a society from becoming too assertively, too hopelessly, itself. (CS,104–105.)

In an essay in *Counter-Statement* devoted entirely to the social role of art as rhetoric, Burke says that "in contemporary America the distinguishing emergent factor is obviously mechanization, industrialism, as it affects our political institutions, as it alters our way of living, as it makes earlier emphases malapropos or even dangerous" (CS,107), and then goes on to point out that

the artist, who is seeking to adjust a vocabulary to a situation (stressing such ways of feeling as equip one to cope with the situation) is necessarily sensitive to both the surviving and the emergent factors in the situation. The contemporary being an aggregate of survivals and possibilities, the artist wholly awake to the contemporary will embody a mixture of retentions and innovations.

His innovations today must be, in some way, the humanistic or cultural counterpart of the external changes brought about by industrialism, or mechanization. The innovations will stress such emotions and attitudes as favor the acceptance of the changes. ("Acceptance of"— not necessarily "acquiescence to." By acceptance is meant an openness to the factors involved. One may accept a situation in thundering against it. . . . Acceptance is exposure. Whether one builds a wall against the new by reaffirming the old, or seeks by a loosening to incorporate the new, he will be "accepting" in so far as his terminology takes the new into account and gives us an accurate workable attitude towards it.) (CS,108.)

The works of various contemporary writers — W. H. Auden, Hart Crane, T. S. Eliot, William Faulkner, E. M. Forster, Aldous Huxley, D. H. Lawrence, Theodore Roethke, and E. B. White — could all be examined for their personal and universal rhetoric, but especially for their historical rhetoric since each of these men has in one way or another dealt with the contemporary situation and has in his works offered us his solution, a set of attitudes which we may take toward the problems it poses for us in our own lives. The work of any author can be examined for its bearing upon the historical situation, as well as for its more obvious bearing upon the personal and universal situation. What is useful in it can be abstracted in the same way and made a part of the rhetoric of rebirth offered to us by poetry as a whole.

In general, poetry considered as rhetoric has two subdivisions which perfectly illustrate the profound pun on form exploited by Burke throughout all of his work. On the one hand there is the rhetoric of catharsis, where the form or structure of the work becomes a magical formula for effecting a catharsis in the auditors; on the other hand there is the rhetoric of statement, where the work is a formula which defines situations, problems, and attitudes, and presents various modes of adjustment to the problems of living. Either way — as catharsis or statement — the rhetoric is corrective in the sense that poetry may act as a counter-force or counter-statement against deviations from the sane moral norm — that ideal humanistic vision of man which Burke has had from the very beginning. Burke's central point is that the poet, and his interpreter, the critic, are (or "should be," for Burke, to borrow a phrase he applied to Freud, frequently takes the optative as indicative) counter-agents who perform a vital social function by perceiving the most serious deviations from the sane moral norm and combating them with the counter-forces and counter-statements of poetry.

It is with this idea in mind that Burke says poetry adds a secular equivalent of "grace" to "the conditions of life" and calls this "grace" the poets' "moral contribution" (*Dial*,LXXXVI,90). According to the dictionary, grace, in its non-religious meaning, is "beauty or harmony of form, attitude," and as applied to rhetoric, means "the element of beauty in discourse that depends on the speaker's power or skill in rendition." But to anyone who has read Burke and noted the degree to which his work is saturated with religious terms, this is clearly not all he means by the word. Again, according to the dictionary, grace is defined as "something added to human nature," "a gift which enables those who have it to do what they could not do without it"; as "gratuitous inward aid," an "influence acting within the heart to regenerate, sanctify, and strengthen"; a "free gift," "assistance," that which is "necessary for salvation"; as that which brings "revelation," "fertility," "joy," "prosperity"; and that which makes man "wise and glorious." As a rhetoric of rebirth, poetry adds the grace of catharsis and the grace of statement to human nature and human living; it gives this inward aid freely, bringing revelation and joy to those who receive it, enabling them to strengthen and regenerate themselves and to save themselves, perhaps, from disorder and disintegration of the self.

As one meditates on the pivotal terms of *Counter-Statement* — norm, form, catharsis, grace, psychological universals, exaltation, eloquence, revelation, ritual, rhetoric, symbol, adjustment to a situation, orientation, formula, psychology of the audience — and thinks about the essays collected in the book, the emphasis of each and the relations between them, and finally on the aesthetic of *Counter-Statement* as a whole, it becomes clear that Burke is equally concerned with two seemingly contradictory areas of investigation: the purely aesthetic and the sociological. In fact, Burke actually seems to contradict himself at certain points in the book, maintaining that poetry is an end in itself which "does not change the mold of our lives" and that poetry is above all a powerful rhetoric, effecting radical changes in the auditor. Actually, there is no contradiction. What Burke maintains is that, ideally, literature is an end in itself, the essence of which is "eloquence"; and that it *can be* studied purely as ritual, concentrating exclusively upon the illumination, appreciation, and enjoyment of the poem qua poem. But in actuality, every ritual may also be a self-revelation (an image of the poet who wrote it), a revelation about the nature of reality itself, and a powerful piece of personal, historical, and universal rhetoric. No poem is either purely aesthetic or purely utilitarian; all poems are both aesthetic and utilitarian, or, both aesthetic and sociological. Every poem is an aesthetic object and has a non-aesthetic function. All poems, like symbols, face two ways, for in addition to being aesthetic objects, they also apply to life (CS,61). And all of Burke's pivotal terms also face two ways: they are Janus or shuttle terms which permit their use in either an aesthetic or a sociological analysis, or in one that combines both. A symbol is both a technical device and a formula for defining our experiences; form is both structure and formula; structure may arouse and gratify emotions to produce either "exaltation" or "catharsis"; a formula is both an aesthetic and a non-aesthetic device. In the aesthetic of *Counter-Statement* there is no dogmatic either/or; there is always the pliant both/and. This is one of the distinctive features of the aesthetic theory developed there and of Burke's literary theory as a whole. Though the emphasis in *Counter-Statement* is primarily literary rather than sociological, and though this primary emphasis changes in Burke's subsequent books to a sociological and finally, in the *Motives* books, to a linguistic one, the pliant both/and attitude characterizes everything Burke ever says about poetry.

· II ·

TOWARDS A
BETTER LIFE THROUGH
SYMBOLIC ACTION

IN THE TWENTIES Burke worked for the *Dial* as contributor, reviewer, translator, and editor. His stories, poems, translations, critical pieces, and reviews of literary and critical works appeared in other journals as well. After 1929, Burke worked for the *Nation* and *New Republic*, primarily as a reviewer, but also as a music critic, and continued to contribute extensively to other journals. During the Great Depression, he moved into new fields, reviewing the works of anthropologists, economists, political theorists, psychologists, semanticists, and sociologists. To be sure, he continued to review critical and creative works and to publish essays of his own, but he finally abandoned his poetic career — a change symbolically re-enacted in the novel *Towards a Better Life* — and moved into the field of social criticism and theory. Though he gave up the writing of poetry as a vocation, he did not relinquish poetry; instead, he turned to it for permanent attitudes toward history which could be fruitfully applied to the problems of living in what he believed was a collapsing democratic society. The turmoil and intensity of this transformation from poet to spokesman for "poetic realism" are evidenced best by such things as Burke's extraordinary productivity between 1931 and 1941 — five books and a large number of still uncollected essays and reviews; by such obvious signs of transition, new vision, and solidification as the nearly hysterical middle part of *Permanence and Change*, the apocalyptic last part of the same book, which is Burke's vision of the new way towards a better life, and the fragmented stylistics of *Attitudes toward History* (parentheses within parentheses, continuous digressions, and long, bewilderingly suggestive footnotes).

What caused Burke's change of direction was the historical situation in which he found himself. In the preface to *Permanence and Change*, Burke says that the book

was written in the early days of the Great Depression, at a time when there was a general feeling that our traditional ways were headed for a tremendous change, maybe even a permanent collapse. It is such a book as authors in those days sometimes put together, to keep themselves from falling apart. (PC,xiii.)

The book is a desperate attempt to locate analytically what is wrong with the changing historical situation by setting it against the permanent universal situation of man as it is revealed in the documents of the present and past. Burke's general conclusion is that certain fundamental needs of man are denied realization and satisfaction by the present scientific, rational, technological, mechanistic, capitalistic orientation. These permanent, fundamental needs — what Burke calls "norms"— are denied realization and satisfaction because the "technological psychosis" is negativistic, dissociative, dehumanized, destructive, combative, deterministic, and selfish; anti-ethical, anti-magical, anti-poetic, and anti-religious. This orientation advocates and actually establishes a conception of self and purpose which leads, not toward the better life of which man is capable, but away from it, toward the terrible holocaust of total war. Burke felt with messianic urgency the need for a new conception of purpose which would counterbalance the dangerously abnormal emphasis of the "technological psychosis." To this end he devoted himself in *Permanence and Change* and, I think, in all the rest of his works.

As Burke has pointed out, neither he nor any of his family ever missed a meal or suffered any kind of physical hardship as a result of the depression; yet so profound was its effect upon his thinking and career that it influenced him in the most complete way during the rest of his life. After the depression began, Burke saw and felt all around him the superstructure of economic, ideological, and political certainties toppling. Always in need of these certainties, always sensitive in the extreme to any weakening of or variation in them, and profoundly aware that man defines and finds himself in terms of these certainties, Burke felt that the very things which gave life meaning and creative purpose were perhaps in the final stages of disintegration. He noted that "when such a superstructure of certainties begins to topple, individual minds are correspondingly affected, since the mind is a social product, and our very concepts of character depend upon the verbalizations of our group" (PC,173). At the time, Burke believed that the social system, or what he calls the "system of coöperation" between individuals and groups, was so seriously impaired that the very structure of rationality itself was threatened. "The mind, so largely a linguistic product," he said, "is constructed of the combined coöperative and communicative materials"; and, if "the system of coöperation become[s] impaired . . . the communicative equipment is correspondingly impaired" (PC,163). The "system of coöperation," the "social structure of meanings by which the individual forms himself" (PLF,108), is what Burke calls an orientation. Any such orientation is dominated by "reigning symbols of authority" which the individual naturally and wholesomely wishes to accept in forming himself. But at certain periods and for many reasons, a whole orientation, or certain key symbols of authority, become "basically unreasonable" (ATH,II,52–53) and the individual finds it necessary to reject the reigning symbols of authority because he loses "faith in the [social] structure's 'reasonableness.'" (PLF, 306.) The painful and bewildering consequence is alienation, or "spiritual dispossession" which causes "nostalgia and emptiness" (ATH,I,116,fn; II,67). Now, something like this is what happened to Burke and a great many other thinkers as a result of the Great Depression. The whole society in which they lived and most of the things for which it stood — in short the national-social orientation — had become unreasonable.

As early as the twenties Burke had characterized this orientation as scientific-technological, as rational-utilitarian, and said that "in contemporary America the distinguishing emergent factor is obviously mechanization, industrialism, as it affects our political institutions, as it alters our way of living, as it makes earlier emphases malapropos or even dangerous" (CS,107). And as early as the twenties, he had argued at length that artists, who are necessarily sensitive to dominant emergent factors in society as a whole because they have the more "barometric minds" (PC,173), must act as counter-agents by stressing the "humanistic" (CS,108), the anti-mechanistic, the anti-industrial (CS,111). Art and criticism should make counter-statements; together they should act as a counter-force to keep society from becoming too much itself. It did not take Burke long to discover that our own national-social orientation was but a part of the larger scientific orientation which began with the Protestant Reformation and, by the eighteenth century, had displaced the old hierarchic or religious orientation. This led Burke to study history and to discover that, preceding the religious orientation, there had been a third major orientation, the magical. He finally decided that each of these major orientations satisfies some of man's permanent fundamental needs, but no one of them satisfies all. In the course of history, which is marked by necessary and inevitable change, one major orientation is established, rigidified, and formulated only to collapse when it no longer satisfies the needs of a given period or is discredited by new knowledge. After a chaotic transitional period, a new orientation is gradually established, rigidified, and systematized. According to Burke, the tendency is for this process to be non-cumulative; often those things in a discredited orientation which actually satisfy fundamental human needs, as well as those things which do not, perish with the orientation. Though a radical shift of emphasis in the new orientation may obscure one or more of the permanent fundamental needs, the needs remain and must be satisfied by one means or another if man is fully and adequately to realize himself. In short, what is permanent, necessary, and valuable may be lost, or lost sight of, or dismissed in the course of the inevitable changes of history. Men often become so absorbed or lost in the historical situation that they fail to remember the universal one. Or, because of what Burke calls the "entelechial" ("to the end of the line") principle, a given orientation, which arose in answer to certain historical and universal needs, becomes too much itself by perfecting its outstanding characteristics at the expense of everything else. This, according to Burke, is exactly what happened with the scientific orientation; it gradually became a "technological psychosis," an aberration, a kind of mechanistic monomania which, absorbed in itself and intent upon its own distorted view of the world, man, and human purpose, could not satisfy some of man's basic, permanent needs, and could not lead toward that better life for which all men yearn.

Crucial to all of Burke's thinking in these matters is the idea of counter-statements, or counter-balances. He says, for example, that "a corrective rationalization must certainly move in the direction of the anthropomorphic or humanistic or poetic, since this is the aspect of culture which the scientific criteria, with their emphasis upon dominance rather than upon inducement, have tended to eliminate or minimize" (PC,65). And he argues that

any point of reference by which a philosophic corrective of the scientific rationalization would be guided must almost necessarily show some superficial affinity with the religious rationalization. For man is essentially human, however earnestly he may attempt to reshape his psychological patterns in obedience to the patterns of his machines — and it was the religious rationalization which focused its purposes upon the controlling of human forces (the organic productive forces of the mind-and-body itself). (PC,63.)

Elsewhere, Burke says that "scientism" needs to be counter-balanced by a stress on "intuition," "imagination," "vision," and "revelation" (*Chimera*,I,24). Those things which have been omitted or de-emphasized in the scientific rationalization must be replaced and re-emphasized in the corrective counter-rationalization; and those things which have been overstressed in the scientific orientation must be unstressed in the same corrective orientation.

For example, Burke speaks repeatedly of scientism's over-emphasis on the profit motive, the competitive aspect of work, and the combative element in general which has "plagued the Western world with increasing violence" and "is a grave stimulus to war" and ultimately to universal holocaust (PC,268; PLF,317,319). Burke calls this "the romantic, 'Faustian' concept of effort that went with the rise of business enterprise," and says that

in contrast with the classical notion that one developed himself by the harmonious apportionment of many different ingredients, you got the notion that development meant the intensification of some one peculiarity or aptitude. Hence . . . there was great opportunity for those warped by inordinate hungers. In the older [religious] frame, they might have tried to *restrain* these hungers — in the new [scientific] frame, they sought only to *embody* them in material attainments. (ATH,I,202–203,fn.)

This "Faustian" concept of effort — "ambition as a disease" — is but part of a larger set of identifications which are characteristic of the scientific orientation. Speaking of the Renaissance and Reformation, which he calls the "watershed" moment in western history, Burke says that

at this point, a *negativistic* [combative] emphasis becomes organized, both in the materials of pure thought and in economic implementation. Beginning with a plea for the separation of church and state, we formally inaugurate the dissociative process that will end with the theoretical separation of everything — a few centuries later, religion will be in one bin, politics in another, art in another, science in another, business in another — and there will be subdivisions, each in its own separate bin. (ATH,I,171–172.)

This particular emphasis of scientism must be counter-balanced in the corrective philosophy by a stress on the "coöperative" and "participant" or non-combative aspects of action (PC,268–270). In the course of his analysis of the scientific orientation Burke concludes that it over-stresses the "rational, scientific categories of linkage" and under-stresses or even ignores the emotional categories. Burke illustrates the point with this example and draws the following conclusion from it:

The lion, if the usual psychoanalytic theory of symbolization is correct, is the male or father symbol *par excellence*. Yet the lion is scientifically included in the cat family, whereas the cat emotionally is feminine. In both great poetry and popular usage, it is associated with female attributes. Here we have, in our rational categories, an association which runs counter to the associations of our emotional categories. A linkage emotionally appropriate becomes rationally inappropriate.

In such cases, where the rational order of symbols would establish a congruity wholly alien to the emotional order of symbols, is it not possible that intense conflicts could arise, with the result that anguish or unrest could follow any really thorough attempt to embrace the rational category? (PC,72–73.)

It is not Burke's contention that the rational categories of linkage are wrong, for he would be the first to admit that in bone structure and in other essential ways, the lion does belong to the cat family; rather, the rational categories are inadequate and may be disastrous, when it is argued that one can *only* define and understand the lion in terms of the rational categories. According to the rational categories of linkage a tree is a tree and is very useful as building material and fuel. But according to emotional categories of linkage, a tree is a parent and usually a father symbol. Hence, Burke argues, if a man takes an axe and fells a great tree,

we need not be surprised to find a strange misgiving permeate him as the noble symbol of shelter comes crashing to the earth. For however neutral his act, though the tree had been felled to satisfy the simple utilitarian needs of firewood, there may also be lurking here a kind of symbolic parricide. Not only firewood, but a parent-symbol, may be brought down in the crash. (PC,71.)

Burke then goes on to make the central point:

It is possible that much of the anguish affecting poets in the modern world is due to the many symbolic outrages which a purely utilitarian philosophy of action requires us to commit. In primitive eras, when the utilitarian processes were considerably fewer, and more common to the entire group, definite propitiatory rituals seem to have arisen as a way of cancelling off these symbolic offenses. In the magical orientation (so close to that of poetry) if the felling of a tree had connotations of symbolic parricide, the group would probably develop a corresponding ritual of symbolic expiation. The offender would thus have a technique for cleansing himself of the sin he had committed. (PC,71–72.)

Finally, Burke says that this radical dissociation between the rational and emotional categories and the tendency in the scientific orientation to deny the validity of the emotional and to ignore what he calls "hidden offenses," has resulted in "the loss of a definite, generally recognized technique for cancelling off these hidden offenses." Burke suggests that "much of the criminality in modern life might be explained psychologically as due to [this] loss" and argues that what we need is "a set of symbolic expiations . . . to counteract the symbolic offenses involved in [the many] purely utilitarian actions" forced upon us by the nature of existence in the modern world. (PC, 74.)

The scientific orientation is inadequate as a description of the scene and the drama of human existence in that scene; it must be supplemented and corrected by a re-affirmation of those things in the religious and magical orientations — what Burke calls the "collective revelation" of mankind — which more adequately locate, describe, and satisfy the permanent, fundamental needs of man. There must be a re-affirmation of the universal situation, of the universals of experience, of what is common to all men in all places; a new attempt must be made to redefine the norms of human existence and, working from them, to find a new way, or rediscover the old ways towards a better life. We must, Burke says,

. . . emphasize the underlying similarities, we [must] return through symbolism to a philosophy of *being*, [to] the Spinozistic concern with man *sub specie aeternitatis*. We [must] replace the metaphor of progress (and its bitter corollary, decadence) with the metaphor of a *norm*, the notion that at bottom the aims and genius of man have remained fundamentally the same, that temporal events may cause him to stray far from his sources but that he repeatedly struggles to restore, under new particularities, the same basic patterns of the "good life." (PC,163.)

To be sure, there was a good deal about the "norms" in *Counter-Statement*; in fact the whole aesthetic theory developed there turns upon the idea that the norms of psycho-physical experience are the materials of art, that these norms link poet and audience and make possible the triple function of poetry as revelation, ritual, and rhetoric. However, in *Permanence and Change* and especially in *Attitudes toward History*, Burke attempts a much more comprehensive and specific treatment of the norms, aiming finally at some kind of description of the permanent fundamental needs of man and their relation to a current historical situation. Later, in the tetralogy of *Motives*, and as the culmination of a continuous effort, Burke arrives at Dramatism, which is offered as a complete system adequately locating what is permanent and fundamental in the drama of human relations. *Permanence and Change* and *Attitudes toward History* are perhaps best understood as stages in this continuous effort to find a way toward the better life through a study of the norms of psychophysical experience.

In *Permanence and Change* and *Attitudes toward History*, as in *Counter-Statement*, Burke starts from the irreducible biological-neurological norm: "situations do overlap," he says,

if only because men now have the same neural and muscular structure as men who have left their records from past ages. We and they are in much the same biological situation. Furthermore, even the concrete details of social texture have a great measure of overlap. And the nature of the human mind itself, with the function of abstraction rooted in the nature of language, also provides us with "levels of generalization" . . . by which situations greatly different in their particularities may be felt to belong in the same class (to have a common substance or essence). (PLF,2.)

The permanent and fundamental biological-neurological similarity between all men results in certain universal situations and certain universal strategies adopted by men as means of coping with the situations. Beyond these rather obvious norms, there are, Burke maintains, three factors at work in every human situation: the threat of disorder, division, and disintegration; "the yearning to conform with the 'sources of one's being'" (PC,69); and the yearning for unity, merger, and integration (PLF,205–206). Existence is a kind of dialectic of division and merger, disintegration and reintegration, death and rebirth, war and peace; the dialectic is the natural and inevitable result of the complex and ever-changing conflict relation between the human agent and his scene. This dialectic of existence — the drama of human relations — centers in what Burke speaks of as every man's attempt to build himself a character in order to establish and maintain an identity. Burke says in *Attitudes toward History* that all the "issues" with which he has been concerned "come to a head in the problem of identity" (ATH,II,138). And this is true not only of that book but of almost everything Burke has written. Man in search of himself and a way toward the better life is, for Burke, *the* universal situation; and the almost unbelievably complex drama of this quest is a major subject of all Burke's work. The mystery of the self in quest is Burke's point of departure; and the ideal self — one which follows uninterruptedly the "transcendental spirals of [its] moral grows" (ATH,I,108) — is his goal. It is the course of the self in quest which Burke charts, endlessly, ingeniously, and with extraordinary perceptiveness; in fact, it would be more accurate to say that Burke attempts to rechart the self, to direct it out of the waste land towards a better life through symbolic action.

As Burke and others have pointed out, the self is usually found and defined in terms of a number of motivational grounds or scenes. Among these are the natural, the biological, the psychic, the personal or reflexive, the familial, the social-political, and the religious or supernatural. The self, some mysterious and irreducible core of being, some changeless yet changing identity, is, in its growth, constantly subjected to radical pressures from within and without in the form of biological and neurological changes, the solidification and dissolution of family ties, sexual initiation and marriage (or vice versa), changes of setting, assumption of social responsibilities, setting of personal goals, religious crises, and the like. The self identifies with one thing or another, consciously or unconsciously; it accepts and rejects various alternatives, merges with and separates from certain things; its growth is the drama of ethical choice and its ideal is that unity of being which constitutes the determined and forward-moving self. Though the search for the self is a universal pattern of experience, though the pattern is almost always similar no matter who undergoes it, and though all selves are basically alike in so far as they have similar biological and neurological equipment, the individual self and the quest are capable of almost infinite variation. So, to say that the search for the self is central to Burke is to add very little unless one goes on to discuss in detail his concept of the self, to lay out Burke's main coordinates — what he later calls the great moments in the drama of human relations.

Burke and the Drama of Human Relations

For Burke, as for Freud, the idea of the self begins with a biological-neurological potential: each individual begins, not with a blank self which is finally completely formed from without, but with a self which has as part of its essence this biological-neurological potential. The self embarks on its quest with something intrinsic to it: it has a certain kind of neurological equipment (the potential for speech and reason); certain permanent fundamental needs; and a certain biological potential (physical growth). In the course of its journey through experience the self builds an identity by making contact with various externals, such as nature and society. This constitutes the drama of the self in quest — the continuous interaction between agent and scene and between the conflicting impulses within the agent. Burke speaks of this gradual evolution of the essential self as "the sojourn of the personality in its different 'glandular [and other] environments' " (ATH,II,97), and points out that the central problem is "how much of one's past identity must be forgotten, how much remoulded, as he moves from one role to the next?" (ATH,II, 98). "The maturing of the individual," for example, "exposes him to 'climacteric stages' of one sort or another." Even if there were no important historical changes taking place in society which called into doubt accepted values and conceptions of human purpose,

the mere changing of one's glandular system would involve him in "new situations." And each change of "situation" [scene], in this purely physical sense, would require a reorganization of the mind with relation to the public, forensic structure. Similarly, a man must be "reborn" in order to fit himself for genuine partnership with a woman — and if this partnership is ended, he must again be "reborn" in order to take new problems of identity into account. (ATH,II, 215–216.)

The drama of the self in quest, then, consists of the self confronting new internal and external factors in the form of radical alterations in its biological, natural, familial, social, intellectual, and religious environments. The new factors and the radical alterations necessitate changes in the self's perspective, in its "structure of interpretations, meanings, values, purposes, and inhibitions" (PLF,270). The self must either confront these issues and adjust to them by making such changes as are necessary or retreat into the abyss of itself and perish.

The drama of the self in quest is an extraordinarily complex life-long ritual of death and rebirth, rejection and acceptance, purification and change, disintegration and reintegration; essentially, it is the drama of moral choice. Confronted by such problems as evil, unchangeable brute realities, the trackless maze of unresolved and even undefined personal and social conflicts, and by an always fundamentally chaotic world, the self attempts to build its individual character and adopt its proper role by constructing a "frame of acceptance" (ATH,I,204–205) — a "more or less organized system of meanings by which a thinking man gauges" the world (ATH,I,3–4). In attempting to build an individual character — to find its real self and live purposefully in the external world, satisfying its permanent fundamental needs by conforming to the sources of its being — the self is almost continually in crisis-conflict situations. In some situations, the choice is simple and obvious and the conflict can be solved by direct physical action; but in others the self confronts "overlapping contradictions," where the choice is enormously complex and direct physical action seems impossible. Where conflicts are not resolvable by direct physical action, one "symbolically erects a 'higher synthesis' . . . that helps him to 'accept' them" (ATH,I,120). According to Burke, this "process of transcendence [is] basic to thought" (ATH,I,113), and is most commonly effected through the symbolic action of language whereby one can erect "a series of transcendental . . . poetic and critical" bridges which produce "a synthesis atop the antithesis by the organizing of a unifying *attitude*" (ATH,I,120). The unifying attitude becomes part of a coherent set of attitudes which make up a "frame of acceptance." With the help of such "transcendental bridges" as are necessary, a man "builds his character"; he attempts to put his self together, to discover and maintain his identity so that he can act purposefully and feel at home in the world. Such, Burke maintains, is man's "natural vocation." The potential for language is built into man's cells and it is natural that a self, which has language as part of its essence, would use the symbolic action which language makes possible to effect some of the transformations necessary to its continued moral growth toward final unity of being.

Burke's main coordinates are essentially moral-ethical, and his drama of human relations is an elaborate and deliberately worked out *secular* version of the Christian drama. Whether fact or myth, Burke says, both the Garden of Eden story and its sequel, the story of Christ, the sacrificial redeemer, are true in "essence," for they state, in narrative terms, certain essential truths about the human condition. By reducing both stories to the level of naturalistic discourse and explaining them in terms of the biological-neurological norms, Burke accepts the essential truths while rejecting both the doctrines and the organization (church) with which the stories are associated. The Garden of Eden, for example, has its biological analogue in the womb; there, "food simply descends benignly . . . and the organism has but to open itself and receive the bounty. There is no competition here. The organism . . . thrives by pure receptivity. It is truly at one with its environment . . . [for] the separation of the part from the whole . . . has not yet taken place" (PC,200–201,fn.). The Fall and expulsion from Eden have their biological and neurological analogues in the birth trauma and the agent's capacity for reason and social intercourse. The separation of the part from the whole, however, does not occur as a result of pride and original sin; it is natural and inevitable: man is not expelled because of original sin, but is expelled into it, for implicit in the nature of reason and the relationship between the individual and society is the potential for "sin" (ATH,I,211,fn.). Reason itself, man's neurological inheritance, is the very factor which causes the "categorical guilt" or "original sin" from which all men naturally suffer. Man "falls" every time he follows the impulse towards abstraction which reason and language make possible, and conceives of ideals ("god-terms") which are incapable of being perfectly realized. Man is naturally of "guilt-laden substance" (PLF,50); guilt as a permanent part of man's condition makes purification and redemption a continuous necessity, for, if unrelieved, guilt fragments and corrodes the self. The secular analogue for Christ, the sacrificial redeemer, is symbolic action; however, the purpose of this secular rhetoric of rebirth is *internal* rather than *eternal* rebirth and salvation, and it leads toward the better life rather than toward Heaven.

One of the most important things the scientific orientation denies to man is some means by which "the sense of the unclean [can be] periodically mitigated by purificatory rituals" (ATH,II,41). This is one reason why Burke believes that the scientific, rational account of the human condition is inadequate; it fails to take into account the fact that man is essentially a moral-ethical animal of guilt-laden substance, in continuous need of purification and redemption. This inadequacy must be remedied, Burke says, by a reassertion of the fundamental truths about the human condition contained primarily in the religious but also in the magical orientations. What the church recognized as well as exploited was the fact that man is essentially a moral-ethical animal. "With astounding exactitude, . . . [the church] built upon the foundations of human guilt, subtly contriving both to intensify people's sensitivity to the resources of guilt (making two opportunities for guilt grow where but one had grown before) and to allay this guilt by appropriate rituals and by acts of loyalty to the social status established by custom" (ATH,I,163). "The church founded the notion of brotherhood on the concept of original sin, the preoccupational basis of a guild of the guilty" (PLF, 50). The church recognized that original sin and the guilt natural to it is a powerful goad to "collectivist" effort; it recognized that "the most normal mode of expiation is that of socialization" (what Burke calls the "socialization of losses") for by sharing, one's guilt is partly absolved. Finally, Burke argues, the church "well understood the disastrous accumulative power of silence. . . . [It] knew that speech [symbolic action] is curative," and invented all kinds of confessional and purificatory rituals whereby a man was able to strip himself bare, periodically and symbolically to slay the guilty part of himself (ATH, I,166,fn.). The church provided man with an elaborate network of "transcendental bridges" which enabled him to cope with one of his most fundamental and permanent conflicts — guilt. Though Burke believes that the church, which he describes as "a big deserted building, with broken windows and littered doorways" (PC,65), can no longer perform this necessary function for man, he does believe that some secular variant of religion must perform it if man is to be saved from the disastrous end implicit in the scientific rationalization.

According to Burke (in 1935) to act in a creative, assertive, synthetic way is man's ultimate motive (PC,259). For these three adjectives Burke uses, almost interchangeably, a whole cluster of others: religious, ethical, volitional, poetic, cooperative; action, communication, participation; unifying, integrating, transcending; and redemptive. The master term — what Burke calls the god-term — is "ethical-moral." "It is the moral impulse that motivates perception, giving it both intensity and direction, suggesting *what to look for* and *what to look out for*" (PLF,164). In typical fashion, Burke takes this "god-term" and links most of his other key terms to it:

Action is fundamentally ethical, since it involves preferences. Poetry is ethical. Occupation and preoccupation are ethical. The ethical shapes our selection of means. It shapes our structures of orientation, while these in turn shape the perceptions of the individuals born within the orientation. Hence it radically affects our coöperative processes. The ethical is thus linked with the communicative (particularly when we consider communication in its broadest sense, not merely as the purveying of information, but also as the sharing of sympathies and purposes, the doing of acts in common, as with the leveling process of communicating vessels) . . . all universe-building [which includes the self] is ethical. (PC,250.)

Having isolated the moral-ethical as the primary "*underlying motive or set of motives that activates all men*" (PC,221), Burke then selects Poetry (symbolic action) as the paradigmatic example of this "ultimate motive" in human experience. The building of a self is compared to the writing of a poem (PC,78); the finding of the true self is compared "to the writing of a great poem," for "the poem is a sudden *fusion*, a *falling together of many things formerly apart*" (PC,158). "All action," Burke says, "is poetic," for "all acts are 'synthetic,' each being a new way of putting things together, quite as each line of a drama is" (PC,215,254). "Life itself," Burke maintains, "is a poem in the sense that, in the course of living, we gradually erect a structure of relationships about us in conformity with our interests" (PC,254). Burke believes, in other words, that poetic

Towards a Better Life through Symbolic Action

symbolic action expresses and embodies the essence of the drama of human relations and that through an intensive study of the nature and function of poetry the moral-ethical part of man denied or ignored by the scientific orientation can be rediscovered and re-affirmed. It is not the church to which we must turn for the way towards a better life, but to poetry, to symbolic action. In a passage which states these central ideas as clearly as anything he has written, Burke asks:

might the great plethora of symbolizations lead, through the science of symbolism itself, back to a concern with "the Way," the old notion of Tao, the conviction that there is one fundamental course of human satisfaction, forever being glimpsed and lost again, and forever being restated in the changing terms of reference that correspond with the changes of historic texture? All that earlier thinkers said of the *universe* might at least be taken as applying to the nature of *man*. One may doubt that such places as heaven, hell, and purgatory await us after death — but one may well suspect that the psychological patterns which they symbolize lie at the roots of our conduct here and now. (PC,183–184.)

The belief that "the way" was to be found in and through poetry appeared in Burke's thought as early as the late twenties. In the middle works (1932–1941), however, Burke takes this essentially Romantic idea and follows it to the end of the line; in his theory of symbolic action he arrives at one of the most extreme defenses of poetry as knowledge and as a rhetoric of rebirth to be found in contemporary American literary criticism. Central to all his thinking about poetry during this period is the premise from the aesthetic of *Counter-Statement* that the poet is a superior man — a kind of ideal norm — with superior knowledge of the psychological universals and superior powers of articulation. These three "abilities" enable the poet to create symbolic structures which "illustrate . . . [the] major psychological devices whereby the mind equips itself to name and confront its [historical and personal] situation" (ATH,I,129). They also enable the poet to have a "clear awareness of the fact that a man's need of 'integration' or 'fusion' involves factors more complex, and closer to 'magic,' than rationalistic oversimplifications of political necessities can reveal" (SoR,I,171). Working from these prem-

[49]

ises, Burke makes a number of additional hyperbolic assertions about the poet and poetry, all of which illustrate the thoroughness with which he developed the Romantic belief in the superiority of the poet and poetry. Burke says that "the devices of poetry are close to the spontaneous genius of man" (PC,66); that "to learn what is really going on in the world" "one must watch the 'poetry exchange' " (ATH,II,240); that poems "are like 'meter readings' " for they are "the dial on which [the] fundamental psychological processes of *all* living are recorded" (ATH,II,35); that "the processes of social commerce operating in life as a whole" are all clearly revealed in poetry (ATH,II,35–36; PLF,308); and that "points of view"— attitudes toward history —"first make themselves apparent in the realm of 'fancy' " (PLF,234). Burke believes that *the* most fundamental psychological process of all living is the "ritualistic naming and changing of identity (whereby a man fits himself for a role in accordance with established co-ordinates or for a change of role in accordance with new co-ordinates which necessity has forced upon him)" (ATH, II,169–170). Poetry not only functions actively in this "ritualistic naming and changing of identity" in the sense that the poet uses it as a rhetoric of rebirth to effect changes in "role," but, Burke asserts, *"the processes of change of identity are* [also] *most clearly revealed by analyzing formal works of art and applying the results of our analysis to the 'informal art of living' in general"* (PLF,308).

All of the above quotations are based upon a single assumption and all of them really affirm the same thing: that the poet is of all men the most extraordinary and that poetry is not only the mirror which reflects and the lamp which lights up the world, but the balm which heals it. Few people have ever taken this assumption and these ideas so seriously as Burke. Working out from them he constructed a poetic orientation which he conceived of as a solution to the historical situation in which he found himself and his society. He proposed the poetic orientation as a counter-statement for the scientific orientation: he asserted that its ideal was peace rather than war, action-without-combat instead of physical violence; he claimed that the poetic orientation gave a more complete account of man, that it was closer to the sources of man's being, that it recognized man as an essentially moral-ethical animal who must move toward the better life through symbolic action. In short, Burke proposed to extract a philosophy of living from poetry itself and with this "fresh unity of purpose" (PC,268) to rechart the self towards a better life. Between 1924 and 1941 Burke moved from writing poetry to theorizing about poetry to converting a theory of poetry into a philosophy of living.

According to Burke — and his own development surely bears it out —"a theory of poetry is likewise a theory of reality, a psychology, and an ethics; and its perspective may even be transferred to an account of historical or economic trends, if the times are such that we ask for the transference" (*Poetry*,XLVII,52). Evidently the times were such, for Burke made his theory of poetry into a theory of everything. In the long summarizing passage at the end of *Permanence and Change*, Burke presents his position as follows:

. . . the ultimate metaphor for discussing the universe and man's relations to it must be the poetic or dramatic metaphor. Many metaphors are possible [e.g., man as warrior, man as machine, man as animal] . . . and though any of these simplifications can serve as a postulate from which important and useful considerations . . . will follow, we suggest that the metaphor of the poetic or dramatic man can include them all and go beyond them all.

In adopting such [a] metaphor as key, we have a vocabulary of motives already at hand, evolved through the whole history of human thought. Indeed, beginning with such a word as *composition* to designate the architectonic nature of either a poem, a social construct, or a method of practical action, we can take over the whole vocabulary of tropes (as formulated by the rhetoricians) to describe the specific patterns of human behavior. Since social life, like art, is a *problem of appeal*, the poetic metaphor would give us invaluable hints for describing modes of practical action which are too often measured by simple tests of utility and too seldom with reference to the communicative, sympathetic, *propitiatory* factors that are clearly present in the procedures of formal art and must be as truly present in those informal arts of living we do not happen to call arts.

Would we not be actually living an onomatopoeia, for instance, if in a moment of anger we abruptly disarranged the furniture in our room or our relations with our friends? Are not such clinical words as fetishism and transference discussing much the same phenomenon

as was discussed in the old books of rhetoric under the name of synecdoche, or part for the whole? Does not the "egoistic-altruistic
merger" involve in practical life that same intimate relationship
which we observe in the identity of poet and material, of internal
attitude and external embodiment? Is not the civic process everywhere marked by acts of ingratiation and justification quite analogous to the motivations of art? Is not the relation between individual
and group greatly illumined by reference to the corresponding relation between writer and audience? . . .

The [poetic] metaphor also has the advantage of emphasizing the
participant aspect of action rather than its *competitive* aspect, hence
offering a prompt basis of objection when the contingencies of our
economic structure force us to overstress competitive attitudes. . . .
Projecting the metaphor by analogical extension, we find that the
entire universe again takes life, as a mighty drama still in progress.
And even if we are led to fear that this drama is essentially tragic,
the poetic metaphor reminds us that in a perfect tragedy there is
"catharsis," hence we may be heartened to inquire what form this
catharsis may take. (PC,263–266.)

The poetic or dramatic metaphor, Burke argues, is a purposive or
teleological one. It stresses man's nature as a moral-ethical animal
and takes into account the drama of choice which the self necessarily
experiences in its quest (PC,260–261). The poetic metaphor is deliberately opposed to the mechanistic, scientific one which treats
human acts and relations in terms of stimulus, response and conditioned reflex. From the poetic or dramatic metaphor Burke proposes
to derive a "*calculus* [a grammar] — a vocabulary, or set of coördi-
nates, that serves best for the integration of all phenomena studied
by the *social* sciences" (PLF,105). In short, he proposes to derive a
view of reality from poetry itself; and at the same time to derive from
poetry an ideal program of action which the self may adopt.

Few people have investigated so thoroughly as Burke the uses to
which poetry can be put for extra-literary purposes. In *Attitudes
toward History*, for instance, he examines the various literary categories to show how "each of the great poetic forms stresses its own
peculiar way of building the mental equipment (meanings, attitudes,
character) by which one handles the significant factors of his time"
(ATH,I,41–42). He begins with the epic, which he calls a "typical

frame of symbolic adjustment under primitive conditions" (ATH,I, 42). "The epic," Burke says,

is designed . . . to make men "at home in" those [primitive] conditions. It "accepts" the rigors of war (the basis of the tribe's success) by magnifying the role of warlike hero. Such magnification serves two purposes: It lends dignity to the necessities of existence, "advertising" courage and individual sacrifice for group advantage — and it enables the humble man to share the worth of the hero by the process of "identification." The hero, real or legendary, thus risks himself and dies that others may be *vicariously* heroic (a variant of the symbolic cluster in Christianity whereby the victim of original sin could share vicariously in the perfection of Christ by his membership in the Church, the *corpus Christi*). The social value of such a pattern resides in its ability to make humility ["peace"] and self-glorification ["war"] *work together*: the sense of one's limitations (in comparison with the mighty figure of the legend) provides one with a realistic attitude for gauging his personal resources, while his vicarious kinship with the figure gives him the distinction necessary for the needs of self-justification. (ATH,I,44.)

The epic, then, promotes the attitudes of humility and resignation, for the flaw in the hero prompts one to seek the flaw in himself, to take "the inventory of one's *personal* limits" (ATH,I,46) and to realize that even the god-like men have their personal and human limitations. In one of his many statements on tragedy, Burke claims that, like the epic, it promotes the attitudes of humility and resignation. Tragedies admonish "one to 'resign' himself to a sense of his limitations." (ATH,I,49.)

This state of resignation is produced through fusing, in aesthetic symbols, mental conflicts which cannot be fused in the practical sphere. The maintaining of a strict family pattern, for instance, gives rise to certain proscriptions or taboos which conflict with desires arising out of the same pattern. One could not practically destroy these taboos without breaking up the family pattern. Hence, by symbolic fusion in tragedy, an ability to "accept one's fate" is established. This, in a general way, is the explanation of the "catharsis" of tragedy, which is the essence of "pure" art. It enables us to "resign" ourselves by resolving in aesthetic fusion trends or yearnings not resolvable in the practical sphere. (PLF,320.)

The "trends" or "yearnings" which are expressed and "resolved" in tragedy are the "criminal" and "expiatory" (PC,195). Tragedy, Burke says, is "a complex kind of trial by jury," and hence is "essentially concerned with the processes of guilt and justification" (PC, 195). All kinds of "secret offenses" and unspeakable conflicts, such as incest, matricide, patricide, and regicide are expressed and purged in the subterfuges of symbolic action. The humility comes from the fact that tragedy universalizes the "trends" or "yearnings" by making them public and by asserting that all men are guilty and must expiate their crimes; the resignation or "acceptance" comes from the fact that the tragic catharsis temporarily or even partly solves (resolves) an intolerable conflict and thus enables one to "resign" himself to himself and life by enabling him once again to "accept" both. Tragedy, like the epic, performs a purgative-redemptive function which can and often does effect a change in attitude.

In *Attitudes toward History*, Burke attempts briefly to show how other poetic categories — notably the ode, the elegy, burlesque, and satire — may help to form our attitudes and become part of the equipment necessary for sane living. Satire, like tragedy, performs a purgative function which enables one symbolically to "sterilize" those trends or yearnings in oneself which might lead to physical violence and war. The satirist "attacks *in others* the weaknesses and temptations that are really *within himself*" (ATH,I,62). Hence, satire "*gratifies* and *punishes* the vice" which one has within himself. The satirist whips himself with his own lash in a kind of grotesque ritual of negative purification. The elegy, Burke shows, functions like homeopathic magic and a vaccination: it helps one to "develop tolerance to possibilities of great misfortune by accustoming him . . . to misfortune in small doses, administered stylistically." The "homeopathic style," which Burke feels is characteristic of all poetry, is "based . . . on the feeling that danger cannot be handled by head-on attack, but must be *accommodated*," controlled by "channelization" rather than by "elimination" (ATH,I,56,fn.). Burke calls this the "lightning rod" theory of art; and some of the ways in which he applies it have been briefly illustrated in the previous paragraphs. To switch the metaphor, Burke believes that "the symbolic manipulations of art [can] supply the vents for 'anti-social' [war-like] impulses, taking up the slack . . . between [a] . . . given society's norms and the individual's necessarily imperfect fit with these norms" (ATH,II,15–17). Now a vent "takes off" impurities and a lightning rod diverts what is dangerous and extremely destructive, rendering it harmless. In a similar way, impurities within the self may be taken off by means of "symbolic manipulations of art," and certain destructive trends may be diverted and rendered harmless through the expression or experiencing of them in the "symbolic manipulations of art." Or, an attitude towards either impurities or dangers expressed in a single work, or category of works, or by a particular author, may be adopted as part of one's equipment for living; and even though the impurity or danger may not be removed, the change in attitude towards it may make it easier to control and live with.

This particular phase of Burke's development of a philosophy or psychology of human relations derived from the nature and function of poetry is perhaps best illustrated in the use to which he puts comedy. "Like tragedy," Burke says,

comedy warns against the dangers of pride, but its emphasis shifts from *crime* to *stupidity*. . . . The progress of humane enlightenment can go no further than in picturing people not as *vicious*, but as *mistaken* [i.e., in need of correction rather than destruction]. When you add that people are *necessarily* mistaken, that *all* people are exposed to situations in which they must act as fools, that *every* insight contains its own special kind of blindness, you complete the comic circle, returning again to the lesson of humility that underlies great tragedy. The audience, from its vantage point, sees the operation of errors that the characters of the play cannot see; thus seeing from two angles at once, it is chastened by dramatic irony. (ATH,I, 51–52.)

The comic attitude, Burke believes, "would enable people *to be observers of themselves, while acting.* Its ultimate would not be *passiveness*, but *maximum consciousness*. One would 'transcend' himself by noting his own foibles. He would provide a rationale for locating the irrational and non-rational." (ATH,I,220–221.) From this attitude Burke develops what he calls a "comic" or "dialectical" methodology which has its final realization in dramatism. Comic or dialectical criticism is a "methodology of exposure"; it attempts to demystify things, or, to use Burke's analogy, like the sun in Aesop's fable, it makes things "strip" and wash in the river. By systematically trying to show that nothing is what it seems to be on the surface, comic criticism tries to get at the full reality of things. Comic criticism, which approaches life in the way a "new critic" approaches a poem, attempts to "provide important cues for the composition of one's life, which demands accommodation to the structure of others' lives" (ATH,I,224).

As I pointed out earlier, Burke makes man as poet the ultimate metaphor for the study of man and human relations. As a result, the poet becomes the ideal man, and living, as well as each individual life, is treated as "a poem in the making." All the acts of a single man, like the parts of a good poem, are treated as if they were necessarily related and organically unified. Acts and things are treated as if they were symbols, and lives as if they were unified dramas of the self in quest. Western history is studied as a drama in five acts. Poetry becomes the expression of the essence of man and human relations and is thus studied as a true image of reality. Oddly enough, and seemingly without worrying about the possibilities of logical contradiction, Burke sees poetry as the expression of the ideal essence of man and human relations and thus studies it as a true image of both the real (or indicative) and the ideal (or optative). Not only does poetry express the real and ideal, but as symbolic action, it mediates between them by performing some of the most complex functions necessary to man if he is to progress toward the better life. Consequently, Burke studies poetry both for a knowledge of how it functions as a rhetoric of rebirth, and so that he may, priest-like, disseminate the good word.

All of these ideas led finally to Burke's theory of symbolic action. Mentioned first in *Permanence and Change* and partly developed throughout the germinal *Attitudes toward History*, the theory is fully developed in the title essay of *The Philosophy of Literary Form*. Ultimately, the theory of symbolic action is developed into a theory of language — dramatism — and is exhaustively worked out in Burke's tetralogy of *Motives*. Though Burke has been defining symbolic action for almost twenty years, he has never, as far as I know, given a concise and complete statement of the complex of ideas which constitutes the essence of the theory. When first introducing the idea of symbolic action in *Permanence and Change*, he makes a distinction between "*symbolic*" and "*necessitous*" labor; "drudgery," he says, "is purely necessitous labor, whereas symbolic labor is fitted into the deepest lying patterns of the individual" (PC,82). " 'Symbolic' acts," however, "are grounded in 'necessitous' ones" (PC,168). Hobbies, for example, "are symbolic labor, undertaken as compensation when our patterns of necessitous labor happen for one reason or another to be at odds with our profoundest needs" (PC,237–238). Later, in *Attitudes toward History*, Burke makes the same kind of distinction between symbolic and other kinds of acts. "If a man climbs a mountain," he says,

not through any interest in mountain climbing, but purely because he wants to get somewhere, and the easiest way to get there is by crossing the mountain, we need not look for symbolism. But if we begin to discuss why he wanted to get there, we do get into matters of symbolism. For his conceptions of purpose involve a texture of human relationships; his purposes are "social"; as such, they are not something-in-and-by-itself, but a function of many relationships; which is to say that they are symbolical. For eventually, you arrive at an act which a man does because he is interested in doing it exactly as he does do it — and that act is a "symbolic" act. It is related to his "identity." (ATH,II,165–166.)

In other words, according to Burke, "there are *practical* acts, and there are symbolic acts" (PLF,9). The distinction between them seems to lie in the fact that symbolic acts are representative, symptomatic acts of the self that performs them and, at the same time, perform some compensating function for that self. What the acts "represent," what they are "symptomatic" of, and their "compensating" function seem to constitute the symbolic or "hidden" meaning of the act. Symbolic action seems to be something which has hidden or private meaning and performs a hidden or private compensating function. Quite obviously almost any act, no matter how practical or necessary, could be a representative, and function as a compensating act. Yet Burke argues that "if one . . . carried out the motions necessary to attain some natural or mechanical end (as when picking up food in order to eat it, when the cells of the body really did need more nutriment), here would be a wholly 'practical' act" (HR,IX,214). The example seems patently absurd in view of the fact that such an act might well be representative and symptomatic of a particular person's essential self, and might be performing some profound compensating function for it. In a recent essay, Burke says that "insofar as an act is representative (or 'symbolic') of an agent, that act is the manifestation of some underlying 'moral principle' in the agent. Insofar as the act does not represent some underlying principle of the agent's character, some fixed trait of his personality, . . . it is not so much an act as an accident." (ChiR,VIII,97.) Certain obvious conclusions can be drawn from these attempts to define a symbolic act. Any act (whether physical or verbal) that is in fact representative of the self which performed it, and any act that has a compensating function for the self which performs it is a symbolic act. But, in vacuo, no act can be said to be purely practical, for, given the complexities of the human psyche and the findings of the psycho-analysts, analysis may show an act to be "symbolic" in either or both of the ways described above.

In view of these conclusions, one of Burke's most concise definitions of symbolic action seems absurd: "poetry, or any verbal act," he says, "is to be considered as 'symbolic action'" (PLF,8). This would seem to mean that all verbal acts are "representative," "symptomatic," and "compensating" acts of and for the person who performed them. The Sears, Roebuck catalogue, newspaper fillers, want-ads, and business letters — all of which strike one as eminently "practical" and "necessitous" verbal acts — become "the manifestations of some underlying 'moral principle' in the agent[s]" who wrote them, and compensate for the frustration of some of the agents' "profoundest needs." Now this is as ridiculous as the example given earlier of a purely practical act. The conclusion to be drawn from setting various definitions of symbolic action side by side is that Burke does not mean the same thing every time he uses the term. Hence, if one wishes to make sense out of the theory, and Burke's applications of it, one must establish the range of meanings it has for Burke and the way in which they are interrelated, and then determine from the context which of the meanings apply.

An examination of the many uses of the term reveals that it has three separate but interrelated meanings. When Burke says that "any verbal act" is "symbolic action" he means this in the most literal way, for words are symbols which stand for things and ideas, and verbalizations are symbols in action. Thus, when Burke speaks of "poetry, or any other verbal act" as symbolic action, or when he runs together "linguistic, or symbolic, or literary action" (PLF,vii), he is not making an absurd statement, but a literal one. All of the literary arts are indeed symbolic action, with symbolic, in this case, being little more than a synonym for verbal. So, when Burke says that "if a man crosses a street, it is a practical act [but] if he writes a book about crossings — crossing streets, bridges, oceans, etc. — that is a symbolic act" (PLF,267,fn.3), the statement, though the term "practical" is misleading, makes perfectly good sense as a superficial distinction between non-verbal and verbal acts. But the statement carries another meaning which helps clarify the "representative" meaning of symbolic action, as well as Burke's consistently misleading use of the word "practical." The opposition between "practical" and "symbolic" suggests that verbal action is not practical, yet even a superficial reading of Burke reveals that he thinks symbolic action the most practical thing in the world. The distinction he is trying to suggest turns on the difference between an act and an accident. If, for example, a man deliberately wrote a book about crossings, or if he were obsessively interested in crossings and collected all kinds of works on the subject, both the verbal act of writing the book and the non-verbal acts of crossing and collecting would be symbolic in so far as they were significant representative acts of the agent or self which performed them. Representative-symbolic acts are images of the self which performs them, and analysis of such symbolic acts will reveal "some underlying principle of the agent's character, some fixed trait of his personality." Just as words are both what they are and what they stand for, so representative-symbolic acts, whether non-verbal or verbal, are both acts and images of the self. They are symbolic autobiography: acts symbolizing the essential self. Though any act may be a static, symbolic representation of some fixed trait of an agent's self, the act may also be performing some profound function for the agent over and above self-expression. For example, Burke says that "going nude" is "a symbolic divesting (unclothing) of guilt, a symbolic purification" (PLF,27,fn.3). He says also that poems function "as a symbolic redemptive process."

In order to be redeemed, one must be purified; according to Burke, "going nude" is a purgative-redemptive symbolic act because previously there must have been "the hiding of the shameful, [and] hence the clothing of the pudenda [becomes] . . . the 'essence' of guilt"; through an associative process, the "covering" takes on the quality of the "covered"; hence, "by removing the clothes, one may at the same time ritualistically remove the shame of which the clothes are 'representative'" (PLF,27,fn.3). These examples give us the clues for another important meaning of symbolic action and explain why it is the "manifestation of some underlying 'moral principle.'" Burke believes that man is fundamentally a moral-ethical animal, that he has built into his system a moral sense and the impulse toward alleviating the guilt naturally produced by moral consciousness. Man must continuously purge and redeem himself from the guilt that is as natural to him as breathing; such highly practical, purgative-redemptive moral action is the third kind of symbolic action. Any act, whether non-verbal or verbal, which performs this function, is a symbolic act.

There are, then, three general meanings for symbolic action; linguistic, representative, and purgative-redemptive. The first includes all verbal action; the second covers all acts which are representative images of the essential self; and the third includes all acts with a purgative-redemptive function. Clearly, symbolic action includes much more than poetry; and clearly almost anything from the full range of human action could be a symbolic act in one or more of the senses given above. As is usual with Burke, he makes his theory broad enough so that it will cover almost everything and permit repeated excursions away from and back to a fixed point. Burke's almost dogmatic assertion that all poetic acts are always symbolic acts in all three meanings is one of the unique features of his system. His argument is that though *any* act may be "symbolic" in one

Towards a Better Life through Symbolic Action

or more ways, all poems are *always* representative, purgative-redemptive symbolic acts. This means that every poem is the true image of the self which created it, and that every poem performs a purgative-redemptive function for the self. A poem, Burke tells us, is "the *dancing of an attitude*"; it is the internal self externalized, enacted in symbolic form (PLF,9,10–11). Poems "symbolically enact" the poet's characteristic "mental conflict[s]" (PLF,10), for "the poet will naturally tend to write about that which most deeply engrosses him — and nothing more deeply engrosses a man than his *burdens*" (PLF,17). And poems, Burke adds, are private rituals of rebirth (ATH,II,37–38), "salvation" devices (ATH,I,173), "purificatory ritual[s]" (PLF,130,131); they are "rituals of redemption . . . a kind of 'private mass' . . . communion services" (PLF,87–88).

Always profoundly personal, always about what deeply engrosses the ideal poetic self, poems (those "charismatic vessels" of grace) function for the poet as a private and, Burke believes, highly necessary and effective purgative-redemptive rhetoric of rebirth. They not only enable the poet to move toward the better life through symbolic action, but they chart the quest of the ideal self with extraordinary exactitude and richness. To use Burke's own word, they not only chart the way, they "dredge" it: they search out the hidden dangers in it and clear the way for others. The theory of symbolic action extends Burke's notion — first developed in *Counter-Statement* — that poetry is a necessary part of one's equipment for sane living. Because poems are the poet's solutions to problems faced in the search for the self and the better life, they may be considered as "charts" or "maps" (PLF,6,294) which one may consult when lost in the wilderness of the world; or they may be used to study the various "routes" which the ideal self takes in its quest, and from such a study one may locate himself and derive some solace from the knowledge that others have traveled the same hard route. Again, since poems are superior solutions to the problems of living, they may be studied as "formulae," as "statements," as "definitions." In this respect, Burke speaks of poems as entries in an informal dictionary, to which we may turn for definitions of, and solutions to, the problems of living (PLF,1,

[61]

283). Poems, he says, are like proverbs: they name the "typical, recurrent situations" (PLF,293), they help one to "organize and command the army of one's thoughts and images" (PLF,298). And since poems are representative-symbolic acts of the ideal poetic self in quest, they provide us with depth knowledge of the self and the way it behaves in various motivational scenes. As representative-symbolic acts, poems should be subjected to the kind of analysis which psychoanalysts use on dreams, and for the same reason, since poems are secular confessions in which one names one's number (PLF,280–281) in the "labyrinthine subterfuges of symbolism" (*Chimera*,I,21).

But this is not all, for poems as purgative-redemptive symbolic acts are "catharsis by secretion," incantations (PLF,281), "salvation device[s]" (ATH,I,173); a poetic symbolic act is like a "private-enterprise Mass" (PLF,286–287), "a strategy for taking up the slack between what is wanted and what is got" (PLF,54). It is a kind of "prayer" in which the poet makes himself over in the image of his imagery (ATH,II,113,fn.). In poetic symbolic action one can place one's burdens on the back of a symbolic scapegoat and whip it out into a verbal desert to die (PLF,45); or one can lift himself up by creating a symbolic hero. Burke thinks of poetry as "prophylactic" or "therapeutic," both for the poet and the reader. Poetry is "stylistic medicine" (PLF,61), and the poet is a "medicine man." As "medicine man" the poet "deals with 'poisons.' . . . [He] would immunize us by stylistically infecting us with the disease," or by providing us with an "antidote." (PLF,64–65.)

The central idea of the theory of symbolic action, and one of the main tenets of the "poetic realism" which Burke hoped would point the way towards a better life, is the belief that "poetry *is* produced for purposes of comfort, as part of the *consolatio philosophiae*. It is undertaken as *equipment for living*, as a ritualistic way of arming us to confront perplexities and risks. It would *protect* us" (PLF,61). Poetry, Burke says, is like the shield of Perseus, for "Perseus . . . could not face the serpent-headed monster without being turned to stone, but was immune to this danger if he observed it by reflection in [his shield] . . . The poet's style, his form (a social idiom) is this mirror, enabling him to confront the risk, but by the protection of an indirect reflection." (PLF,63.) The poet is like Perseus: his superiority is equivalent to the sword, shield, and winged shoes which Hermes and Athena gave to Perseus. His superiority enables him to do what Perseus was able to do with his gifts. Though Burke mentions only one of the gifts — the mirror-like shield which he compares to the poet's style and form — he must certainly have been aware of the others, for without the winged shoes Perseus never could have reached or left the island, and without the sword he could not have slain the serpent-headed monster. Poetry is not just an indirect reflection; it is symbolic *action*. The sword and winged shoes are as important as his shield if one is to take Perseus as Burke's figure of the poet. In moving from the poet-poem to the poem-audience relationship, Burke reverses the Perseus myth, for he contends that symbolic action is the poet's gift to humanity. The first gift — the verbal sword — enables man to do his symbolic slaying of the real or imagined monsters which menace him; the second gift — the verbal shield or mirror — enables man to observe and confront indirectly the monsters which might turn him to stone if they were observed and confronted directly; and the third gift — the verbal winged shoes — enables man to travel to and from the dangerous island and, ultimately, to return home. Together, the three gifts enable man to progress toward the better life.

As wise man, prophet, and medicine man, the poet will perform those charismatic symbolic acts which are the means of man's salvation; priest-like, the critic will mediate between the redeemers and those seeking redemption, interpreting the holy texts and preaching the gospel of the new secular religion. In this way, Burke hopes to effect a cure for the technological psychosis, directing the self away from the universal holocaust which he envisions as the ultimate end of the scientific orientation and toward the better life of purified war which he envisions as the ultimate goal of the poetic orientation.

·III·

THE ANALYSIS OF
POETRY AS
SYMBOLIC ACTION

i

THE ASSUMPTIONS

BURKE DEFINES POETRY as symbolic action, which means it is symbols in action, verbal action that is symbolic of something, and verbal action that performs a vital psychological and physical function for poet and reader alike. To consider poetry as symbols in action is to study it as poetry, more or less for its own sake; to consider poetry as verbal action that is symbolic of something and that performs some vital function is to study its extra-literary meanings and functions. The first approach Burke calls "intrinsic," and the second "extrinsic." The intrinsic approach is necessary because one ought to study something in terms of what it is and because much poetry obviously is created and read for its own sake; but the extrinsic approach is also necessary because, for writer and reader alike, poetry is often a means to some other end. Burke believes that both extreme positions are unrealistic. A purely intrinsic approach tends to deny the many rhetorical functions which poetry performs and to look with incredulity upon the notion that poetry transmits knowledge of many kinds. A purely extrinsic approach is finally inadequate because it denies — or will not deal with — poetry itself; such an approach systematically reduces poetry to statement, attitude, archetype, or some kind of statistic, and totally disregards what is unique

The Analysis of Poetry as Symbolic Action

to the literary mode of discourse. For Burke, an ideal theory of literature accepts both approaches and makes them interdependent; this is the reason why he thinks of his own theory as an "ideal" one. The analysis of poetry as symbols in action requires a focus on the techniques of poetry and permits one to do justice to poetry as poetry; the analysis of poetry as verbal action that is symbolic acknowledges the importance of technique (verbal action) but shifts the focus to the content of the symbols; and the analysis of poetry as verbal action that performs a vital function for poet and reader also acknowledges the importance of technique but shifts the focus to the psychological and physical function of the verbal act.

Even though an "ideal" theory of literature were to deal adequately with the nature, meanings, purpose, and function of poetry, it would still have to be selective; one of the areas would receive greater emphasis than the others, one of them would be selected as the generating principle and would control the specific applications of the theory. Sometimes Burke seems to take "the substance of the act within itself" and sometimes he seems to take "the substance of a literary act as placed upon a scene" as his generating principle (PLF,viii). Actually, however, Burke believes there is no act without a scene, and that no analysis of a poem is complete until one has shown how the act functioned in the scene for the agent, or how the act reflects either the scene or the agent or both. Furthermore, Burke maintains that if one takes purpose and function as his generating principle, and approaches "poetry from the standpoint of situations [scenes] and strategies [acts upon a scene], we can make the most relevant observations about both the content and the form of poems. By starting from a concern with the various tactics and deployments involved in ritualistic acts of membership, purification, and opposition, we can most accurately discover 'what is going on' in poetry." (PLF,124.) This is so because

when you begin to consider the situations behind the tactics of expression, you will find tactics that organize a work technically *because* they organize it emotionally. . . . Hence, if you look for a man's *burden,* you will find the principle that reveals the structure of his unburdening; or . . . if you look for his problem, you will find the lead that explains the structure of his solution. His answer gets its form by relation to the questions he is answering. (PLF,92.)

Thus, Burke causally links problem, solution (or poem), structure, purpose, and function, making the last two the pivotal terms. His claim is that "we cannot understand a poem's structure without understanding the function of that structure. And to understand its function we must understand its purpose." (PLF,286.)

A poem for Burke is always designed to "do something" for the poet: it enables him to express himself, it helps him to solve his problems, it purges and redeems him from guilt, and it enables him to effect one of the many changes of identity necessary to the continued growth of self. So when Burke speaks of "purpose" and "function," he has in mind the poet's private purpose in writing the poem and the personal and private function of that poem for the poet. If the critic can "discover what the poem is doing for the poet, [he] . . . may discover a set of generalizations as to what poems do for everybody," and "with these [generalizations] in mind," the critic would "have cues for analyzing the sort of *eventfulness* that the poem contains" (PLF,73). Thus, though Burke thinks of his theory of literature as an "ideal" one, it is still highly selective, for he takes the poet's private and personal purpose in creating, and the private and personal function of the creative act for the poet as his generating principle, and argues that this point of departure will enable one to deal most adequately with the nature and meaning of poetry and with the function of poetry for the reader. This Burke calls the "functional approach" to literature.

Actually, Burke is even more selective. He not only takes purpose and function as his point of departure, but also tells us what the general function of all poetry is. Because all men are naturally "guilty," Burke believes that all poetry acts as a mode of "purification," and an "expiatory strategy." He isolates "evidences of guilt, with corresponding modes of purification, as the major cue leading . . . into the tactics of poetic socialization" (PLF,92). If all poetry functions as purgative-redemptive symbolic action, it follows that the general purpose of all poetry is individual "salvation" and that the general subject of all poetry is the drama of the individual self in quest. Poetry becomes creative moral action and poems become images of the moral self — records of the moral life of the ideal poetic self. It turns out, then, that Burke's "ideal" theory of literature is highly selective, for though it does indeed combine the intrinsic and extrinsic approaches, the theory is built upon the idea that the essence of poetry is the function which it performs as purgative-redemptive symbolic action. Since poetry is not *either* end *or* means, but *both* end *and* means, the true essence of poetry is best derived from a study of it as a purposeful and functional verbal act which had its origin in a number of specific scenes.

Burke's commitment to this "functional" "scenic" approach imposes upon him the necessity of developing a critical method which will enable him to apply the theory of symbolic action fruitfully and convincingly and also permit the application of the theory by others. The theory presents the critic with seemingly insurmountable obstacles; it makes the analysis of any poem as symbolic action turn upon the specific purgative-redemptive function of that poem for the poet. This means that one must correlate scene or agent and act in order to determine purpose (motives and function). Though Burke asserts that the general purpose of all poetry is salvation, that the general function is purgative-redemptive, and that the general burden which all men naturally bear is guilt, salvation, purgation, and guilt are all ultimately private specific variables, buried deep within the individual self. Yet it is these very secrets which Burke must have for the analysis of poetry as symbolic action. Where there is ample biographical material upon which Burke can draw, as in the cases of Hart Crane and Keats, the problem is not especially difficult; but where there is no, or very little, biographical material, as in the cases of Shakespeare and Spenser, the problems of the critic of symbolic action are acute, for he is confronted by symbolic acts written in the secret language of a kind of formalized dream, and, unlike the psycho-analyst, he cannot interview the dreamer. How, then, is the critic to deal meaningfully with poetry as symbolic action? Burke does not say that some poems are symbolic acts; he says that all poetry is symbolic action. What the critic needs is some reasonably accurate — or, as Burke would have it, empirical, scientific — way of extracting the specific motives for a symbolic act from the act itself. Obviously, one cannot do this without making certain basic assumptions about the nature of the poet, the relation between a poet and his poetic acts, the way in which the creative imagination works, and the nature and function of symbols.

These four interrelated groups of basic assumptions are the bridge between the theory of symbolic action and the dramatistic critical method Burke develops to apply it. The first group of assumptions has to do with the nature of the poet. Like Wordsworth, Burke believes that the poet is similar to other men but superior in every way. Thus, though the poet is the ideal self, his problems are the same as other men's and his solutions (poems) have relevance for other men. The similarity of all men is the point of contact between poet and reader; the poet's mind and body are made and work like those of other men. This difference in degree rather than in kind makes possible the assumption that what you find in yourself and other men you may find in the poet, and *vice versa*. Pursued long enough and hard enough this assumption tends to blur distinctions and obscure the real complexity of experience because it sets up a quick and easy shuttle service between the one and the many. However, the assumption is fundamental for Burke; without it he could not move so easily from poetry to non-poetry, from function for some poets to function for all poets, from function for poets to function for readers, from parts to the whole, from particular examples to all-inclusive generalizations.

The second group of assumptions has to do with the relation between the poet and his poetic acts. Since the poet is superior in every way, it follows that what he says is likely to be very valuable. This is so, Burke asserts, because all poems are presumably deeply personal and about what profoundly engrosses the poet. Poems spring from the very sources of the poet's being, and in the course of the creative process there is a transfer, or transmutation, of this being into symbolic form. Hence every poem is charged with the being of the poet and becomes part of a symbolic autobiography. Burke assumes that the essential self of a poet at a particular stage in his quest is contained, in symbolic form, in any substantial poem he wrote at that particular time. All poems are metaphors of the self. Assuming that a man wrote for most of his mature life, as Yeats did, the whole quest, and all of the transformations which the self underwent as it moved toward unity of being, would be faithfully recorded in the symbolic language of poetry. Theoretically, at least, it is possible that one could reconstruct the individual drama of a self in quest from the poems.

The third group of assumptions has to do with the workings of the creative imagination and explains why poems are *always* charged with the being of the poet and hence are symbolic autobiographies. Though Burke has never claimed that creating a poem is the same as dreaming or that a poem is the same as a dream, he believes that creating and dreaming are, in many ways, very similar. According to the psycho-analytic theory of dreams, every act of the dreaming self is purposeful and meaningful in some way; the dreaming self spontaneously generates images and symbols to express or embody certain ideas, emotions, fears, and conflicts; the linkages or associations of images and symbols which the dreaming self makes are always true (if one but knows how to read the language); all dreams are necessarily related to the dreamer and are therefore charged with his being; if one could read them, all dreams would be true images of the dreamer's essential self; and no dream is meaningful when divorced from the dreamer. Burke acknowledges the fundamental dissimilarity between dreaming and creating: the first is primarily unconscious and uncontrollable, whereas the second is primarily conscious and controllable. Still he believes that the dreaming self and the creative imagination are alike in certain respects. Every act of the creative imagination at work is purposeful and meaningful; the creative imagination spontaneously (as well as consciously) generates images and symbols to embody the self's moods and ideas, and like the dreaming self, the creative self cannot lie in the depths of its imagery. (ATH,II,104–105.) The selection and arrangement of images and symbols are thus charged with the secrets of the self: Burke, in fact, assumes that selection and arrangement are partially determined by the most profound, compulsive needs of the self, and hence believes that no poem is finally meaningful when divorced from the self.

The final group of assumptions has to do with the nature and function of symbols. According to Burke, all of a poet's symbols are "charismatic": they glow with the secrets of the self which the poet inevitably infuses into them. Symbols and symbolic structures are charged, not only with public but with private meaning; each symbol has implicit in it an almost infinite number of public and private identifications. Symbols are mergers, marvelous syntheses, which fuse in a single word, act, or work "a complexity of factors that could not be verbally extricated in a lifetime" (ATH,II,31–32). "A symbol," Burke says, may "fuse an author's attitude toward his parents, his friends, his state, his political party, his métier, his memories of childhood, his hopes for the future, etc." (ATH,II,28). To take one of Burke's favorite examples, a house as symbol (and for Burke any house in a poem is symbolic) could mean security, mother, father, privacy, sexual pleasure (or the reverse), love, hate, imprisonment, kingdom, chaos, failure (as a child, husband, or father), achievement, creation, and the like, depending upon the poet who used it and the way in which he used it. A house as symbol could mean any or all of these things because it is conceivable that a poet could have identified or fused all of them with house.

All symbols, then, are charismatic; they glow with the secret identifications of the self which used them; they function as "vessels" which can fuse or merge a myriad of ideas, attitudes, feelings, and meanings (ATH,II,77–78). And all symbols are mysterious, both in the way they function and in the totality of their meaning, for, theoretically at least, every complex symbol an author uses has implicit in it the totality of that author's self. If one could track down (or reconstruct) all of the associations which a symbol has for a particular poet, the total meaning of the symbol would be equivalent to the poet's essential self at the time the symbol was used. Like a snowball which has been rolling down a hill as long as the poet's life, the symbol gets bigger and bigger with meaning. If the poet uses it on a certain occasion in a particular poem, it is as big with private meaning as it has had time to roll; if the poet uses the symbol at a later period, it still has implicit in it all of its previous meanings and all that it may have picked up as it continued to roll. Thus, if a house at one time meant hate, terror, and incest for a poet because of a particularly unhappy childhood, trouble with his parents, and basically erotic love for his sister, house would always have this as part of its total meaning, even though the poet later married happily and house came to mean love, joy, blessing, and normal sexual fulfillment to him. In this way symbols are charged with the secrets of the self and become iridescent with the mysterious glow of the poet's self.

These four groups of assumptions are fundamental; they support Burke's theory of symbolic action and determine the critical method developed to apply it. The superiority of the poet and of poetry as a way of knowing and acting answers the first of the ontological questions which Burke says the critic of literature must ask himself. It indicates why one should study the poet and poetry: one is the ideal self and the other is the ideal self in thought and action. All of the other assumptions, as well as the theory of symbolic action, answer the second ontological question: they tell one what to look for. What Burke looks for, of course, is the drama of the self in quest, and all that this implies for him. The two ontological questions — why and what — must be followed by the three methodological ones — how, when, where — if the critic is to ask and answer the five fundamental questions about literature (PLF,68). The critic must know what to look for, and why; and how, when, and where to look for it. When and where are easy: one always looks for evidences of representative and purgative-redemptive symbolic action in poetry, and one looks for it everywhere in poetry. How is not quite so easy; in fact it is enormously difficult and calls for the most ingenious and crafty methodological maneuvers. At best, poetry as symbolic action is a kind of private code, and the critic of symbolic action a kind of cryptologist whose main object is to break the code so that he can understand and make public the vital secrets being transmitted.

Somewhat facetiously, Burke once said "cryptology is all." This is a wonderfully accurate remark about Burke's own endeavor; it tells one that the end — breaking the secret code of poetry in order that we might all be saved — both generates and justifies the means. As

[71]

a cryptologist, Burke himself is remarkably inventive and ingenious; he is also brilliantly intuitive, making the leaps to perception which no statistics and no critical apparatus, however formidable, can make. Any critical method is systematic and inductive only up to a point; by emphasizing certain things, it can coach certain kinds of intuitions, certain startling and illuminating insights into such things as the author's self, a given work, even a whole body of works. But, finally, a methodology has the limitations of a machine; it is impersonal, and only most productive when it is applied by an intuitive critical intelligence. Though Burke surely realizes this, and in his own applied criticism illustrates it, he sometimes writes as if it were not true and makes extravagant claims for what he likes to call his "statistical," "empirical," "inductive," and "scientific" critical method. He assumes that if we master the method we can *always* break the code. Often, after a brilliant assault on a work which bewilders the reader with insights into its structure and meaning, Burke says, "see what the 'statistical' 'dramatistic' critical method can do!" What he should say, of course, is "see what *I* can do with this method." Where "cryptology is all," any method can take one only so far; the rest is Burke — a wonderfully perceptive mind contemplating a work of literature.

This does not mean that Burke has no critical method which can be taken over by others and profitably applied, or that no one but Burke can fruitfully analyze poetry as symbolic action; it means only that no study can do justice to a first-hand Burke analysis, and that in spite of what Burke says, a critical method is finally inductive only up to a certain point. If cryptology is all, a Burke analysis of a poem as symbolic action is method plus hunches, guesses, intuitive leaps, and sheer speculation.

In order to break the code and get at the secrets, Burke starts with the methodological proposition that "the main ideal of criticism . . . is to use all that is there to use" (PLF,23). Though Burke has never explicitly stated it, there is a second methodological proposition which he follows in practice. Using one of Burke's own syntactical maneuvers, one has only to transpose two words to make the first proposition read: "the main ideal of criticism . . . is to use all that there is to use." These two propositions, when properly understood, state the central tenets of the dramatistic critical method which Burke developed for the analysis of poetry as symbolic action. According to Burke, a work of literature is an act; about this act the critic can ask himself five general questions: where, when, and under what circumstances was it enacted; what is it in itself and what does it mean; who enacted it; with what was the act performed; and why was the act performed? Translated into the language of dramatism, the five questions become: what is the *scene* of the *act*; what is the nature and meaning of the *act*; what *agent* performed the *act*; what *agencies* did he use; and for what *purpose* did the *agent* in the particular *scene* perform the *act* using the *agencies* he did? Depending upon the circumstances, what "is there to use" varies greatly. With an anonymous poem arbitrarily dated, one has only the single poem and the agency — in this instance, words. There is no specific scene at all, and no agent; lacking these, one has no hints as to what the private, extra-literary purpose may have been, beyond, of course, what can be extracted from the poem. Given a poem by a known author who wrote a number of poems and for whom we have some fairly exact biographical information, the amount of what "is there to use" increases. The poem now has a number of known scenes, for it can be placed historically, perhaps regionally, perhaps even socially; there is a known agent whose life might help elucidate the poem; besides the poem there are other similar acts by the same agent which can be used to analyze the one act; the agency, words, remains known and constant, and whatever special meanings some words had during the given historical period would now be available; and anything from the various scenes, the agent, the other acts of that agent, and the agency can now be used to help determine the private, extra-literary purpose. With any poem, there are two things which are always given: these are the agency, which is always words, and the characteristics of the act, which include such things as plot, structure, imagery, genre, and prosody. There is almost always one unknown, which is the private, extra-literary purpose. The two remaining factors — scene and agent — may or may not be known; if they are known at all, the amount of knowledge that one has of them can vary enormously.

So, when Burke says that the main ideal of criticism is "to use all that is there to use" he literally means what he says. However, there is much more "there" than meets the eye because of certain relationships which necessarily exist between the various terms of the pentad (scene, act, agent, agency, and purpose). Burke calls these "ratios"; and they constitute a kind of Burkean logic. Here again, what Burke starts with is the act — that is, the poem — and what he wants to know is the purpose. No act takes place in a vacuum: it has a scene, or scenes, an agent, an agency, and a purpose. Hence, there are various relationships which must exist between the act and the other four terms in the pentad. The most obvious of these ratios are scene-act, agent-act, agency-act, purpose-act, and act-act. The other possible ratios are scene-agent, scene-agency, scene-purpose; agent-purpose, agent-agency, and agency-purpose. Altogether there are eleven ratios, and probably only with act can there be a reflexive ratio. Each ratio contains two terms and each asserts a causal or equational relation between them. For example, every poem is written at a certain time in a particular place or places in a certain climate of opinion; these scenes, or physical, psychic, and historical environments, influence the poems enacted in them in the most profound way and, according to the scene-act ratio, are alway reflected in the poem. Actually, the scene-act ratio establishes a number of causal relations between scene and act: any scene, from a university campus to a whole culture, is characterized by a particular orientation; this orientation tends to generate problems because it automatically limits the range of acts by approving of some and disapproving of others; accordingly, one gets acts (poems) of acceptance and rejection. In the first, the positive values of the orientation or scene are carried over and directly reflected in the poem, and usually the negative values are either implied or directly reflected. A classic example is Tennyson's *In Memoriam*. In the second, the positive values of the orientation are explicitly rejected and their opposites, or some new set of values, affirmed, and, as in the first, both are directly reflected in the poem. A classic example is *The Waste Land*. Either way, as with the self of the poet, the act always contains the scene in which it was enacted. In fact, according to the Burkean logic of the scene-act ratio, the act contains ingredients of all the scenes in which it was enacted, for every poem has implicit in it a set of ideas, moral values, a social system, and the like. They are there, in the imagery and structure, if one wants to look for them. Thus, the scene not only controls the act to a certain extent, but often generates the problem for which the poem is a solution, and often provides the values which the poem affirms.

Just as any poetic act is charged with its scene, so also is it charged with the self of the agent. The agent-act ratio is but a variant of the scene-act ratio, though there are key differences between them. In the agent-act ratio one has to deal with both a causal and an equational relation which exists between the poet and his poems. A poem, Burke says, is the "dancing of an attitude." This is not only a stunning phrase but a loaded one, especially if analyzed in terms of the logic of the pentad, and particularly the agent-act ratio. The phrase makes an assertion about what is "there" in a poem to use; it says that, like the poet who wrote it, a poem is both body and mind; moreover, the poem is body and mind in action. Poems do not state attitudes; they dance them. Though Burke never actually uses the phrase, he believes that a poem is also "the dancing of a self." Thus, for Burke, a representative selection of a man's poems would be a symbolic equivalent of the man himself; or, in some cases, because of the operation of Burke's favorite trope, synecdoche, a single representative act might be equal to the man himself. Since a poem is the dancing of an attitude or the dancing of a self, it is going to contain both psychic and physical terms, both mental and physiological processes and conflicts. If, for example, a man had some physical disease, one would find signs of it in the imagery, structure, and prosody of the work.

According to Burkean logic, the poetic act is charged with both the scene and the agent; both are "there to use" in the analysis of poetry as symbolic action. A third key relationship exists between agency and act, which is expressed by Burke as the agency-act ratio. Just as an act derives part of its substance from the scene in which it is enacted and the agent who enacted it, so it derives part of its substance from the agency used to enact it. In literature, the agency is always words, either written or spoken; sometimes music is added when a poem is set to music, and in drama physical props and bodily movement are added. Agency, like scene and agent, initially limits or controls the act: one cannot do with tools what one can do with words. But each agency, like each scene and agent, has a certain potential, certain essential characteristics which are inherent in it. According to the agency-act ratio, these characteristics of language as a whole are inherent in any single poetic act. Again employing Burke's favorite trope, the part contains the essential ingredients of the whole. For example, verbal action is an externalization of the internal, an expelling and a release; in this sense, it is like other excretions of the body, such as urine, semen, feces, and sweat. For Burke, then, speech is essentially cathartic and curative. By the logic of the agency-act ratio, all verbal acts contain this cathartic, curative ingredient. It is "there" to be used in the analysis of poetry as symbolic action. There is also in language and the use man makes of it, a driving tendency toward higher and higher levels of abstraction, culminating finally in "god-terms" and the idea of god — the term of terms. A simple example would be biological and zoological classification and a complex example would be Plato's *Phaedrus*. According to the logic of the agency-act ratio, all poetic acts contain this movement toward higher and higher levels of abstraction. Finally, verbal symbols for Burke are miracles of synthesis; they can unite logical opposites. In fact, Burke believes that because all symbols unite logical opposites each symbol contains its opposite. For this reason, another of Burke's favorite tropes is the mystical oxymoron. Just as an act contains its scene and agent, so a symbol contains its opposite. This essential characteristic of complex verbal symbols is, by the logic of the agency-act ratio, also "there to use" in the analysis of poetry as symbolic action.

Thus far, the poetic act has been charged in various ways and degrees by scene, agent, and agency; in a somewhat similar way, a poetic act is also charged with its purpose. According to the logic of the act-purpose ratio, the kind of act (poem, play, prose-fiction)

The Analysis of Poetry as Symbolic Action

as well as the selection and arrangement of detail within the act are largely controlled by the author's conscious purpose. But since the creative imagination sometimes spontaneously generates images and symbols to express itself, the selection, and sometimes the arrangement of detail, must be controlled by the author's unconscious purpose. Since Burke seems to believe that the creative imagination is invariably right, guided as it is by a deeper logic of the self which gives it an almost unfailing sense of unity, it does not really matter whether the purpose is overt, covert, or both. Burke's own analyses show that he feels both kinds of purpose are usually operating all the time and that somehow, quite miraculously, they complement each other. What Burke is really interested in is the author's private purpose — what the poem does for the poet — so that purpose tends to shade off into function. The result of this is that Burke tends to use purpose and function interchangeably — the purpose of a poetic act is always the private function it performs for the poet. The act-purpose ratio therefore is really an act-function ratio. Whatever the author says, a poem is never written *purely* for its own sake. Even if there is no overt function, there is a covert one. Every poem is something of a compulsive act, performed in response to some of the poet's deepest needs. A poet writes because he has to, because there is something curative about poetic action itself. Now if, as Burke says, the selection and arrangement of detail — that is, the imagery and structure — of a poem are largely controlled by the author's covert as well as overt purpose, it follows that the poem will be charged with this covert, private purpose, and somehow, in the symbolic subterfuges of poetry, it will be "there to use" in the analysis of poetry as symbolic action.

Milton's overt purpose in *Lycidas*, for example, was to write a pastoral elegy commemorating the death of his friend, affirming God's grace and his friend's immortality. Along the way, also as part of his overt purpose, he interjected some social criticism which, according to the tradition of the pastoral elegy, was quite proper. But Burke notes that Milton also had a covert purpose — the poem performed a vital purgative-redemptive function for him — and this, as well as the overt purpose, controlled the selection and arrangement of detail. As Burke explains this covert purpose:

"Lycidas" was written in 1637. Milton traveled in 1638 and 1639. And for the next twenty years thereafter, with the exception of an occasional sonnet, he devoted all his energies to his polemic prose.

These dates, coupled with the contents of the poem, would justify us in contending that "Lycidas" was the symbolic dying of his poetic self. It was followed by a period of transition (the "random casting" of travel). And then he focused upon the work of his "left hand." During this prose period, except for the occasional sonnet, he hid "that one talent which it is death to hide."

. . . in "Lycidas" he testifies that he is holding his dead self in abeyance, and that it will rise again. For after the funereal solemnities of his catalogue of flowers, he adds a coda:

Weep no more, . . .

So the poet remained, for all his dying; and at the Restoration, after the political interregnum of Cromwell, he would be reborn. "Paradise Lost" is the fulfilment of his contract, though he returns to the poetic matrix as one of the "blind mouths" he tells us about in "Lycidas." (ATH,I,111–113,fn.)

Even if one did not have the biographical material here used, Burke would still maintain that the private function which the poem performs for the poet is contained in the poetic act itself, and that an analysis of the structure (which moves, with only a single interruption devoted to a polemic against the church, from death to rebirth) and of the imagery, would yield the same results. By the logic of the act-purpose-function ratio, it has to be there.

The poetic act is charged, controlled, and limited in various ways and degrees by scene, agent, agency, and purpose. Each of these relations is described by Burke in one of the ratios, which is sometimes causal, sometimes equational, and sometimes both. One final ratio remains, the reflexive act-act ratio. In *Counter-Statement* this matter was discussed as "conventional form," and treated as one of the five kinds of form which an author may use to arouse and gratify emotions and to unify his work. In *Permanence and Change* and *Attitudes toward History*, Burke renames the idea and deals with it as "the recalcitrance" inherent in certain materials, forms, and situations. Burke's point is that certain things make demands of their own which one cannot deny without destroying either them or himself. Finally, the idea is again renamed in the *Grammar of Motives* and there dealt with under "Pure Act." In a typical Burkean maneuver, the ideas of "conventional form," "recalcitrance," and "pure act" are combined into a single complex concept which can be called the reflexive act-act ratio. A pure act is one in which the sole purpose is the performance of the act for its own sake. Burke's example is God's creation of the world and man. Under these circumstances the pentad becomes a reflexive duad, the essence of which is pure action: all causal factors are internalized, for God is his own scene and agency, the act is its own purpose, and the agent's motive is action for its own sake. Stated as a formula, one gets the great Burkean reversible paradigmatic ratio: agent is act, act is agent. Sometimes, though the meaning remains the same, the formula is expressed as scene is act, act is scene. The formula states as equational what is primarily causal; and it reduces the pentad and ratios, which seem to be machinery for studying the multiple causes of an act, to a single reversible equation, which in essence makes the four outside causes equal to the act. In other words, it internalizes them so that theoretically (that is, ideally) the act *is* or *equals* the scene, agent, agency, and purpose which caused it.

The reflexive act-act ratio has two seemingly contradictory implications for the study of literature. The first has been partly covered, but deserves a brief restatement here. Burke maintains that what is true of the pure or paradigmatic act is true of all specific poetic acts. Stated as formula, this means that poetic act equals scene, agent, agency, and purpose. Stated in the metaphor used throughout this section, it means that the act is charged with its scene, agent, agency, and purpose and that they can be induced from it. Stated in terms of the two methodological propositions, it means that "all that is there to use," like the ratio itself, is reversible and therefore equal to "all that there is to use." The second implication is the one suggested by the reflexive act-act ratio itself. When a man writes a poem, prose-fiction, or drama he is partly motivated by the poetic act as an end in itself, and partly limited by the formal, conventional demands of the act. For example, a man may write a sonnet or, as in Milton's case, a pastoral elegy, partly because he wants to write such a poem. Once committed to either prose or poetry, to the lyric, dramatic, or narrative mode, and to a particular genre, the author finds that the act not only makes demands of its own, but has certain built-in resources of its own which beg to be exploited. At a certain point, Burke says, the work of literature partly begins to write itself. He is not talking about automatic writing, but about the fact that any work of literature, and especially those cast in some conventional form, generates demands of its own which the author must meet.

The two implications are then joined by Burke and may be stated as follows: though the poetic act is partly undertaken as an end in itself, and though the poetic act makes formal demands of its own which may have nothing to do with the author's private purpose and, in fact, may be in violent conflict with it, the work is still the symbolic act of the agent who wrote it and is therefore equal to him. For example, consider the sonnet: if one begins to examine the variations within this "set form" Burke's point becomes immediately obvious and relevant. Though the form makes demands of its own, each creative agent uses the form in his own way; thus, though the general form of the sonnet is set, the particular form of an individual sonnet or group of sonnets becomes symbolic of the poet. Sometimes the poet breaks the form, and this in itself is symbolic. Meredith is particularly interesting because he obviously had a sonnet sequence in mind when he wrote *Modern Love*, but wrote extraordinary sixteen-line sonnets made up of four quatrains (or two octaves) rhyming in the Italian manner. Merrill Moore compulsively wrote sonnets (forty-five thousand, at least) and worked so many variations on the form that he all but destroyed it. Cummings often wrote sonnets and then visually destroyed the form by typographical eccentricities. All of this is not just technically interesting, it is symbolically "loaded." Burke would say that Spenser varied the rhyme scheme and tended to write sonnets with interlocked rhymes and no divisions at all for profoundly personal reasons; that he met the demands of the set form in his own way, and this being so, the very form of his poem, the structure, is symbolic.

The Analysis of Poetry as Symbolic Action

Assuming that a good poet knows what he is doing, every variation within a set form becomes significant in the analysis of poetry
as symbolic action. Though the conventions themselves are impersonal, the variations are not. They constitute the personality of the
work; they glow with the secrets of the poet's private self. Hopkins'
metrical and rhythmical experiments, and his tendency to pack a
sonnet to the point where the fourteen-line structure cannot contain
the subject; and Wordsworth's peculiar inability to make his sense
divisions coincide with his rhyme divisions: all these may be dealt
with not only in technical terms, but in terms of personality. They
are all reflections of the artist's constant battle with his recalcitrant
material, his battle to shape an impersonal body of material to meet
his personal needs. According to Burke, no poem is anonymous.
Though a man may want to be a poet above everything else, his personal and private needs will partly control even his principal mode
of expression, such as lyric, narrative, or dramatic; the repeated use
of particular conventional forms, as with Auden and the sonnet;
the refusal to use any conventional forms, as with Whitman and
Roethke; the use of only very strict conventional forms, as with
Dylan Thomas in his later poems; the tendency to write in only one
form as with Frank O'Connor and the short story; and finally, the
tendency to destroy deliberately the very form one has chosen, as
with Joyce in *Finnegans Wake*, and Thornton Wilder in *Our Town*
and *The Skin of Our Teeth*. Thus, though the poetic act is partly
undertaken in and for itself, and though it makes demands of its
own, the form of the work is still charged with the secrets of the
self which produced it.

An enormous amount of material, then, is "there to use" in the
analysis of poetry as symbolic action. Two very concrete things are
always there: the act and the agency. Two rather general things are
always there: the poem as an expression of self, and the poem as
purgative-redemptive symbolic action. Two other things are usually
there in varying degrees: the poem's scene, and other acts by the
poem's author. Originally Burke meant by this proposition that it
was unrealistic to deny the critic the use of extrinsic sources in the
analysis of poetry, and that the critic ought to be able to use all that

was there to use. In Coleridge's case, for example, this meant such things as all the other poems, the letters, all the biographical material, and all the varied prose works. An example of how this approach works can be found in Burke's scattered remarks on Coleridge in *The Philosophy of Literary Form*. Though some of Burke's conclusions are perhaps suspect, his approach is, as he says, scientific, statistical, inductive. The material is there to use, and when Burke says that a particular image has these meanings in Coleridge, he can cite the various contexts in which the image occurs to show that it does indeed have those meanings. It is, therefore, perfectly legitimate to use whatever outside material is available in the analysis of a poem. As everyone knows, however, there is often little or no outside material; rather than drop the principle, Burke converted what is essentially a method into a theory. He did this by making everything extrinsic intrinsic. That is, he argued from the evidence derived from cases where all the outside or extrinsic material was there and could be used that, even where there is no actual extrinsic material, it was there once and is somehow buried in the poem. So, "to use all that is there to use" theoretically means to look for all that should be there, or, as Burke would have it, must be there. Theoretically, at least, Burke moves from the assertion that the act is caused by the scene, agent, agency, and purpose to the assertion that the act is equal to the scene, agent, agency, and purpose. The logic is: since "caused by" therefore "equal to." This reductive or synecdochic logic is thoroughly characteristic of Burke.

Burke reduces the number of things to look for but increases the number of ways in which to look for them. In order to analyze a poem as symbolic action one must use all that is there to use in order to get at all that should be there; actually, however, in order to dredge the poem of its secrets, one must use all that there is to use. For example, since the poetic act contains its scene, and the scene may be natural, familial, economic, social, political, philosophical, or theological, coordinates from these areas may be used in the analysis of poetry in order to determine its scene. Since the poetic act also contains its agent, and the agent is both psychic and physical, coordinates from neurology, biology, and psychology may be used in the analysis of poetry in order to correlate agent and act. Since a poem is a verbal act, the coordinates of semantics, rhetoric, and grammar may be used in the analysis of poetry as symbolic action. Since the poetic act contains its purpose (function) and since Burke maintains that the general function of all poetry is purgative-redemptive, the religious and non-religious terminology of sin, guilt, purification, and redemption may be used in order to determine the specific purpose and function for the agent. Similarly, the coordinates of ethics, anthropology, comparative religion, and mythology may be taken over and used in the analysis of poetry. Finally, since the poetic act also "contains" itself, that is, has poetry as one of its scenes, whatever is known and relevant about poetry may be used.

No one can master all of these fields. A critic cannot possibly use all that there is to use. As is Burke's practice, however, one can use whatever is available to him for a single purpose. That single purpose for Burke is the drama of human relations as it is recorded in literature. It is in this way that Burke reduces the number of things to look for and expands the ways of looking. In order to determine the specific purgative-redemptive function which a poem performs for the poet, Burke believes that the critic should use all that there is to use, for ultimately he is not just concerned with the formal beauty of a verbal structure, but with its function as an agency of "human rescue" (PLF,260).

ii

THE METHOD

Burke's critical method is deceptively simple. One begins with an analysis of "structure," which Burke defines as "what follows what and why." Every kind of progression is covered under structural analysis. The most important of these are plot (sequence of external events); action ("spiritual movement," or sequence of internal reactions); pattern of experience (the simple and complex patterns of psychic and physical experience resulting from conflicts within an agent and the interaction between agent, other agents, scene, and the like); spatial movement (up, down, in, out, north, south, east, west); tonal progression; chronological progression (seasonal progression, biological growth, historical change); scenic progression; and qualitative progression (from dark, to gray, to light imagery; from rot, to purgation, to redemption imagery; from innocence to corruption to depravity). The first step in the analysis of a poem as symbolic action requires an exhaustive descriptive and analytic study of its structure in order to determine what follows what, and why.

An analysis of the progressive forms of a work leads quickly to the realization that all works have other kinds of form as well, and that to do a structural analysis one must also do a cluster analysis. The object of a cluster analysis is to find out what goes with what, and why; it is done by making an index and a concordance for a single work or group of works by the same author. The index is necessarily selective; one is guided by terms that are either of high intensity or high frequency. The former are terms which are naturally charged, such as love, sex, society, or are particularly significant in a given author, such as the rose garden in Eliot; the latter are frequently repeated terms or groups of terms. Whereas the index is selective, the concordance aims at being exhaustive; every context in which a term either implicitly or explicitly appears is listed. An index of the significant repetitions in a work or group of works often only reveals what is fairly obvious to any attentive reader; recurrent settings, themes, characters, types of characters, pairs of characters, progressions, contrasts, and images. An index is primarily statistical and descriptive. For example, it would tell you that flower is a significant repetition in Cummings. If one pursued this lead in order to find out what was repeatedly associated with flower in various contexts he would find that flower and enjoyed mistress are linked again and again in the same context. Sometimes, however, he would find flower in very strange contexts which do not seem to make any sense, such as "petal-drops — flower falling," or "your house — this brightly flower." According to Burke, there is really nothing very puzzling about these linkages, for a concordance would provide the critic with an equation which may be used to help explain the meaning of flower every time it occurs. In Cummings, flower equals enjoyed mistress, and so in the first line Cummings is talking about rain that reminds him of his mistress, and in the second he is talking about a house where he would like to make love to his mistress (ATH,II,98–100).

The same method of analysis may be applied to a very different poet, with rather different results. In Wordsworth's *Tintern Abbey*, the obvious pivotal terms revealed by an index are nature, society (the city), the self, and God. A cluster analysis of the poem discloses that society (the city, non-nature) is surrounded in its various contexts by the following terms: lonely room, weariness, mystery, burden, heavy, weary weight, unintelligible world, darkness, joyless, fretful, unprofitable, fever, evil tongues, selfish, dreary intercourse of daily life. Nature is surrounded in its various contexts by the following terms: repose, beautiful, sweet sensations, felt in the blood and heart, purer mind, tranquil restoration, pleasure, kindness, love, blessed mood, sublime, lightened, serene ecstasy, harmony, deep power of joy, knowledge of reality, animal joys, dizzy raptures, joy of elevated thoughts, God, Prime Mover, anchor of purest thoughts, nurse, guide, guardian of heart, soul and moral being, fidelity, quietness, lofty thoughts, cheerful faith, and healing thoughts. Once finished with the concordance, and working only with this poem, one would have a number of general equations: society equals a crushing burden, sickness, chaos, worthlessness and evil; nature equals a burdenless life, health, order, everything that is valuable, moral goodness, guidance, and so forth; God equals nature; the self equals nature. Without being excessively reductive, one can say that in this poem society equals everything bad, and nature equals everything good. This is surely a great oversimplification of life, but it is what the poem says. Whether consciously or unconsciously, Wordsworth associated everything negative with society: loud noises, physical fatigue, being overburdened, unintelligibility, blackness, physical illness, monetary loss, dreariness, moral evil. And, whether consciously or unconsciously, all of the opposites plus a good deal more, he associated with nature. From nature, the self receives every kind of sensory pleasure; it receives as well moral truths, psychic health, knowledge of reality, knowledge of God, faith and harmony; it is nursed, guided, healed, anchored, ordered, blessed, and continuously regenerated by nature. One can say that the self is passively overpowered by nature, quietly persuaded to everything that is good. Nature is consistently linked with feminine qualities and given the attributes of a mother, nurse, and wife. Nature, like the self, is passively active, which perhaps accounts for the great stillness at the center of Wordsworth; the self is quietly, even gently nursed to self-discovery, moral direction, and integration by a benevolent nature. Though a great many other conclusions could be drawn from the evidence presented by the concordance, and really penetrating conclusions could be drawn if a concordance were made of the other major poems so that a larger body of evidence could be examined, enough has been said to demonstrate the method of cluster analysis and the kind of conclusions it leads to. Essentially, it is a way of finding out what something means by finding out what the term is associated with in the poet's mind.

The third major methodological approach which Burke uses is one immediately forced on the mind by the results of a cluster analysis. "A total drama," and by drama Burke here means any complete work of literature,

is analytically subdivided into competing principles, of protagonist and antagonist. . . . each of the "principles" possesses satellites, or adjuncts, some strongly identified with one or another of the principles . . . whereas other characters [or images] shade off into a general overlapping background . . . Such a set of "mediating" characters [or images] is necessary, as a common ground of persons [or images] through which the coöperation of the competing principles can take place. Hence, no matter which of the three the . . . [poet] begins with (agon, protagonist, or antagonist) he cannot give us a full drama [or poem] unless he imaginatively encompasses the other two. (PLF,76.)

Sometimes Burke calls this the principle of the "agon," sometimes "dramatic alignment," and sometimes simply "what vs. what." The difference between cluster analysis and the analysis of the dramatic alignments is like the difference between the gathering of evidence and the interpretation of it. In *Tintern Abbey*, a cluster analysis reveals that certain things equal nature and certain things equal society and suggests, because of the obvious loading of terms by Wordsworth, that the two are in conflict. An agon analysis converts nature into protagonist, society into antagonist, and locates the drama in the self of the poet; the poem is treated as a dramatic lyric in which the conflict is worked out in images rather than through characters. Though the lyric, unlike a drama, has no plot to give it forward movement, it does have progressive form in so far as it charts the spiritual movement of the self in conflict. Though the self may perform no external act in a lyric poem, it does react by lamenting, praising, meditating, praying, and coming to knowledge, and these movements of the self constitute the progressive form necessary to drama. The implicit or explicit opposition of terms constitutes the conflict necessary to drama and the self of the poet provides the necessary human agent. An agon analysis treats all lyrics as mono-dramas of the self in quest.

Since all narrative and dramatic works have characters, an agon analysis of them is slightly different. Drama itself provides Burke with the paradigm for agon analysis, and its application to this form is more obvious. For example, a cluster analysis of *Othello* reveals three major clusters or "principles," headed respectively by Desdemona, Othello, and Iago. The first is characterized by whiteness, by heavenly images; the third is characterized by blackness and hell images; and the second is characterized by mixed black and white images and movements towards and away from heaven and hell. A superficial structural analysis shows that the mixed character, or the one in whom the drama is centered and the actual protagonist of the play, moves towards and actually merges with the first cluster, then gradually moves away from and actually merges with the third by destroying the main representative of the first; then, finally, rejects the third and re-accepts the first by making public his terrible error and killing his contaminated self. An agon analysis, which would have been preceded by an exhaustive cluster and structural analysis, would work out in detail the nature and implications of the dramatic alignments and the introduction, development, and resolution of the dramatic conflict. It would investigate the principal satellite or adjunct characters, such as Emilia, Cassio, and Roderigo, the fact that each of them, though obviously belonging to one cluster rather than another, is mixed, and like the protagonist (Othello), but not the protagonist principle (the Desdemona or heaven cluster), moves towards and away from the heaven and hell clusters. It would investigate other facts turned up by the intensive cluster and structural analyses, such as the monetary imagery used by Iago; the obscene animal imagery used by Othello; the shifting settings, such as Venice, the sea, and Cyprus; and the significance of the progression from one setting to another. Finally, to suggest a few other things, it would investigate the fact that though, in terms of characters, Othello is the protagonist and Iago the antagonist in the play, Desdemona actually represents the protagonist principle, Iago the antagonist principle, and the play is really about a man (that is a self) torn apart, and finally destroyed, by the internal conflict between the two principles.

An agon analysis of a novel, though much like that of a lyric and a drama, is different because, for one thing, there are more things to work with, the most notable being point of view. However, the method is the same in all cases. For example, a cluster analysis of *Madame Bovary* would turn up some rather interesting facts. In spite of all its seeming objectivity and realism, the novel is a fantastic distortion of the world as one experiences it because, with one or two exceptions, there is only one explicit cluster in the whole novel — the romantic-bourgeois-country-town cluster. Whatever other cluster there is in the novel is there, once explicitly in the person of Dr. Larivière, and the rest of the time implicitly in the person of the omniscient narrator. The only alternative (that is the protagonist principle) offered the reader is Flaubert's attitude toward his subject which is embodied in his polemical and didactic treatment of the subject. Since what happens to Emma, Charles, and Bertha Bovary is hardly drama at all, the real agon of the novel is the artist against middle-class society; the resolution of the drama comes when the artist destroys Emma and Charles and transcends Homais Lheureux and Yonville by savage ironic contemplation.

In Meredith's *The Ordeal of Richard Feverel* there are three main clusters: one headed by Sir Austin Feverel and the system, one by Lucy Feverel and "nature" or "human nature," and one headed by the narrator, or Meredith himself. Sir Austin is the antagonist principle and has as his adjuncts Mrs. Doria, Hippias, Adrian, Heavy Benson, pure reason, science, and super pride (wanting to play god, or providence, using reason as the instrument); Lucy is the protagonist principle and has as her adjuncts Mrs. Berry, Clare, Austin Wentworth, Tom Bakewell, nature, poetry, the heart, natural instincts, love, marriage, humility, beauty, and an enormous number of allusions to myth, pastoral romances, and some of the great figures of innocence in literature. Richard, the protagonist character, is, like Othello, mixed, and in the course of the novel moves towards and away from the antagonist and protagonist clusters; this movement gives the novel its structure. The main drama of the novel is centered in Richard, who, like Othello, mediates between the two clusters. Lady Blandish performs a similar function, and like Emilia, finally migrates from one cluster to the other. After Richard, the principal mediating device is the author, who narrates the novel from a point of view shifting from third person to omniscient first person. Meredith not only mediates between the two clusters, but actually fuses the best elements of both to form a third. Meredith incorporates into the style and frequent interruptions of the forward movement of the novel both reason (comedy, ironic detachment, reflection, analysis) and emotion (feelings of the heart, instinctive compassion, "poetry"), in this way offering an alternative to the other two partly defective clusters in the novel. Lucy, like Desdemona, is naively innocent and lacks both the strength and rational power to defend herself against the combined onslaughts of nature, chance, and the system; consequently, she is destroyed by Sir Austin and Richard, the first of whom lacks the necessary instinctual or acquired compassion to control the inherently destructive powers of reason and pride, and the second of whom has been rendered permanently defective by the misdirected idealism of the first.

These examples of structural, cluster, and agon analysis are, at best, superficial, but they should give some idea of the directions in which such analyses would take one. Essentially reductive, the method approaches all works, whether lyric, dramatic, or narrative, in the same way, looking for the same things. Every work is first indexed and then schematized in terms of the opposed principles or image clusters; then the structure is carefully charted and the work is again schematized in terms of the interplay between the opposed principles and the tonal, plot, or spiritual forward movement generated by the interplay. At this point, an intensive agon analysis can begin, for the critic has now prepared the work so that it can be analyzed as a document of and in the drama of human relations, and more specifically as a literary embodiment of the drama of the self in quest. The opposed principles represent the self's choices, and the movement towards and away from them — the progressive form of the work — represents the quest, the self's journey toward unity of being. The drama of the self in quest, of course, is the idea that lies behind the whole theory of symbolic action, for poetry considered as symbolic action is both a verbal image of this quest and one of the agencies which the self uses in its quest. It is this focus on the self in quest and the insistence on the purgative-redemptive function of poetry which leads Burke to the other techniques of analysis which may properly be said to belong to his critical method. These are pun analysis and "joycing"; archetypal analysis, or what Burke often calls "levels of symbolic action"; and the analysis of the structure as symbolic and purgative. All three methods are designed to get at the same things: the ways in which the self and the quest are symbolized in various kinds of imagery and structure and the ways in which literature functions as purgative-redemptive symbolic action for the self.

In many ways pun analysis is the most characteristic of the three methods because it shows Burke's real center of interest in the analysis of literature as symbolic action. Burke believes that all poets consciously or unconsciously pun all the time, and that usually the concealed or covert meaning of the word is scatological. As Eric Partridge's *Shakespeare's Bawdy* makes clear, what Burke maintains is often true, and the first type of pun analysis which Burke uses is indeed a valuable and legitimate tool. It deals with phonetic puns and all kinds of generally recognized double meanings; it is well illustrated in Partridge's book and in Empson's *Seven Types of Ambigu-*

The Analysis of Poetry as Symbolic Action

ity. A classic example of the first is the following sequence of French words: *mer*, *merde*, *mère* (mother), *Mère* (mother of Jesus), *mère* (mother earth), and *mère* (pure). According to the "logic" of pun analysis, any one of these words covertly contains the meanings of all the others, and the use of any one of them may be examined in context for any of the other possible meanings. The range of meanings, of course, is quite extraordinary: *mer* refers to nature and natural phenomena, and includes all of the many symbolic meanings attached to the sea, such as the uncharted, the unknown, the uncontrollable, death, water as a cleanser, hence purification; *merde* refers to excrement and a physiological process, and includes in it a great many symbolic meanings, such as filth, purification by elimination (catharsis), the value of waste products (fertilizer), disgust and shame produced by filth, abhorrence of the biological; *mère*, as mother, refers to the familial, and suggests childhood, the passive euphoria of the womb, early (and late) sexual attachment to the mother, love, authority; *Mère*, meaning the Virgin Mary, refers to the religious and supernatural, and suggests Mariolatry, morality, the humanization of god; *mère*, as mother earth, refers to nature and natural phenomena, and suggests support, roots, growth, natural laws; finally, *mère*, as purity, refers not to a person, place, or thing, but to a quality, and hence has a social and moral/ethical reference. As the analysis shows, any one of these words contains a multiple pun, for it might refer covertly to any or all of the following points of reference: supernatural, natural, familial, social, and biological. Since any of these covert meanings is always in the offing, at least in French, it is possible that when a poet speaks of the sea he is actually talking about his mother or the Virgin Mary; or when he talks about his mother he may actually be talking about excrement. Because similarity of sound constitutes an identity or association which may exist in the poet's head as well as in fact, a critic would be foolish to take the word *mère* at is face value, for a careful examination of the work in which it appears and the other contexts in which the poet uses it might reveal that the poet really means mother-excrement, or mother-god, and this clue might provide the critic with the lead (or motive) that would explain many of the poet's works. A pun analysis, in other words, provides the critic with quick clues which he can follow up and either accept or reject depending on what other evidence he turns up.

Burke happens to believe that most puns are really scatological ones, and it is this kind that he looks for and usually follows up. In the above example, for instance, Burke would immediately seize on *merde* as the concealed meaning in all the other words, for filth (and its various analogues, such as sin, guilt, crime, shame) is something that needs to be purged and transcended; it is what Burke calls the "fecal motive" which must be expressed (covertly or overtly) before any purgation and redemption can be complete. Since one's "fecal motives" are not usually something one likes to brag about, they are often expressed in a pun. According to Burke, there is never any question that the fecal motive is there; the only problem is how to find it. One method is through pun analysis. Consider, for example, the key word in the title of the Meredith novel discussed earlier: Feverel. The name has two puns in it, the first on fever, the second on the over-all sound of the name, which suggests something like "fever all." There are a number of generally accepted meanings of fever: the first is a "morbid condition of the body characterized by undue rise of temperature, quickening of the pulse, and disturbance of various bodily functions"; the second is "intense nervous excitement"; and the third is sexual burning or fever. Fever may also be a verb, meaning to "affect with or as with fever." Were Burke to make a pun analysis of this name, he would point out that the pun links bodily, psychic, and sexual fevers, and that every member of the Feverel family probably suffers from all three kinds of fever, though one of the three is no doubt the cause of the other two. Before even reading the novel, Burke would select sexual fever as the primary cause, and as he read would examine the novel for sexual guilt, sexual denial, or what he might call "pudenda anxiety." Given the second pun on Feverel, Burke would examine the novel for instances of the ways in which this "pudenda anxiety" renders the Feverels defective in some way, and for the ways in which, as carriers of some disease, they infect and destroy others.

Cryptology is all, Burke says, and so he advocates pun analysis as a means of breaking the symbolic code which the poetic self uses to express its secrets. Aside from phonetic puns which permit a poet to say one thing and mean or suggest another, there are also non-phonetic puns made possible by the double or multiple meaning of various words. All language is full of euphemisms for various things which people will not or cannot talk about directly. Most of these are such things as sexual organs, excretory functions, and sexual intercourse. These three things (urinating, elimination of feces, and sexual orgasm) and everything connected with them, Burke calls the "Demonic Trinity," because from them come most of the sin and guilt which need to be purged. Though pun analysis has many uses, its primary one is to discover the presence of the Demonic Trinity where one least expects it. Elizabethan literature, and especially Shakespeare, is rich in such scatological puns; in fact, scatological is itself such a pun, for it suggests eschatological, and the reason why Burke discusses these matters under the heading of Demonic Trinity. For example, to die is such a pun, for it means both to die physically and to have an orgasm. As Donne, and others, go to great lengths to explain, sexual dying is like physical death because each orgasm deprives you of part of your substance and hence hastens your actual death. The sexual pun on "to die" suggests the sin and guilt associated with sex, for the pun makes sexual intercourse a kind of suicide. Purse and jewels are other sexual puns, which this time link the Demonic Trinity with money; both of these puns appear extensively in *Othello*, Goethe's *Faust*, and *Madame Bovary*. In *Madame Bovary* Emma's money difficulties coincide exactly with the final, frantic sexual expenditure of herself with Léon; and in the novel, whenever Flaubert talks about Emma and money he is also talking about Emma and her voracious eroticism. This kind of pun analysis, which quickly shades off into a study of the various ways in which the Demonic Trinity is expressed in metaphors, deliberately opens up all kinds of passages as well as complete works to sexual interpretation by discovering "fecal motives" everywhere.

Nowhere is Burke's ability to find the "fecal motive" where one least expects it so well illustrated as in the final kind of pun analysis named, appropriately enough, after Joyce's habit of tampering with sounds, sometimes for the sheer delight of it, sometimes to pun by phonetic distortion. A critic "joyces" a word when he phonetically tampers with it to see what other meanings (primarily scatological) are suggested, however remotely. Of all the techniques Burke uses in the analysis of poetry as symbolic action, "joycing" best illustrates what he means when he says that, in the analysis of literature, cryptology is all. Although there are a great many examples of this technique in Burke, one extended application of the principle will serve to illustrate them all.

For many years now Burke has been meditating on and tampering with Keats's "Ode on a Grecian Urn." In *A Rhetoric of Motives*, he finally got around to stating his results, but, somewhat coyly, modestly, and "scientifically," in terms of certain phonetic "laws." With apologies beforehand to the reader, the results, in rather plain English, are as follows: "urn" is "joyced" to read "urine," and the oracular statement which ends the poem is "joyced" to read "body is turd, turd body" (RM,204). Burke's explanation for such tampering is as follows: "Since death, disease, the passions, or bodily 'corruption' generally (as with religious horror of the body) may be variants of the fecal, their transcending may involve a corresponding translation of the fecal." Keats's *Ode*, Burke believes, is a poem about such a transcendence, and in it Keats splits a "distraught state into active and passive, so that the evil element (the suffering) can be abstracted and eliminated, while only purified spiritual activity remains" (RM,317,fn.). It is the body, represented by the sexual and bodily fevers in the poem, which causes the suffering, and by "joycing" Burke attempts to include the other two members of the Demonic Trinity to round out, as he would say, the motivation.

Joycing differs from the first two kinds of pun analysis because it depends on wild guesses and deliberate distortion by the critic. Actually, for Burke, it is often a way of forcing a work to mean what he thinks it ought to mean. Sometimes, however, it is a most useful technique, for poets often deliberately use words which need to be joyced in order to get at their full meaning. Such an example is Prufrock in Eliot's poem, which readily joyces to prude frock and provides one with a valuable insight into the poem. Like joycing,

The Analysis of Poetry as Symbolic Action

the first two kinds of pun analysis are valuable methodological devices, for poets are specialists in words and often consciously use phonetic puns, words with double and multiple meanings, and words whose covert meanings can only be got at by phonetic tampering. However, when pun analysis becomes what one critic has called "peeping thomism," it sometimes becomes obscene, not because Burke so upsettingly reminds us that the mind has a sewer running through it, but because he argues and attempts to demonstrate by means of unbelievable forcing that the sewer is always full of unspeakable filth.

There is a certain amount of forcing in all of Burke's applied criticism; it is the result of messianic zeal and a reductive theory which limits the general content of literary works to the drama of the self in quest and the general function to a purgative-redemptive one. Convinced that the theory of symbolic action (and, later, the dramatistic theory of language developed out of it) can somehow save man in society, Burke zealously applies the theory and sometimes forces and distorts. In this respect, Burke is like the medieval Christian interpreters of literature who took the Christian orientation as the basis of all symbolism and meaning and somehow referred everything back to it, or like the Freudian, Jungian, or Marxist critics of our own time who have done the same thing with their orientations. When Burke makes a pun analysis of a work, experimentally substituting and joycing to get other meanings, he is not just disinterestedly exploring a work for its multiple meanings, but is deliberately tampering to see if he cannot make it another document in and of the Burkean version of the drama of human relations. Joycing, which up till 1945 Burke used primarily to "discover" scatological meanings, and after that to "discover" both scatological and "hierarchic" meanings, is the extreme example of a method created to make a theory work. The method, which Burke applies with a great deal of linguistic mumbo jumbo about cognate sounds and metathesis, is based on the highly suspect assumption that any remote similarity of sound constitutes a similarity or even identity of meaning which the collective conscious or unconscious mind is aware of because the human psyche "works" that way. Unfortunately, every time Burke joyces a word there remain a number of alternative meanings which could also be got by joycing but which Burke arbitrarily rejects because of another suspect assumption: that the covert meaning is always one of the "unspeakables," or one of the ten thousand things which Burke regards as sinful and hence contaminating and hence guilt-inducing and hence in need of being purged. Pun analysis is, therefore, one of the many shuttle devices Burke uses in the analysis of poetry as symbolic action for getting from any kind of subject, diction, imagery, and structure back to the self in quest and the purgative-redemptive function of poetry.

For such an analysis, the critic needs many shuttle devices, because the theory itself maintains that all poetic journeys are purgative-redemptive, and that it is always the poet's self which is purged and redeemed. And the theory itself, which conceives of life as a series of purgative-redemptive dramas, with the self split into various competing identities, moving from conflict to resolution, offers Burke a number of fixed points to which he can always return and from which he can spin out a terminology for analysis. His version of the drama of human relations gives him a means of positing certain archetypes of the self and experience which ultimately become the basis of all symbolism and meaning. What is true of all fundamentally archetypal theories is true of Burke's: it is reductive. The method constructed to apply it is also reductive, for all roads finally lead to the same place.

But the first three parts of Burke's critical method (structure, cluster, and agon analysis) are not reductive in the same way the fourth, fifth, and sixth parts are. The first three can be used by anyone for any purpose, but the last three, though they could be used by anyone, are best used for the analysis of poetry as symbolic action. One of these, joycing, has been discussed. The fifth might be called archetypes of the rhetoric of rebirth and the sixth the dialectic of the Upward or Mystic Way. The fifth part of Burke's method, the analysis of poetry as a rhetoric of rebirth, is primarily a method of relating all images, terms, and subjects to certain archetypes in the purgative-redemptive quest; the sixth, the analysis of poetry as a dialectic of the Upward Way, is primarily a method of relating all progressive

The Analysis of Poetry as Symbolic Action

form to two similar but slightly different archetypal progressions or patterns of experience, the paradigmatic forms of which are to be found in Plato's *Phaedrus*, Dante's *Divine Comedy*, and any classic tragedy, such as the *Oresteia*, *Oedipus Rex* and *Oedipus at Colonus* considered as a single play, *Othello*, and *King Lear*. The fifth and sixth parts of Burke's method overlap to an extraordinary degree and actually complement each other. One deals with what Burke often calls repetitive form and is an extension of cluster analysis, and the other deals with what Burke calls progressive form and is an extension of structural analysis. For convenience, they can be split and discussed separately.

The theory of symbolic action has as its central tenet the idea that all poetry is a rhetoric of rebirth which enables the poet to purge and redeem himself. Thus, the analysis of poetry as symbolic action is hardly possible without some universal grammar of rebirth which enables the critic to name what was purged, examine the mechanics of symbolic purgation, and discuss the process of redemption or rebirth. In the drama of human relations as Burke conceives it, every man has his burdens; and though specific problems outnumber the stars, in general there are two basic kinds: guilt and identity. On the one hand, poetry is a ritual of cure which enables the poet to purge his guilt or, since Burke sometimes uses the word to mean tension or anxiety of any kind, to resolve his tensions and be redeemed; on the other hand, poetry is a ritual of rebirth which enables the poet, by means of symbolic identification, to effect permanent changes of identity. Either way, poetry is essentially persuasive action because it enables the poet to effect a change in himself by means of symbolic manipulation. In a sense, all poetry considered as symbolic action is rhetoric addressed to the self — or the self persuading itself — the purpose of which is individual salvation. So every poem is really a "from-to" affair; by means of the poem the poet moves from burdened to unburdened, from problem to solution, from guilt to expiation, from filth to cleansing, from one self to another, from death to rebirth. Every poem is really a purgation of some kind, an unloading, an unburdening in which something undesirable, filthy, or abhorrent is transferred to a symbolic equivalent and expelled; and every poem is

[97]

really a redemption of some kind in which what was purged is replaced by something new and better or in which the redemption comes simply from the fact that what was undesirable has been expelled. The substance that is continuously purged and redeemed by means of this symbolic rhetoric of rebirth is the author's self, a partly psychic, partly physical entity which is forever in quest of unity of being.

If poetry is in fact a rhetoric of rebirth, and if all men have their burdens (and hence are guilty) and if all men are continuously in search of themselves, then it follows (as Burke maintains it does) that there are going to be certain archetypal motives, images, terms, characters, and structures which will appear and reappear in all poems in varying specific guises. In the analysis of poetry as symbolic action, the problem is not to determine empirically whether the various archetypes of the rhetoric of rebirth are present — they are always present — but to determine by means of what Burke calls "free association" in what particular, specific form they appear. Burke points out, for example, that in most rituals of purification there is a transfer of some kind from the polluted, burdened person to some other person, place, or thing. In almost every purification there is victimage of some kind: some thing, person, or place is contaminated in order that another may be purified; someone dies in order that another may live; someone suffers in order that another may be happy. Because of this there are a number of closely related archetypes which are central to the analysis of poetry as a rhetoric of rebirth: the scapegoat, the sacrificial agent, the victim, the polluted person, place, or thing. These archetypes, of course, appear in various guises in or out of literature. Their presence in any form shows a concern with the polluted-purified-redeemed "cluster of motives"; and because all works are deeply personal expressions of the author's inmost self, their presence in the work automatically shows the author's private problems, albeit somewhat enigmatically, and his solution of them. So, in proceeding with the analysis of a poem as symbolic action, one starts with the proposition that all men experience the polluted-purified-redeemed pattern of experience and that all poetry is an expression of it. The rhetoric of rebirth pattern is itself an enormously complex archetypal pattern of experience which is made up of many other archetypes; like all truly complex patterns, it is capable of being expressed in an almost infinite number of different specific forms, depending upon the content of the individual writer's experience. The real problem in the analysis of poetry as symbolic action is to make an intelligible connection between the highly personal secret language of the individual writer and the archetype; even when using the polluted-purified-redeemed pattern as a key to the basic meaning of the symbolic language of poetry, this is no easy task: the pattern, like the Marxist doctrine or the Jungian orientation, tells one what he is looking for, but it does not make all the connections.

Consider, for example, a poem like Matthew Arnold's *Sohrab and Rustum* (RM,7–10). If the critic starts with the assumption that the poem performs some purgative-redemptive function for the author, his first task is to check the poem for specific forms of any of the archetypes of the rhetoric of rebirth. Sohrab, for example, is a sacrificial agent who dies in order that (1) his father may live, (2) there may be a reconciliation between father and son, and (3) there may be peace between the two armies. Rustum, at the end of the poem, is the polluted person, for both Sohrab's burden and the guilt of having killed his own son are transferred to him and he carries them off with him as his perpetual burden; Sohrab's noble sacrifice of himself is at once a purification and redemption for him, an act which enables him to find himself by finding his father. The poem moves from war (pollution, anxiety, guilt, chaos) to peace (redemption) via sacrificial death (purification); the end of the poem is dominated by river and sea imagery, two common forms of expression for both physical and spiritual cleansing.

To move from the poem itself to the poem as a rhetoric of rebirth for the author is the next task of the critic. According to the theory of symbolic action, the poem *must* be symbolic autobiography and hence must deal with some deeply personal problem which the author faced and solved or tried to solve in the poem. The central problem dealt with in the poem is a familial one: a son searching for his father, a father's refusal to recognize his son, a father's fear of being

[99]

displaced by his son, a son rendered incapable of action by father-awe, a son racked by a sense of inadequacy because he has been rejected by his father without knowing why, a son's terrible longing for and need of his father. Read as symbolic autobiography, the noble, Christ-like Sohrab would be a surrogate for Matthew Arnold, and the god-like, club-wielding Rustum would be a surrogate for his father, Thomas Arnold. Presumably, the poem deals with a problem that cannot be solved in a non-symbolic form in the realm of actual experience and requires a single or repeated solution in the form of symbolic action if the author is not to be corroded by the insoluble problem. Read as symbolic autobiography, the poem tells us that the following problem existed and that it had the following effects on the author: a god-like, seemingly invincible, arrogant father, for reasons which he does not understand and in ways which he is not aware of, rejects and permanently impairs his son by forcing upon him a problem which he never wanted and which he cannot solve; rejected, misunderstood, and mocked as an upstart who thinks he is his father's equal, the son is yet filled with a terrible longing for respect from and recognition by his father; so terrible, in fact, is this need that the son cannot be complete without it. A hero in his own right, the son cannot understand why he has been rejected, and hence feels guilty because he must have failed his father in some way.

Read as a purgative-redemptive symbolic act, the poem solves the problem in the following way: though the son is completely blameless in the poem, he is the one who carries the burdens of longing, anxiety, guilt, inadequacy, and incompleteness because he is fatherless; since the son is surrogate for Arnold, the solution will require a transfer of burdens from Sohrab to some other person and place, preferably Rustum, since, in the poem at least, he is the real guilty party. In the poem, the purification and redemption is effected for Arnold by having Rustum commit the culminating act in a long series of arrogant and ignorant acts: the enraged and blind murder of his own son. By recognizing his terrible error, Rustum assumes the burden of guilt, thus absolving the now noble, sacrificial son; through Rustum's acceptance, Sohrab's long anxiety, guilt, and incompleteness are over, and he dies redeemed and at peace. As a result of the side effects of his sacrifice (peace between the warring armies) Sohrab is further exalted; and through having to bear the burden of his terrible guilt till he dies, Rustum is finally adequately punished for the unjust agony he caused his son. At the end of the poem, through his sacrificial act, Sohrab is rewarded by being symbolically joined with the great river and sea, the compulsive and recurrent images of blessed oblivion in Arnold. In summary, the poem as symbolic autobiography presents the conflict between Arnold and his father, and as purgative-redemptive-symbolic action, it solves the problem by absolving and exalting Sohrab (Arnold) and punishing Rustum (Thomas Arnold) for his ignorance and cruelty.

In *Sohrab and Rustum*, the purifying and redeeming act is a dying, an actual physical change; at the end of the poem Sohrab's new state of being — his redeemed, new self — is indicated both by the river flowing into the maternal sea, and by the state of peace now existing between the previously warring armies. The pollution — generally anything needing to be expelled, changed, or transcended — is indicated by the war generally, by the "ignorant," "blind" combat between father and son, and by all the bad attributes which Rustum possesses. All of these signs can be considered images of the rhetoric of rebirth, Arnold's specific images of Burke's archetypes. In one way or another all of them can be taken back to the trinity of terms which constitutes the essence of symbolic action: pollution-purification-redemption. In analyzing poetry as symbolic action one looks for specific images of these three archetypes; and usually, because of Burke's synecdochic logic, the presence of any one of the three suggests the implicit presence of the others. Burke himself says, "no purification is complete until the fecal motive has been expressed and redeemed." Now fecal is simply another word which Burke uses to indicate the pollution archetype — that which needs to be transcended, expelled, changed, expiated, or solved. Analyzed as symbolic action, the fecal or pollution archetype is indicated by all the negatively charged persons, places, things, and ideas — by all that the author wishes to reject. Almost at random, here are some of the hundreds of fecal images which Burke has, or might have, cited; the list, with the running commentary, will show as well as anything how Burke employs the archetype idea, shuttling always from an extraordinary variety of images back to a fixed point.

Any one of the Demonic Trinity in any form is a fecal image: this would include the fecal, sexual, and urinal orifices; the products of all three; anything resembling them in shape, size, or color; the clothing that covers them, which, Burke feels, is contaminated by proximity; the acts themselves, and especially defecation, which is the physical counterpart of symbolic action; and its opposite, constipation; various perversions of the sexual act which are indications of special kinds of pollution — masturbation, for example, indicates an obsession with the reflexive self; incest indicates an obsession with the family, or the oedipal situation; sodomy indicates an obsession with the same sex, or unisexuality, and so forth. As with any really complex set of motives, the possibilities here are nearly endless, especially when one remembers that talk of sex or elimination may be symbolic of something else, and that talk of something else may be symbolic of sex or elimination. For example, in treating *Ethan Brand*, Burke suggests that the kiln in which Brand immolates himself is really partly a fecal image, the opening at the bottom being symbolic of the anus (HopR,V,45–65). At the very least the kiln is an enormously complex symbol, for in shape it is slightly phallic; as a kiln it is a purifier by means of fire; as the place where Brand returns it represents a return to origins (the womb); as an instrument of his death by his own hand, it represents a paradigmatic reflexive act. As a symbol, it has implicit in it both the pollution or fecal archetype and the purification archetype; and possibly, since Brand eliminates himself from the world in order to rid the world of his polluted self, it contains, implicitly, the redemption archetype. The presence, therefore, of any one of the Demonic Trinity, in any size, shape, or form, indicates the presence of the pollution or fecal motive and the probable presence of the purification and redemption motives. In Ethan Brand's case, the real pollution comes from the absolute love of the reflexive self, the continuous in-turning and in-growing which produces a man so selfish or self-centered that not even fire can touch his heart. This is the unpardonable sin, the monstrous perverted transcendental self, which Melville also represented in Ahab, who, unable to get out of himself, is finally capable only of destroying both others and himself. In *Ethan Brand*, and everywhere in Hawthorne, this is the negatively charged fecal or pollution image and represents that which needs to be purged. Various images drawn from the Demonic Trinity are used in *Ethan Brand* to symbolize Hawthorne's kind of pollution, which is basically spiritual and psychological rather than physical. The unseeable and internalized cancerous rot of the self is symbolized by various physical representatives of the Demonic Trinity, as well as by many other concrete persons, places, and things which suggest Brand's particular kind of pollution. Among these are the man in fecal brown, the dog chasing his tail, and the fact that the story takes place almost entirely at night.

The Demonic Trinity, then, as well as anything related however remotely to any part of it, is both an indication of the pollution or fecal archetype and a means of expressing the abhorrent and unclean generally. One could, of course, call the fecal or pollution archetype the Hell archetype, for though there are radical differences between it and Dante's Hell — the one having a psychological reality and the other a metaphysical one — there are striking similarities between the two. When Burke speaks of the Demonic Trinity, he deliberately intends to suggest its opposite, the Divine Trinity of redemption, and to suggest that where there is pollution there is need of purification and the possibility of redemption. He means also, in speaking of the pollution archetype as the Demonic Trinity, to call up the central idea of Christianity: purification and redemption, and to suggest that, unlike the damned Christian who once in Hell is always in Hell, there remains for others the possibility of exploiting the rhetoric of rebirth and moving, via symbolic action, from hell to purgatory to the heaven of symbolically resolved conflicts. For a Christian, Hell is a place; for Burke it is a state of mind, something psychological which is capable of being cured and changed. As a place, Hell is somewhat fixed; though the imagination is capable of conceiving it in many different ways, it is usually always "down there somewhere," hot or cold, and full of people who are there for specific reasons. But as a state of mind, as a condition of the individual self, hell is something quite different. Each man has his own hell, his own secret sins, crimes, guilt, and burdens; he may be polluted in ways that no one else knows about, and he may require modes of purification as peculiar and private as his burden. Thus when Burke speaks of the pollution or fecal or hell archetype and when, in the analysis of a literary work as symbolic action, he charts the fecal images, he is attempting to locate what, for the particular author, are the negatively charged persons, places, things, and ideas and to see if he can, in this way, locate the author's specific form of the archetype. Since the theory of symbolic action turns on the notion that every man has a burden, no analysis of a poem as symbolic action is possible without a fecal motive which the author must purge, transcend, or expiate. This is the reason for the enormous amount of prurient peering, the lists of images of the Demonic Trinity, and the endless discussions of guilt and its causes that one finds in Burke.

The three main archetypal clusters are pollution (hell), purification (purgatory), and redemption (heaven). The movement from the first to the last through purification constitutes the pattern of the rhetoric of rebirth and is the prime function of symbolic action. Burke contends that no redemption is complete unless the fecal motive is first expressed and then transcended or purged. Hence, no symbolic act is complete unless it contains images from all three of the clusters in the pattern. Accordingly, just as Burke's analyses catalogue fecal images, so they catalogue purification images. Purification is always a process — movement and change — something is always expelled or sloughed off, and the end is always a change of some kind, whether physical, spiritual, or psychological. Of necessity, purification is almost always depicted by "active" or "process" images. In Dante's Purgatory, for example, nothing is fixed; everything moves, ideally, upward and changes as it is gradually purified. Pollution may be regarded as a *state*, and purification as the enabling *act* which permits one to move from hell to heaven. The second Burkean archetype, then, is almost always symbolized by something which implies movement and action of some kind, though, as Burke points out, it is sometimes symbolized by "static" images which have implicit in them the notion of process. For example, Burke cites a can of dutch cleanser as a purification image, because it suggests the notoriously clean

The Analysis of Poetry as Symbolic Action

Dutch, the process of cleansing itself, and the act of making the dirty clean. But most often Burke concentrates on such things as fire and the chemical process of purification and organic change produced by fire; on journeys of all kinds, such as pilgrimages, quests; on crossings; on movement of any kind from negatively charged to positively charged, such as from black to white, night to day, down to up; on the act of unburdening or divesting in any form, such as going nude; on the imagery of ascent (mounting) in any form, such as mountain climbing; on outpourings, such as confession; and finally, on dyings and killings of all kinds, because he believes that, in literature at least, dying and killing frequently symbolize change, either from one self to another, or from polluted to redeemed.

Purification is always a process of moving from one thing to another, usually from polluted to purified, from crime through punishment to redemption. Purification is usually painful and involves one in suffering, often both physical and psychological. Raskolnikov, for example, during the long ordeal which is his purification, is almost continuously physically and psychologically "ill"; Dostoevsky depicts his movement from crime through punishment to redemption in the commonly employed images of disease, cure, and health, as well as in religious terms, mainly Christian. *Crime and Punishment*, in fact, provides a plethora of images from all three parts of the rhetoric of rebirth, for it deals almost exclusively with the central ideas of the theory of symbolic action: the problem of selfhood and pollution-purification-redemption. A careful analysis of this novel is an excellent way of discovering what the theory of symbolic action is all about and of realizing that Burke's theory is not so eccentric as it may appear to be at the outset. The novel charts in great detail Raskolnikov's decision to commit a crime to prove his theory of the superman. Gradually he becomes that self which can commit the crime, though the terrible struggle within him between the completely rational self-ish, isolated, and would be self-dependent self goes on. At the same time that he prepares himself to commit the crime, and actually does so, Raskolnikov's other (and for Dostoevsky, ideal) self performs various acts which are always impulsive and charitable. The pollution archetype is symbolized by Raskolnikov's

[105]

superman self, by Luzhin and Svidrigailov, who are two of the many "static" images of pollution, by the murder of the horse in Raskolnikov's dream, by the murder of the pawn broker and her sister, by Svidrigailov's dream of the child who becomes a French harlot, by what Luzhin tries to do to Sonia, and by what Svidrigailov tries to do to Dounia — to mention just a few. The terminal point in the pattern, the redemption archetype and also, for Dostoevsky, the ideal self, is symbolized by Raskolnikov's other impulsive charitable self which gives money to Marmeladov's family and for the ravished drunken girl, and again, by a number of static images, such as Sonia, Dounia, and Razumihin. The purification archetype is symbolized by many different kinds of movement on the part of Raskolnikov but, basically, it is a movement toward the ideal self and away from the superman. It is worked out in the novel in terms of physical and psychological movement towards and away from, or acceptance and rejection of, various persons, places, things, and ideas. The final purification is effected after Raskolnikov's nightmare about a world full of supermen, each of whom is sure he is right and has the "right" to do exactly as he pleases; after this dream in prison, the superman self "dies" and Raskolnikov is redeemed by the rebirth of the self he tried to reject when he committed the crime, that self being most perfectly symbolized in the novel by the sacrificial agent, Sonia, a kind of female Christ. The central idea of the novel, as in Christianity and in Burke everywhere, is that the miracle of regeneration is possible, and that even if the necessary knowledge can only come through the most terrible suffering, the end result, the attained ideal self and unity of being, is worth the ordeal.

Redemption, the terminal point, is also conceived as a state and often depicted in "static" images. A psychological rather than a metaphysical reality, Burke's heaven is almost infinitely variable. One locates it by cluster and agon analyses of a given work; heaven carries the positive charge and will always be the desirable end, that which is "good." In a particular work, whatever "heaven" is represents the specific expression of the redemption archetype, whether or not the author's conception of what is good and desirable is, in any absolute sense, good and desirable. In Byron's *Manfred* and *Don*

Juan, for example, the good is "natural," absolutely free, spontane-ous — and ultimately completely "selfish." Dostoevsky's hell is By-ron's heaven. Though the redemption archetype may be expressed in a variety of ways and may represent, depending upon the author, diametrically opposed things, there are, as with the pollution arche-type, certain more or less universally used forms of expressing the archetype which are the reverse of but analogous to the Demonic Trinity. Certain kinds of women are universally used as symbols of the redemption archetype. Usually they are naively innocent, and often they become sacrificial agents or innocent victims; they are usually naturally good, have always been and will always remain this way. Shakespeare's Lucrece, Desdemona, and Cordelia; Jane Austen's Jane Bennet; Dostoevsky's Dounia and Sonia; Alain-Fournier's Yvonne De Galais; Meredith's Lucy Feverel; and Byron's Haidee are examples of such women.

Just as the three separate stages of the purgative journey are arche-typal clusters, the three taken together in their proper order form an archetypal structure, or pattern of experience. Like the three arche-types of the rhetoric of rebirth, the pattern is capable of being ex-pressed in an extraordinary variety of ways. Burke discusses this archetypal structure in many different forms: sometimes he calls it the dialectic of the Upward Way, the Mystic Way, the tragic pattern, the search for the self, the dialectic of the platonic dialogue, the grammar of rebirth, the ladder of abstractions, or simply the sin–guilt–expiation–redemption pattern. He has analyzed the pattern as it appears in lyric poems, novels, plays, symphonies, philosophical tracts, political documents, theological systems, religious thought and practice, magic and magical rites, and many other human experi-ences and writings. He has worked out its physiological and chemical analogues, and examined the many analogues which occur in the natural world. From first to last, the nature and function of this ar-chetypal purgative-redemptive pattern of experience have been one of Burke's central concerns and an area in which he has done some of his most brilliant work.

Though individual experiences differ enormously depending upon individual range and content, the pattern, its variations, and the logic of the movement within the pattern, remain basically the same. That is, the pattern always has the structure of a purgative journey. Consider, for example, some of the variations within the pattern. What Burke calls the tragic rhythm and what Francis Fergusson has perceptively analyzed in *The Idea of a Theatre* and elsewhere, is made up of the following parts: action, passionate suffering, coming to knowledge, change, redemption or restoration of order. The pattern begins with an initiating act of some kind performed by the tragic protagonist in some kind of blindness which in some way disturbs a divine, natural, political, social, or familial order. This act is always polluting; it contaminates the doer himself and always has extensive consequences. Always irrevocable, the act leads inevitably to passionate suffering. Though all who are directly involved suffer, it is the doer himself who suffers most; the suffering — the purgative agony — produces a prolonged in-turning or, as in Othello's case, a brief but intense one, which, if the pattern is to complete itself, always results in a regenerative revelation of some kind. From this knowledge comes the change necessary for a new act by the protagonist which restores order. Usually, the tragic protagonist comes to the knowledge of his pollution, acknowledges the terrible nature of his act, reaffirms the principle of order violated, and dies in order that the world may be purged and redeemed.

The tragic pattern is but one of the many variations of the purgative journey. The search for the self is another. Though the ideal self to be achieved as well as the self or selves to be "killed" always vary according to the individual author, the pattern is more or less fixed. The plot almost invariably takes the form of a journey or quest; the searcher starts out in quest of something (himself) which often he will only recognize when he finds it. Frequently, as in Chrétien's *Percival*, the first book of the *Faerie Queene*, and *Portrait of the Artist as a Young Man*, the searcher finds what seems to be his proper self, defines himself in those terms, and begins to act; it soon becomes apparent, however, that this is not the true self, and there is a gradual, agonizing in-turning and loss of self which culminates either in madness or some kind of symbolic dying. As the old self dies a new one is born and the searcher, now equipped with some knowledge he did not previously have, can continue, both to build and test his new self. Although I have greatly schematized the pattern here, it should be clear that it deals, like the tragic pattern, with Burke's pollution-purification-redemption archetype. Though basically similar, the two patterns differ in that the search for the self deals primarily with individual salvation, with the pollution-purification-and-redemption of a single person as he tries to find a set of values and a self which will order experience and the world for him; whereas tragedy, though it deals with individual responsibility, is primarily concerned with some larger principle of order and disorder, and with the relation between the individual and some generally accepted principle of natural, social, cosmic, and divine order.

The manifestation of this driving impulse in man for regeneration and order can be seen in various other purgative structures. The Mystic Way, which receives its most perfect literary expression in such dream visions as the *Dream of the Rood* and the *Pearl*, and also provides the unifying form for such poems as Marvell's *The Garden*, Donne's *The Ecstasy*, and Keats's *Ode to a Nightingale*, is another of these purgative structures. It begins with the pure soul and impure body joined; then, due to an often indeterminate cause, the ecstasy, or Way Up, begins, where the pure soul is separated from the impure body and ascends; the separated and pure soul then has a revelation or vision of some kind, usually of God, absolute purity, or absolute truth; after the revelation comes the Way Down where the soul, equipped with its new knowledge, rejoins the impure body in the finite and impure world; the final stage is reached when the soul, with the new knowledge gained from its vision, attempts to effect changes at an earthly level, attempts, that is, to make its complete self and the world in which it lives approach the perfection perceived in the vision. Only in Donne's poem, of course, is the pattern completed; Keats's poem ends with the Way Down, and Marvell's with the vision itself; however, each of the poems, as well as the pattern itself, follows the movement of the pollution-purification-redemption archetype and the form of each may be regarded as a purgative journey.

Burke and the Drama of Human Relations

The dialectic of the Upward Way or, as Burke sometimes calls it, the dialectic of the platonic dialogue, is similar to the pattern of the Mystic Way, the central difference being that one is essentially lyric and the other dramatic. Plato's *Phaedrus* is probably the most perfect example of the form that we have. In literature, E. M. Forster's *A Passage to India* provides a good, though not perfect example. In structure, the dialogue is characterized by a movement from error through dialectic to absolute truth, and thence to summary of the particular truth and the translation of the Idea or Ideas into mythic images. Platonic dialogues deal, generally, with the ascent of the mind, via dialectic, from error to truth, from particulars to high-order abstractions, from appearances to "reality," and the subsequent translation of the system of abstract ideas, and the way to attain knowledge of them, into a concrete myth. Error, ignorance, appearance, and particulars are here equivalent to pollution; dialectic is here equivalent to and the means of purification; and the apprehension of absolute truth is equivalent to redemption. The movement, as in the Mystic Way and the *Divine Comedy*, is upward; as is true of all variations of the pollution-purification-redemption archetype, the whole turns upon the coming to knowledge-rejection-change cluster, that moment when half intuitively, half consciously, some process occurs internally which permits an almost simultaneous rejection-ejection, acceptance, and new forward movement. In *A Passage to India*, the over-all movement is from mosque to caves to temple, or from widespread ignorance and a glimmering of knowledge (Aziz and Mrs. Moore in the mosque), to abysmal ignorance and near total division (Adela and Mrs. Moore in the caves), to revelation (Adela in court), to the knowledge necessary for unity between the races, to the mythic, visionary representation of a means of unity (the festival in part III). In the novel, the dialectic results, not only from interplay between two or more people, as in a platonic dialogue, but from the interplay between East, West, and author. The structure of the novel resembles that of a dialectic, because from the interplay between the two forces, both of whom are partly in error, and their various representatives in the novel, there is, first, a gradual downward movement into greater and greater error and stupidity,

[110]

and then a gradual upward movement (for some of the characters, and for any perceptive reader) toward truth, sanity, and unity. Even though the novel ends with the phrases, "No, not yet . . . No, not there," or with four flat negatives, the dialectic of the novel, exposing, as it does, the source and nature of the error, the ignorance, and stereotyped blindness which prevents unity for both sides, moves also toward the revelation of the way to unity – a passage to India; the dialectic of the novel brings the reader to a realization that even though man and nature are by nature divided, the right kind of men (Stella and Ralph, Godbole), through knowledge, compassion, and understanding, and through various man-made systems of thought, such as religion, can transcend nature and effect the unity for which the whole novel yearns. The dialectic of the novel is designed to carry or move the reader to this truth, and it is this truth which is translated into myth in those extraordinary chapters devoted to the Hindu Festival in the Temple section of the novel.

Like the tragic pattern, the search for the self, and the Mystic Way, the dialectic of the Upward Way follows the pollution-purification-redemption archetype; and any work which has this kind of a structure enables the author and/or reader to go on a purgative, albeit symbolic, journey, for if he submits himself to the work, the progressive form of the work will, ideally, induce in him a similar kind of progression and his reading self will undergo the purgative journey the author has prepared for him.

iii

THE APPLICATION

Burke's remarks on symbolic action in the poetry and prose of S. T. Coleridge provide one with an excellent idea of his theory and method, even though they have never been collected in a single place and do not make up a single, self-contained essay. For years Burke has promised a monograph on Coleridge, and for just as long (since 1941) he has made scattered remarks on symbolic action in the works of Coleridge, concentrating primarily on *The Rime of the Ancient Mariner* and drawing heavily upon Coleridge's other works and what is known of his life to help him in his analysis. For Burke, Coleridge is an ideal subject because it is not necessary to go grubbing for the problem; it is there, in the open, and one can concentrate on the consequences of the problem as they are reflected in the life and works of the man himself. "In the case of Coleridge's enslavement to his drug . . .," Burke says, "you get an observable simplification, a burden the manifestations of which can be trailed through his work — yet at the same time you have him left in all his complexity, and so may observe the complex ways in which this burden becomes interwoven with his many other concerns" (PLF,22). Burke's point of departure for all of his remarks on symbolic action in the works of Coleridge is the "sin" of drug addiction; he is primarily interested in tracing how it led to other problems for Coleridge, how the drug addiction and all other problems produced in Coleridge an overpowering sense of guilt, and, finally, how both the sin and guilt were translated into the symbols of poetry and how *The Rime of the Ancient Mariner* in particular, but all the poems generally, functioned for Coleridge as rituals for the redemption of his drug addiction (PLF,96). Burke, then, is primarily interested in Coleridge's private drama of the self in quest as it is manifested in his public (verbal) actions; he is interested in showing how *The Rime of the Ancient Mariner* is a representative, purgative-redemptive symbolic act. In the course of his often very detailed and complex analysis, Burke uses all six parts of his critical method in an attempt to illustrate both the nature and scope of his literary theory and method. In what follows I have sometimes greatly expanded Burke's points and have often added further illustrations, but, in the main, I have followed his analysis very closely.

That *The Rime of the Ancient Mariner* follows the sin-guilt-punishment-coming to knowledge-regenerative new act-expiation-redemption pattern of experience is almost too obvious to mention were it not for a number of striking oddities in Coleridge's version of the archetypal purgative pattern. The sin, for example, is completely unpremeditated and involves the slaying of a seemingly insignificant albatross; the act, however, causes terrible consequences which are completely beyond the control of both the mariner and his shipmates; the change within the mariner, which results in a regenerative new act (the blessing of the water snakes) is, like the initiating act, impulsive, spontaneous, and seemingly insignificant; the act, however, produces two extraordinary changes: what was before malign suddenly becomes benign as a result of the mariner's altered attitude, and the uncontrollable force which punished the mariner reverses itself and now begins to "bless" and reward him; though the mariner has suffered beyond all reason for his sin, he must continue spontaneously, compulsively to do penance and purge himself by hypnotizing various people (even if it means keeping them from a wedding) whom he recognizes only when he sees them, and then quite literally ejaculating his confession, releasing the "unwilling" confessor only when the moral of this story has been stated.

Aside from the striking oddities in Coleridge's version of the archetypal pattern, there are certain striking and significant characteristics of the over-all structure of the poem. Since the poem is a symbolic rather than a literal narrative, the structure is generated by the author's intended meaning rather than by fidelity to a sequence of events that actually happened or to a sequence of events that might happen in the world of everyday experience. Consequently, the events depicted in the poem are not really so important for their own sake as they are for their symbolic meaning; the same is true of the over-all structure, for the movement is from one symbolic event to another, and the meaning of the poem can only be derived from an understanding of the logic of this symbolic progression. The poem, for example, begins in the present very suddenly when the "grey-beard loon" of an ancient mariner with his "glittering eye" hypnotically detains the wedding-guest and partly through the spell and partly through the story he tells, forces him to a "willing suspension of disbelief" which keeps him listening to the mariner's confessional story; the poem ends when, the wedding now over, the mariner finishes his story, delivers the moral, which makes a pointed contrast between "the marriage feast" and universal brotherhood, and releases the wedding-guest, who is now, as a result of hearing the story rather than going to the wedding, "a sadder and wiser man." Though a certain shock effect and a certain tone of mystery are achieved by the spellbinding mariner's detention of the wedding-guest, and though these do add to the power of the narrative to interest us, the symbolic progression from wedding-feast, to the detention of the wedding-guest, to the mariner's story, to the moral, to the contrast, to the release of the wedding-guest after the wedding is the important thing, for it indicates the real hierarchy of values and points to the central meaning of the poem. The contrast in the poem is between one kind of love and unity, symbolized by the uniting of an individual male and female in a holy ceremony, and another, larger, better kind of love and unity, symbolized at length by the mariner's story and stated explicitly in the moral which ends the poem.

To get at what this other, larger, better kind of love and unity is, one must examine the symbolic progression within the mariner's story. The over-all story deals with a symbolic journey which begins and ends in the same place: geographically, the mariner goes to the South Pole (that is, the ends of the earth) and back. Symbolically, however, the mariner goes from ignorance, indifference, and a "sinful act" which is the product of this state (the killing of the albatross); to guilt and the punishment meted out by the spirit of the universe itself for such crimes against the universe, universal brotherhood, and harmony; to an unconscious realization that even the meanest, ugliest things in the universe are beautiful and worthy of love; to the regenerative act which is the product of this new state (the blessing of the snakes); to the reward meted out by the spirit of the universe for such blessed acts (rain, sleep, movement, reversal of direction, return home, etc.); to the gradual realization that even so small a crime against the universe as he committed partly contaminates him forever (reaction of the pilot and pilot's boy); to the gradual realization that no priest can ever completely cleanse him (hermit episode) and that he will have to do perpetual penance (compulsive confessions, preaching the moral) for his sin; to the gradual realization of the great truth (the other, larger, better kind of love and unity described in the moralistic quatrains which end the poem and embodied in the very structure of the poem) he must disseminate, even if it means deliberately detaining a wedding-guest.

This over-all symbolic progression — a movement of the self — is the generating "idea" of the poem; it controls the selection and arrangement of all the details within the poem. Meditation upon the progressive forms to be found in the poem reveals, for example, that aside from the sin–guilt–penance–redemption progression, which is indicated very forcefully in the poem by the movement from sinful act (killing) to regenerative act (blessing) to expiatory act (public confession), there are a number of other very significant corollary progressions. To mention only the most important: there is the progression from movement ("quickness"), to absolute immobility, to movement; the "reductive" progression which begins with the killing of the albatross and ends with the blessing of the snakes, followed by the "expansive" progression which begins immediately after the blessing; the progression from society, to absolute isolation and aloneness, back to society; the progression from life and healthful growth, to death and rot, back to healthful growth; and the progression in the quality of the imagery from positive to negative to positive to mixed (the hermit on the rotten stump).

All of the progressions in the poem are of a piece, even that movement of self-perception which occurs within the wedding-guest. In the most general sense, the movement is from happy ignorance through suffering to saddening knowledge, the two specific forms of the purgative journey being that of the mariner and that of the wedding-guest. What is purged out of the wedding-guest in the course of his journey is a specious view of the world which, in the case of the mariner, led to terrible consequences; the mariner, who is trying to save the wedding-guest from a fate similar to his own, acted on the specious view and underwent at first hand the whole pattern resulting from the act; now burdened with a perpetual guilt, he must undergo continued purgative journeys by telling his story and transmitting the "true" view of the universe which he has gained. Since the mariner already has his knowledge when the poem begins, it is only his guilt which is purged in the course of the poem, though we do learn, from his story, how he was purged of his specious view of the world; that is, he actually undergoes one purgative journey during the course of the poem while he reconstructs another one for us and simultaneously forces on the wedding-guest a third kind. A structural analysis, filled out where necessary by cluster and agon analyses, tells us at least this much about the poem's meaning. As a poem which is obviously primarily concerned with journeys of various kinds, both internal and external, it is not surprising that so much should be revealed by a structural analysis.

But, for Burke, such an analysis is just the beginning, just a way of discovering certain "leads" or "clues" which may be followed out and later used in the analysis of the poem as symbolic action. For example, the detained wedding-guest and his movement of perception suggests some opposition (agon) between marriage and universal brotherhood as a way to the better life; the forceful detention of the wedding-guest suggests some compulsion away from marriage and, for Burke, the guilt naturally associated with this; the mariner's story suggests a sin or sins so great that they permanently impair; the mariner's actions in regard to the wedding-guest suggest some profound and compulsive need to expiate via public confession; the over-all structure of the poem suggests a messianic urge to announce the "good word." Not content simply to analyze the poem in vacuo, or even to analyze it in the context of Coleridge's other works, Burke follows these leads backwards in an attempt to show how the poem is at the same time a representative and a purgative-redemptive symbolic act:

The Albatross . . . came through the fog "As if it had been a Christian soul," and the Sun that avenges the murder is . . . "like God's own head." In "The Eolian Harp" we are told that Sarah, the poet's wife, who biddeth the poet walk humbly with his God, is a "Meek Daughter in the family of Christ." Sarah and the Albatross are thus seen to be in the same equational [image] cluster. The drug, however, is in a different cluster. As he tells us in his letters, it is responsible for "barbarous neglect of my family." As for its affinity with pure or metaphysical evil, we have that explicitly in his letters: "I used to think St. James's Text: 'He who offendeth in one part of the Law, offendeth in all,' very harsh; but my own sad experience has taught me it's [sic] awful, dreadful Truth. What crime is there scarcely which has not been included in or followed from the one guilt of taking opium?" And when he suffered from its malign effects, we are told in the same letter, "An indefinite indescribable Terror as with a scourge of ever restless, ever coiling and uncoiling serpents, drove me on from behind" (as the Mariner's ship was driven). (PLF, 71–72.)

Through an analysis of the equational clusters in Coleridge as a whole, and working on the assumption that in the depths of his imagery (his unconscious identifications) a poet cannot lie, Burke makes the following connections between the symbols of the poem and Coleridge's life. The albatross is a surrogate for Sarah, and since marriage and Christian duty are linked in Coleridge's mind, the albatross and the detained wedding-guest are symbolic of what Burke calls Coleridge's marital-religious problem (PLF,94–95). The snakes are a surrogate for his drug addiction, or what Burke calls the drug problem (PLF,96–99). The drug and marital-religious problems are causally related in two ways: the drug had both malign and benign effects on Coleridge (symbolized in the poem by the use of malign and benign images for the snakes) and both of these caused him to neglect his wife and family. The compounded results of the malign effect of the drug and neglect of his wife and family are symbolized in the poem by what happens to the mariner after he kills the albatross up to when he blesses the snakes, and by the residual, permanent effects of the act on the mariner; the benign effect of the drug was a "kind of impulsive oneness" with the universe, a sense of universal brotherhood and cosmic unity; this state, or sense of unity, was so superior to anything Coleridge felt with his wife that it in turn caused him to neglect his wife and family; in fact, to deny the latter as inferior to the former. In the poem, this is symbolized by the movement from specious to true view of the universe for both wedding-guest and mariner, by the mariner's pointed contrast at the end of the poem between the pleasures of marriage and the pleasures of universal brotherhood, by the benign effects that result from the blessing of the water snakes, and by the terrible punishments visited upon the mariner and his shipmates for the act against the universe. The drug addiction, though, since it has both malign and benign effects, is in itself evil-good; consequently, it is symbolized in the poem by ambivalent or mixed images, such as the water snakes, the sun, and by the fact that out of evil (the killing of the albatross) comes good (knowledge of the true nature of the universe).

[117]

Burke and the Drama of Human Relations

It would, perhaps, not be so difficult to work out an analysis of the poem as symbolic action if one had only to work with the three "burdens" Burke mentions above: the drug addiction, the offense against Sarah, and the offense against the universe. But Burke further complicates the matter by arguing that much more than this is actually symbolized in the poem and that the poem as a whole really functions as solution for a complex of interrelated problems which Coleridge faced and which were brought on, primarily, by his drug addiction — that small offense which had enormous consequences. As a symbolic act, the poem is a miracle of synthesis; each symbol is charged with multiple secret identifications which the author has made in the depths of his psyche; the structure of interrelationships in the work, if one can but work it out, is a psychograph of the author; and the various progressions in the work are typical movements of the author's self, his recurrent patterns of experience. According to Burke, then, there are, aside from the drug and marital-religious burdens, three other interrelated problems reflected in and symbolically "solved" by the poem. What Burke means is that the drug-wife-evil nexus could not possibly have remained isolated from Coleridge's other central concerns, even though the drug-wife problem is essentially a private and in some ways surely a bodily-sexual one, and the others are more public, and more psychic than physical. The three other problems reflected in the poem are aesthetic, political, and metaphysical.

Burke's usual practice when he is trying to show how the law of synecdoche works is to bridge, by means of equational logic, the gap between the part and the whole. Two examples of this procedure appear in the long quotation above: there, Burke argues that since the albatross and Sarah appear in the same equational cluster, the albatross symbolizes Sarah; and he argues that since Coleridge described the effect of opium on him in terms of snakes, the snakes symbolize the drug addiction. Through the use of this equational logic which moves effortlessly from similarity to identity, Burke is able to link seemingly unrelated things and establish the connections between the part and the whole which he requires. The spontaneous, impulsive, uncontrollable killing of the albatross and blessing of the

The Analysis of Poetry as Symbolic Action

snakes are very like the taking of a drug by the addict. If the albatross is Sarah, then the killing of the bird represents Coleridge's neglect and rejection of his family brought on by the drug addiction; but the drug, Coleridge tells us, had a benign effect as well, and hence the same "kind" of an act could lead to different results, symbolized in the poem by the blessing of the snakes and the "impulsive oneness," the sense of communion between the mariner and the universe which follows the act. The impulsive, uncontrollable act of killing and the ensuing results represent the extreme of evil or pollution; the impulsive, uncontrollable act of blessing and the ensuing results represent the extreme of good, or redemption. In the poem, which surely makes use of the paradox of the fortunate fall, the mariner must sin before he can be redeemed, so that out of evil comes good and good and evil seem inextricably mixed. Burke also suggests that out of Coleridge's drug addiction came his metaphysical views on the nature of and relation between good and evil which are embodied in the concrete images of the poem. The benign effect of the drug produced a sense of oneness, of integration and communion with the universe as a whole; in this attitude, which is the one advocated by the mariner at the end of the poem, evil would cease to exist by being included in the universal embrace of the mind—it would be dissolved in an attitude of love towards everything in the universe. This attitude of universal love and the state of universal harmony produced by the drug provided Coleridge with his idea of the good; and Coleridge's ideas of the political good and the aesthetic good bear a striking resemblance to this drug-induced vision of perfection.

The aesthetic ideal, which Burke says is embodied in *The Eolian Harp* and exemplified in the "perfect communion between the individual and the universe," turns upon the distinctions Coleridge makes between imagination and fancy and the primary and secondary imagination. Greatly oversimplified, the distinctions are: the fancy, a mode of memory, simply stores things as they come in from the outside world and recalls them; the secondary imagination "dissolves, diffuses, dissipates, in order to recreate"; the primary imagination performs the final, "dim analogue of creation"; it infuses the "organic unity," and "forms all into one graceful and intelligent whole." As contemporary critics have reminded us, the primary imagination is the "shaping spirit" which effects that miraculous change symbolized by the mariner's internal change, which in turn changes the water snakes from malign to benign: out of dissolution, diffusion, dissipation; out of chaos and suffering, it makes order by means of a central intuition into the nature of experience and the universe. The end product of the primary imagination is, like the benign effect of the drug and the metaphysical ideal, essentially "unitary." It reduces the many to the one, to a vision of "the All which is at the same time One." It is the kind of vision which produces the mariner's seemingly platitudinous remark "He prayeth best who loveth best / All things both great and small," and the kind of vision which does not deny the value of marriage but places it in a larger, more inclusive system of values which diminishes its importance.

Finally, there is the political ideal, exemplified in Coleridge's "Pantisocracy" project. Coleridge's "Utopian plan for a communistic colony in America" was based on the notion that "in this colony, given an adequate property structure, virtue would be inevitable." According to Burke, the political problem is related to the aesthetic, marital, metaphysical, and drug problems as follows: for one thing, "Pantisocracy perfectly exemplified [Coleridge's] ideal of imaginative unification" (PLF,96); in the colony each individual would be in perfect communion with the others and all would be in perfect communion with the universe; in this way, the many would be one and the colony as a whole would be a concrete embodiment of the unitary ideal. The colony would be a living, human poem — poetry in action. As a living embodiment of the unitary ideal, the colony would solve the metaphysical problem, for when people were put in a scene where virtue is inevitable, evil would cease to exist. The marital problem figures in all of this since Coleridge was "engineered into marriage because it was agreed that each of the colonists should be married," presumably because marriage was not an end in itself, but a means to a larger, nobler end. But, Burke adds, "the project fell through soon after his marriage, so that the focal reason for his marrying Sarah at all was removed" (PLF,96), and coupled with an extreme disappointment over the collapse of the project was a complex attitude toward his wife, made up of resentment, disappointment, and guilt. Coleridge's unitary ideal could not be attained through marriage; in fact, the ideal itself made necessary the reduction in importance of a wife and family — perfect communion and unity with the universe at large was more pleasing and important than communion and unity with a wife and family.

At this point, Burke might say, Where are we? Lost, it seems, in the almost trackless maze of private symbols, trying to see how, in a single, rather short narrative poem, are stated and resolved five enormously complex problems, some physical, some psychic, some psycho-physical; trying to see how, for Coleridge, *The Rime of the Ancient Mariner* functioned as a purgative-redemptive symbolic act. Burke believes the poem *is* a ritual for the redemption of Coleridge's drug addiction, a "private-enterprise Mass, with important ingredients of a black Mass" in it (PLF,287). As such, the poem is a kind of religious service in which some private version of the Eucharist is celebrated, with the poem as viaticum for the self's journey from pollution through purification to redemption.

The ancient mariner represents Coleridge the poet (hypnotic teller of autobiographical tales which alter the hearers' attitude by re-ordering experience); Coleridge the drug-addict, the sinner, the man of "guilt-laden substance" (the mariner as unintentional "murderer," as compulsive confessor, as someone who must do perpetual penance by publicly confessing his own misdeeds and pointing the moral of his story); Coleridge as reluctant and guilty husband (the mariner as deflector of wedding-guests who pointedly says "O sweeter than the marriage-feast / 'Tis sweeter far to me, / To walk together to the kirk / With a goodly company! —" and the mariner as "slayer" of the loving Albatross); Coleridge as visionary, if somewhat saddened, idealist (the mariner who, in spite of his nightmare memories has had a benign vision and passes "from land to land" teaching his tale of universal brotherhood which shows how out of dissolution, diffusion, dissipation; how out of evil, chaos, and suffering came the regenerative visionary knowledge of the "All which is at the same time One"); and finally, the ancient mariner represents Coleridge the performer of poetic purgative-redemptive acts (the mariner must tell his story, for the telling is not only penance but purgation, the enabling symbolic act which keeps him going until the next curative unburdening).

As symbolic action, the poem functions first of all as a public confession which enables Coleridge to speak the unspeakable, to unburden himself at the public's expense of all those polluting elements which, if left unspoken, rot and destroy the self. Though the confession is public and makes use of a public idiom (language), many (probably most) of the pollution symbols are private, for only in disguised form can the unspeakable be spoken. However, since the poem is a public document, designed for public consumption as well as private confession and purge, Coleridge uses symbols with obvious public as well as disguised private meanings: the Albatross, the snakes, rot, the mariner himself. The poem's function as private-public confession, or simply as an externalizing of what can no longer be borne internally without serious damage to the self, is revealed in the various specific expressions of the pollution archetype which Coleridge uses. All together, these make up the content of the confession or, as Burke would have it, the fecal motive which must be expressed and transcended. In Coleridge's case, the poem as confession permits him to unburden himself of a monstrous guilt complex brought on by various "sinful" acts (or thoughts) against his wife, his family, himself, his visionary unitary ideal, society, nature, and "God." Though it is not really clear whether Coleridge's drug addiction was primarily cause or effect, or whether the real guilt-producing failing lay somewhere else and was simply symbolized by the drug addiction, Burke takes it (on Coleridge's own word) for *the* polluting act which led to other polluting acts which led to the monstrous guilt complex.

Confession itself is curative; simply verbalizing the pollution is the beginning of the purgative action. The whole poem, of course, performs a scapegoat function, for Coleridge loaded it with his burdens and sent it off into society at large. This is another part of the purgative action. But the main purgative action is to be found in the progressive form of the poem, which expresses Coleridge's variant of the purgative journey. Of course, there are a great many forms of purgation, but all of them usually involve suffering of some kind and many of them involve self-inflicted punishment. The classic example is Oedipus, whose awareness of his own psychic blindness and its consequences leads him to blind himself as symbol and punishment. Though the whole of the *Ancient Mariner* functions as a purgative for Coleridge, with the agony of creation as part of the punishment and suffering, there are particular parts of the poem which function in special ways as part of the purgative punishment and suffering. From the killing of the Albatross to the blessing of the snakes, Coleridge presumably reproduces in symbols and in the progressive form of that part of the poem, the malign psychic and physical effects of the drug addiction as well as some of the other consequences brought on by the drug addiction. These include social and familial failures, a cacophonous relation with the universe, a kind of searing loneliness, and manic depression. To recreate is in a sense to relive, and to relive the old or recurrent agonies is to punish oneself by suffering again one's sins and their consequences. And so, as another part of the purgative action, there is the punishment and suffering, which is a way of earning the redemption that terminates the journey.

In Coleridge's case, the redemption seems to come from the emergence of some good from so much evil; this, in general, is the solution which the poem as symbolic action arrives at. To be sure, the confessional unburdening, as well as the punishment and suffering, is a kind of solution. Coleridge is "relieved" by the symbolic action itself, by the sheer performing of the act. But there is another sense in which the poem is solution, another sense in which it redeems Coleridge. As symbolic action, the poem should "solve" Coleridge's drug, familial, aesthetic, metaphysical, and political problems. Burke does not mean by this that the poem solves them once and for all; rather, it temporarily resolves them so that as long as they exist and cannot be solved by some other means, repeated symbolic solutions-resolutions will be necessary. Either the author must effect another psychic and physical catharsis through the actual experience of writing the poem or he must invent another symbolic solution for transcending the problem; actually, according to Burke, he probably does both.

But to return to the poem as solution: the drug addiction is the offense against the part which is an offense against the whole; but from the offense against the part comes the revelation that salvation lies in encompassing the whole through love, and the realization that so great a truth ought to be disseminated. This sequence from offense to revelation to dissemination is what redeems the drug addiction, for out of evil comes knowledge of the greatest good; and disseminating the truth is a good act in itself which helps to counteract the evil out of which everything came. If one can't live the ideal, be poetry in action or a living poem, he can at least preach it, he can tell others (Coleridge as poet–critic–philosopher–public lecturer) who will perhaps be able to live the ideal. Again, though preaching is not doing, at least some good is extracted from an evil, if uncontrollable, act.

The poem, then, is the realization of the aesthetic ideal. In the poem the metaphysical problem is solved. The poem also indicates the means to the realization of the political ideal. And finally, the whole poem is a ritual for the redemption of the drug addiction. There remains, then, only the family problem, which is solved by the hierarchy of values arrived at by the mariner. The drug caused Coleridge to neglect his wife and family; but the drug-induced vision of perfection, the unitary ideal which is the central idea of the aesthetic, metaphysical, and political ideals, relegates the wife and family to what would seem to them an inferior position, for the ideal states that all things "both great and small" are equal and worthy of equal love. Furthermore, in its benign effect, the drug produces in Coleridge a state of cosmic unity which is so superior to anything experienced with his wife and family that he cannot help but prefer the drugged state. The problem, then, is how to justify (rationalize, perhaps?) the preference for communion with the universe over communion with the family. In the poem, the solution is explicit: the mariner deliberately stops the wedding-guest and tells his story in order to point out that loving a wife to the exclusion of other things in the universe would be a sin against the part which would be a sin against the whole; that is, the larger ideal of universal brotherhood would include the smaller ideal of marriage and is thus better and more satisfying, but the smaller one excludes the larger, and this is, in the mariner's terms, "sinful." To this realization the mariner brings (forces) the wedding-guest, and presumably it is in this way that Coleridge, though he still feels guilty about neglecting his wife and family, justifies his attitude and actions toward them and presumably solves the problem.

As Burke is quick to point out, this does not remove the problem, it merely solves it by an alteration of perspective or a shift in attitude. Since the whole poem turns, not upon any alteration in external reality, but upon an internal change which alters the way in which one views external reality, the poem provides Burke with an ideal illustration for the workings and importance of symbolic action. The motto of symbolic action is "change or perish" and it may be interpreted in a number of ways: "purge or perish," "transcend or perish," "alter the self or perish." Essentially, all these variations amount to the same thing, for all are based on the same premise: man, Burke believes, is equipped with two most extraordinary instruments for effecting beneficial changes — reason and language, or, more accurately, reason and symbolic action. Many problems cannot be solved through direct, "practical" action; in these instances, man has at his disposal the miracle of symbolic action, best practiced by the poets of the world; and with, or more properly, through, symbolic action, man can solve problems "peacefully" which might otherwise lead to his own or another's destruction. Presumably, in Coleridge's case, his poems and other writings were "salvation devices" which enabled him to go on living by helping him cleanse and order himself. As Burke says of his own *Permanence and Change*, Coleridge put his poems and essays together in order to keep himself from falling apart.

Briefly and without benefit of his own brilliant texture, that is what Burke does with the poem as poem and symbolic act. Much of what he says is not new, though some of it sounds new because it is written in the language that Burke created. What is unique — and enormously suggestive — about his approach is the insistence upon always examining the works as representative and purgative-redemptive symbolic acts, his insistence upon returning always to the self of the poet and the drama of that self's quest for the better life as a basis for the interpretation of the poem's images, structure, conflict (agon), and function. Though Burke attempts to do justice to all three parts of the aesthetic trinity — creator, creative process; created object; audience — it is the first which he takes as essence, arguing that if we regard the poem as a symbolic act of and for the poet who made it, more can be learned about the poem as poem and the poem-audience relationship than if we adopt some other approach. Burke's approach — up to the mid-forties — is what he likes to call a "functional" one, emphasizing the symbolic function of the creative and created act for the creator, on the assumption that a great deal of depth knowledge about poetry, the human psyche, and human relations generally can be acquired from such a perspective. In the jargon of contemporary criticism, Burke's approach is basically an extrinsic one, built upon those two most heinous of sins, the affective and intentional fallacies; or, to invent a new term which would include both, the functional fallacy. Actually, as the term symbolic action suggests, Burke has attempted to fuse the extrinsic and intrinsic approaches; to study the poem as a verbal act is to study it as a poem in and for itself and to study it as a symbolic act is to study it as symbolic autobiography and as a ritual of cure. Burke's method, like his theory, also attempts to fuse the two approaches, for structural, cluster, agon, and pun analysis are neutral methods which may be used by anyone for the analysis of a poem as poem; but the extensions of them — the dialectic of the Upward Way (form as a purgative journey), the rhetoric of rebirth (pollution–purification–redemption archetypes), and joycing for the Demonic Trinity — are loaded methods which, though they can be used by anybody and might be used for some other purpose, were specifically designed, and are best used, for the analysis of poetry as symbolic action. Burke's critical method is such that he can use the neutral part of it to make what he calls a technical or formal analysis of the work and then, since the loaded part is simply an extension of the neutral part, move effortlessly from the poem as verbal act to the poem as representative and purgative-redemptive symbolic act. What is really involved is the shift to another orientation and another set of referents for an exegesis of the poem's images, structure, agon, and function. The orientation is a kind of secular Christianity where Hell, Purgatory, and Heaven have been replaced by their psychological equivalents, and where the redemptive Christ has been replaced by the miracle of symbolic action, the great rhetoric of rebirth.

·IV·

DRAMATISM: LANGUAGE
AS THE ULTIMATE
REDUCTION

i

THE DRAMA

THE PROGRESSIVE FORM of the title essay in *The Philosophy of Literary Form* is symbolic of Burke's whole development. The essay begins with a consideration of poetry as symbolic action, and then moves to a consideration of symbolic action as drama, to all poetry as drama, to ritual drama as the essence of poetry, to ritual drama as the paradigm of all linguistic action. In typical fashion, Burke reduces the many to the one. In the above progression, all verbalizing is reduced to symbolic action; symbolic action is then reduced to its most perfect or ideal form, which is poetic symbolic action; all poetic symbolic action is then reduced to its essence, which is the purgative-redemptive ethical drama; ethical drama is then reduced to its most perfect or ideal form, which is ritual drama; Burke then takes the final step and equates the point of departure — linguistic action — with the terminal point — ritual drama — and ends up with the proposition that the essence of all linguistic action is to be found in ritual drama.

This drama becomes the archetype in the Burkean version of the drama of human relations, the essential characteristics of which will necessarily be reflected in all linguistic acts, poetic or otherwise. Since ritual drama is the essence of all linguistic action, it follows

[128]

Dramatism

(Burke says) that a dramatic perspective is best suited to the study of language and linguistic action generally. In systematizing "dramatism" and the "dramatistic" methodology Burke extends his reductive generalization about language and ritual drama one step further and arrives at what is to be his final, total vision: he defines man as "the essentially symbol-using animal" and makes linguistic action the essence of man. As a result, the central, generating principle of everything Burke has written since 1945 (including *A Grammar of Motives*) is the proposition that man is the specifically language-using or symbol-using animal, and that somehow the essences of man, human relations, and ultimate reality are to be derived from the dramatistic study of language and the various functions it performs for man.

One movement in Burke's curve of development thus comes to a close in *The Philosophy of Literary Form*, and another begins in *A Grammar of Motives*. The stages in the first are from creative artist to literary critic to social critic to the fusion of literary and social criticism. The result is a theory in which the purgative-redemptive function of the creative act is the vehicle whereby every man can move toward the better life, and in which poetry is used as the source of both the archetype of the drama of human relations and the methodology for the analysis of this drama. The second movement begins where the first ends. This time it is from literary and social criticism to the discipline which Burke believes will include all others: the analysis of language and linguistic action — what he has recently called "Logology," and proposed as a complete system, a total vision of man and the universe. Starting from the definition of man as the symbol-using animal, Burke spins out a language-oriented system, complete with methodology, which follows to the end of the line the implications of the definition; at the same time he applies the system and method in as many areas of human relations as possible, attempting to show the universality of his vision and the many uses to which it can be put. The system is a coherent and total vision, a self-contained and internally consistent way of viewing man, the various scenes in which he lives, and the drama of human relations enacted upon those scenes. In dramatism, Burke has reached a terminal point, a resting place beyond which he has no desire to go. All that now remains is the rounding out of the dramatistic system and methodology in the last two volumes of the tetralogy of motives.

Like Aristotle's definition of man as a rational animal, Burke's definition of him as a symbol-using animal is simplistic, but with enormously complex ramifications. Logically, the first ramification is presented in a long, four-part essay published in 1952 and 1953 called "A Dramatistic View of the Origins of Language." Here Burke works out one of the central coordinates of his system, the theory of the negative. "*The essential distinction,*" he says, "*between the verbal and the non-verbal is in the fact that language adds the peculiar possibility of the Negative*" (QJS,XXXVIII,252). What Burke means by this is that before man added the verbal to non-verbal nature, there were no negative acts, states, or commands. The negative is the very essence of language and the ability to use it is one of the distinguishing characteristics of man. To a positive, amoral, and fundamentally innocent nature, man, with language ("reason"), adds the negative and all of its products — such things as property rights, moral and social proscriptions of all kinds, law, justice, and conscience. Man not only adds these to nature, but he infuses them as a substantival ingredient into all non-verbal and extra-verbal reality. For example, a "No Trespassing" sign on a piece of property is the infusion of a linguistic negative into nature; and the proposition that adultery and fornication are sinful is the infusion of a linguistic negative into pure sensory experience — what Burke calls "sheer animality." Because of this unremitting tendency on the part of man to make the world and himself over in the image of his distinctive trait, man has a language-ridden view of himself, his products, and the universe; and language acts as a key motive or scene for all of man's acts. Every aspect of non-verbal, socio-political, and extra-verbal reality is viewed by man through a fog of symbols, and human relations are at every point complicated by the linguistic factor that is intrinsic to the human mind.

In the theory of the negative Burke reduces reason and morality (conscience) to language (symbol-using). In this way he opens up man's rational and moral life to what he calls linguistic analysis.

Dramatism

Burke thinks of those things which we normally consider the products of reason and conscience as the products of language, because without language there would be no reason, and without language and reason, there could be no morality: "eliminate language from nature," Burke says, "and there can be no moral disobedience" (RR, 187). With and because of language, man transcends his "sheer animality," for language makes possible the ethical drama of human relations. According to Burke, this drama is made up of seven "interlocked" moments and the whole drama is either directly or indirectly caused by language and the negative. The great moments of the drama are the Negative, Hierarchy, Guilt, Mortification, Victimage, Catharsis, and Redemption; they are "interlocked" because all of them belong to the "Order" or "Covenant" cluster of terms and any one of them "logologically" implies all the others. Briefly, the seven moments are related to each other in the following way: the whole drama is made possible — or inevitable — by language, which introduces the negative into human experience; with language and the negative man creates various kinds of hierarchic orders, all of which have hundreds of "thou-shalt-nots" in them; every hierarchy is experienced by man as a kind of covenant, but no man is capable of meeting all the terms of the agreement and in some way he will fail or disobey. Failure and disobedience — the "fall" — cause guilt, which in turn makes necessary the whole machinery of catharsis. The two principal means of purification are mortification and victimage; and the end result of both is redemption, or the alleviation of guilt.

The two key moments of the drama are the negative and hierarchy, primarily because they are the principal guilt-producing factors, and guilt — Burke's all-purpose word for moral guilt, all kinds of tensions, and any uneasiness from whatever cause — is the "without which not" of the whole system in the sense that the other moments either explain why all men are guilty or how all men cope with their guilt. In the most general sense, hierarchy is any kind of order; but more accurately, it is any kind of graded, value-charged structure in terms of which things, words, people, acts, and ideas are ranked. Any hierarchy is simultaneously unifying and divisive in so far as it orders the whole by ranking according to some value-system and in so far as the ranking is a division into different classes of being. All hierarchies have inherent in them a progressive form which comes from the nature of language itself: the upward movement from lower to higher and the downward movement from higher to lower. Thus, any hierarchy generates for those who participate in it what Burke calls the "hierarchic motive": on the one hand people are goaded by the desire to mount the hierarchy, either through action or possession; and on the other hand people are goaded by the threat of descending the hierarchy, again either by action or possession, but also by failure to act or inability to possess certain things. From hierarchy and the hierarchic motive inherent in it, comes what Burke calls the "hierarchic psychosis" and explains as "any uneasiness stemming from the social order." Quite conscious of the meaning of the word, Burke calls it a "psychosis" because it is incurable; it can be relieved, but not cured; it is inevitable, ubiquitous, and eternal. It is part of man's natural condition and constitutes what Burke calls "categorical guilt"— his version of "original sin" (PC,274–294). The hierarchic psychosis, Burke says, is "inevitable in social relations," and man, by nature a social animal, inherits this "categorical guilt" at birth, when he is unavoidably born into a pre-existing hierarchically ordered social, political, economic, and religious structure, with each hierarchy, as well as the over-all hierarchy of his historical orientation, interwoven with thousands of moral, social, familial, economic, and religious negatives. So every hierarchy, which is a "good" in that it makes orderly what otherwise might be chaotic, is a "goad" in so far as division into higher and lower is inevitable wherever there is ordering, and such division makes inevitable the hierarchic psychosis and categorical guilt engendered "spontaneously" by any "social order" (PC,294).

As Burke explains it, these pre-existing orders are equivalent to the "covenant." The pre-existing orders tell man what he should and should not do and be: they provide him with his ideals (economic, sexual, social, familial, intellectual) and with a number of alternative selves from which to choose; they offer a complete set of values in terms of which he can find himself, measure success and failure, goodness and evil. The first or original "temptation" and "fall" are automatic; that is, they are inherent in man's nature as a symbol-using animal, for language, which has imbedded in it a driving impulse towards abstraction, enables man to construct ideal selves and ideal modes of behavior which are never capable of attainment, but on the basis of which he nevertheless judges himself and others. So, just as Christians say that all men suffer from "original sin," Burke, in his secularized, dramatistic version of the Genesis "myth," says that all men suffer from "categorical guilt"; and just as all Christians begin in a fallen state, needing and yearning for the redemption made possible by the sacrificial Christ, so all men, according to Burke, begin in a fallen state brought on by their distinctive trait — language — needing and yearning for the redemption made possible by the dramatistic equivalent of the sacrificial Christ, symbolic action and the rhetoric of rebirth.

Language, one might say, is the equivalent of the fortunate fall; it not only makes redemption possible, but provides the means to that end. The notion that all men begin in a fallen state, burdened by the hierarchic psychosis and categorical guilt, both of which belong to the Burkean hell — the pollution, war, division, disorder, corrosion, disintegration, alienation, fragmentation cluster — is central to all of Burke. Without it, his own obsessive concern with pollution, guilt, and disorder, his almost monomaniacal emphasis on modes of purification, on mankind's vast and complex rhetoric of rebirth, and on redemption as an achieved state, would be meaningless — save, perhaps, as his own purgative-redemptive symbolic action. As it is, the categorical guilt and the emphasis on pollution–purification–and–redemption indicate more clearly than anything else the fundamentally moral and ethical center of Burke. What he has finally done in his dramatistic theory, after many years of moving steadily in that direction, is to systematize a naturalistic, linguistically oriented, secular variant of Christianity. Burke has retained the principal ideas of Christianity and worked out dramatistic equivalents for them with astonishing thoroughness. The whole dramatistic system is laid out on a moral-ethical, Christian-Catholic bias, and is presented in such a way as to make perfectly clear Burke's belief that he has developed a new "scientific" religion which twentieth-

century man can "believe" in, but which, unlike the old one it re-
places, is designed to save man in this world.

Though the similarities between Burke's version of the drama of
human relations and the Christian one are striking — in both the
drama is moral and the sacrificial redeemer is the central figure —
the differences between them are radical. Burke has reduced God to
an idea (or term), Heaven and Hell to psychological states, Purgatory to symbolic action, Christ to the dialectics of redemption, and
the grammar of Christianity to a rhetoric of rebirth, with the whole
transformation culminating in the reduction of theology (discourse
about God) to logology (discourse about discourse). As "logologer"
and "logologist," equipped with his "logologic," Burke has spun out
a "logological" "dramatistic" view of the world and man's place in
it. (See RR,7–42,172–272.) He has begun at the beginning — in the
beginning was the Word — and has explained how with the word and
its peculiar genius, the negative, man built on the natural, biological,
animalistic base the symbol systems, the familial, socio-political, and
religious orders which, along with nature now viewed through a symbolic fog, become the logological scene in which the drama of human
relations is enacted. One of the most striking things about Burke's
system, and what differentiates it from Christianity and almost any
other systematic view of the human drama, is the insistence that the
human agent cannot do otherwise than always act upon a logological
scene. Whereas a Christian might say that God is the scene and operates as a motive in all men's acts, Burke says that language is *the*
scene and operates as a motive in all experiences possible to man.
Even if the act is non-verbal, it must be affected in some way by the
symbolic ingredient that is intrinsic to the human mind and constitutes part of man's essence.

ii

THE INTERLOCKED MOMENTS

Language, which is usually thought of as an agency, but is treated
by Burke as an act, is also, in terms of the pentad and its ratios, always part of the scene or motivational ground of any human act, is

always in the agent as a substantival ingredient, and is, in very complex ways, always involved in the purpose of the act as well as *any* purposive human action, whether verbal or non-verbal. Burke's explanation of language as the ultimate reduction is based on three of the main coordinates of dramatism — the nature of language, the negative, and hierarchy — and the relations between them. Language, Burke believes, is by nature "transcending," for it has in it as part of its "entelechy" the motive of transcendence, an upward movement towards abstractions (god-terms) and abstract thinking (dialectics) (PC,184–185,fn.). Language is also by nature hierarchic, for the end result of the driving impulse towards abstraction is an ascending order of terms headed by a god-term and many ascending orders of terms headed by *the* god of god-terms. As a final step, one arrives at the idea of god which heads and orders the whole hierarchy of terms. Since language is part of the essence of man, these qualities of language become essential attributes of man, with at least the following results. According to Burke, "there seems to be in man an unremitting tendency to make himself [and the world in which he lives] over, in the image of his distinctive trait, language" (PC, 184–185,fn.). In man are abstract and hierarchic modes of thought and action which Burke derives directly from the nature of language and discusses as linguistic traits or as evidence of man's "language-ridden view" of the world and human relations. Man exfoliates socio-political hierarchies modeled "of necessity" on the structure of language: instead of an order among terms one has an order of social classes; instead of the impulse towards abstraction, one has social and ethical climbing; instead of god-terms one has rulers, heads of family and state, even "living gods"; imbedded in every complex socio-political hierarchy, and again as a kind of inevitable outgrowth of the abstract and hierarchic modes of thought and action intrinsic to the mind of the "typically language-using species," are hundreds of smaller hierarchies and patterns of abstract thought which reflect man's distinctive trait and make it inevitable that he should experience the world in the image of that distinctive trait.

For example, Burke says that due to this "tendency to abstraction" man separates himself from his "natural condition" (ATH,

Burke and the Drama of Human Relations

2nd ed., dust jacket). By "natural condition" Burke means "nature" — the positive world of the biological, of sensory perception; and by "separates" he means "alienates," which for him is a loaded, dyslogistic term belonging to the pollution, war cluster. The separation occurs as a result of what can be called a "movement of abstraction." In this process man moves first from thing to word, from positive to negative, from image to idea; then he regards the thing in terms of words, the positive in terms of the negative, and the image in terms of the idea. This process separates man from his natural condition until one half of man's nature (the animal) is dominated by the other (symbol-using); the result is not only a perversion of the natural but an almost psychopathic denial and distrust of "natural impulses." An extreme manifestation of the process is the systematic destruction and desecration of nature and the natural by the engines of industry in the exalted name of "Progress," with the very idea of progress as well as the engines of industry being products of "reason" (or, as Burke would have it, "symbol-using"). The most extreme manifestation, and the end toward which the whole process seems to be moving, is the total separation and desecration that would result from the use of a few hydrogen or cobalt bombs, both of which are among the really great achievements of the rational, scientific, symbol-using mind. This example illustrates as well as anything the paradoxical condition of man which fascinates Burke. Though man's specific differentia is symbol-using, he is still generically an animal; as such, he is almost mystically bound to the biological and natural by the most profound, if sometimes unconscious, needs and by the biological processes which govern his body. The abstraction from the physical — the central theme of D. H. Lawrence — and its effect on man is perhaps best illustrated in what Burke calls "psychogenetic" illness and explains as linguistically caused physical disorders. Sometimes the linguistic cause seems remote until one remembers that all hierarchies are linguistic products, and that social and linguistic are interchangeable terms in Burke. A businessman's ulcer, for example, is linguistically caused because economic and social hierarchies are symbol-systems; false pregnancies, stigmata, and all kinds of sexual disorders not attributable to biological malformation can also be accounted for by man's tendency to abstraction and hierarchic modes of thought and action.

Nothing is ever merely simple in Burke. He takes this same impulse towards abstract and hierarchic modes of thought and action and shows how it can also redeem man from the very effects it causes. The process of abstraction leads, finally, to the dialectic of transcendence, a purificatory process best illustrated in Plato's *Phaedrus*. The end result of this dialectic is a vision of oneness, of an ultimate order among all terms which has the effect of unifying everything in the vision of a universal hierarchy. The movement of abstraction, the dialectic of transcendence, and the ultimate hierarchy are all, according to Burke, linguistic resources; they are among the many "modes of *symbolic purification* ingrained in the nature of symbolic [linguistic] action" (MPE,269). *From* language, then, comes man's separation from his natural condition, his abstraction from the physical, the hierarchic psychosis, categorical guilt, and a great many other results; but *through* and by means of the various modes of dialectical, rhetorical, and symbolic purification ingrained in language, man can unify himself and the world, treat his hierarchic psychosis, and expiate his categorical guilt.

One consequence of this line of thought is the reduction of all modes of purification either to "verbal resources" or analogues of "verbal resources." Thus, man's great drive for perfection, which is self-evident, and the various modes of action which he adopts in trying to achieve this ideal, become either verbal resources or are traceable to a verbal cause. The drive for perfection — Burke calls it ethical striving or mounting — is set in motion and fed by the impulse to abstraction, for transcendence is implicit in language-using, and language itself provides (or constructs) the hierarchy of values which one must mount in order to achieve or approximate perfection. Heavens are built of symbols, and language, that great purgatorial agency, provides man with the means of ascent. This is what Burke means when he says that the motto of dramatism is "By and through language, beyond language" (MPE,263). Redemption as an achieved state is a moment of stasis, the still moment following the fusion and release of a symbol-induced catharsis, or the still moment of vision when, after the furious activity of dialectic, a fusion at a higher level of discourse takes place to produce a perceived unity among many previously discordant ideas and things.

In describing this language-caused and language-resolved movement of man from alienation through purification to redemption, Burke deliberately alludes to Dante's *Divine Comedy* to identify the characteristic movement of all his works and thinking. He divides the "divine human comedy of language" into three stages corresponding to the three books of Dante's poem. The first is the inferno which, Burke says, is the realm of "abysmal problems" brought on by the use of language; it is the realm of "the great deceptions of speech," the realm that breeds neuroses; in this realm man wanders lost through a "forest of symbols," "stumbles" through a "fog of words" (JGE,V,202). Here man is alienated, not from God, as the people in Dante's Inferno are, but from his natural condition; and not because of "sin," but because of words — because, as in E. B. White's "The Door" (that representative anecdote for our time), nothing is what it seems to be, everything is "koid" and "tex." Burke's equivalent of Dante is Everyman, and his equivalent of Virgil and Beatrice is himself, Hermes, the messenger of the gods, who, with dramatism, leads man out of the abyss.

The movement from hell to purgatory is the "movement of transition, whereby the very sources of lamentation [language, symbols] could, if beheld from a different angle, be transformed into the promissory." This different angle of vision is achieved by exploiting the resources of the "dialectic of the Upward Way" until one arrives at the "principle of oneness," "the vision of unity." In more detail, Burke describes this "dialectic" as the "linguistic devices whereby we may move from a world of disparate particulars to a principle of one-ness, an 'ascent' got, as the semanticists might say, by a movement toward progressively 'higher levels of generalization.'" After the ascent, there would be "a descent, a Downward Way, back into the world of particulars [what *was* hell], all of which would now be 'identified' with the genius of the unitary principle discovered en route." As a result of this verbal journey, "all would be thus made consubstantial by participation in a common essence, as with objects bathed in the light of the one sun, that shines down upon them as from the apex of a pyramid" (JGE,V,202–204). Purgatory, then, is the realm of dialectic; Burke calls it Socrates' realm and in his work it is best exemplified in *A Grammar of Motives*, whose subject and method is dialectics itself. Dialectics, Burke says, is a verbal resource which can be exploited to transform any "troublesome *either-or* . . . into a *both-and*" (MPE,293); or, it is a resource which can be used to take "A" on a verbal journey from which it returns as "non-A." Finally, "the real world of action [and experience]," which "is so confused and complicated as to seem almost formless," is made orderly (to the mind, at least) by the miracles of dialectical transformation (MPE,263–264). This is what Burke means by "different angle" of vision; and it is only by means of this altered angle of vision that man can get out of the inferno-like "forest of symbols."

For Burke, no journey, verbal or otherwise, would be complete if it terminated in purgatory; though this is the realm of purification, it is also the realm of pain and endless activity. *A Grammar of Motives* is purgatorial; it is a perpetual-motion machine, in itself dialectical as it develops and illustrates a method of dialectical analysis. Nowhere in it, really, is there an ultimate hierarchy of values which would permit both the furious purgatorial activity and the moment of stasis which comes from a fixed point toward which the whole activity moves. It is fine to subject everything to the whirligig of dramatistic dialectical analysis; and such analyses are curative, leaving one with the sense of completion that comes from systematizing anything; but when finished, where are you? Still in purgatory, ready to take the formidable method and apply it again to another text, with the same results, forever taking apart and putting together again, with the method as an end in itself.

The next step in *The Divine Comedy* analogy, the changing of guides and the final ascent from purgatory to heaven, is taken by Burke in *A Rhetoric of Motives* and constitutes the completion of his journey and system. The completion of the system provides him with the doctrine of dramatism (lately called "logology") which, as Hermes, he will convey from the gods to man in order that he might finally find peace. The final step is from dialectics to hierarchy, from order among terms to an over-all order among all terms, to a "vision of Oneness," a cosmological vision of universal order. The eloquent passage which brings *A Rhetoric of Motives* to a close is the best description of what hierarchy is and why it permits the furious activity of dialectics and yet provides one with a fixed goal and those moments of stasis which are heaven's reward. "But since, for better or worse," Burke chants,

the mystery of the hierarchic is forever with us, let us, as students of rhetoric, scrutinize its range of entrancements, both with dismay and in delight. And finally let us observe, all about us, forever goading us, though it be in fragments, the motive that attains its ultimate identification in the thought, not of the universal holocaust, but of the universal order – as with the rhetorical and dialectic symmetry of the Aristotelian metaphysics, whereby all classes of beings are hierarchally arranged in a chain or ladder or pyramid of mounting worth, each kind striving towards the *perfection* of its kind, and so towards the kind next above it, while the strivings of the entire series head in God as the beloved cynosure and sinecure, the end of all desire. (RM,333.)

The hierarchy which Burke envisions is compounded of movement and rest, flux and fixity, division and merger; the whole is a monolithic structure of ascent headed by the heavenly idea of "universal Justice" which, for Burke, is the noblest ideal ever conceived by the mind of man. It is toward this ideal, toward "the purification of war," that all dialectics should move by following the grammar of ascent inherent in the hierarchy. Persuasion to this ideal – in the sense of bringing man to knowledge through theoretical discussion and applied criticism, with the knowledge designed to effect a change in attitude, and the change in attitude eventually to result in an altered course of action – is the principal motive behind all of Burke's recent effusive and often extraordinary rhetoric. Like all persons who see "god," Burke has been made ecstatic and messianic by the power of the vision, by the sense of completion and ultimate unity among all terms, which he has quite obviously experienced.

The idea and principle of hierarchy enabled Burke to end what Austin Warren aptly called his sceptic's progress, because it allowed him to order the world in a way that was both final and fluid. The idea itself is so fertile that one could not exhaust it in a lifetime, even if one worked in only one of the four major hierarchic orders Burke has settled on: the natural, verbal, socio-political, and religious. If one moves to the analogical relations among the four orders and their various suborders and to the cause-and-effect relations among the four, the whole of nature, human relations, and supernature is opened to linguistic analysis. Though he often simply investigates the wonders of hierarchy and the hierarchic principle, the term has a specific meaning in Burke and all his investigations are really guided by this meaning. Though he studies — especially in his literary analyses — the metaphor-and-symbol-making process made possible by the analogical relations among the four major hierarchies, and the complex implications of such cross-breeding of terms, he is particularly interested in two things: reading the socio-political hierarchy backwards into the natural hierarchy and forwards into the supernatural one. To the study of these phenomena, Burke has given the deliberately cacophonous name of socioanagogic criticism.

In Burke's scheme, there are four major and a great many minor hierarchies. The natural order can be divided into animals, natural things, natural places, and the biological. The socio-political can be divided into such minor orders as the familial, the economic (property and property structure), the social, and the political. And the supernatural can be divided into myth, religion, and cosmology. In dramatism, where language is the ultimate reduction, another kind of ordering is also possible: the division of everything into non-verbal, verbal, and meta-verbal. One of the principal objects of dramatism is to study the cause-effect relation between the non-verbal, verbal, and meta-verbal as it is manifested in the natural, socio-political, and supernatural orders. By cause-effect relation, Burke means the ways in which language as cause affects man's views of and relations to the non-verbal and meta-verbal, and the natural, socio-political, and supernatural hierarchies.

Socioanagogic criticism is one way of studying this cause-effect relation. In order to understand socioanagogic criticism one has to remember that according to Burke all socio-political hierarchies are linguistic products in so far as they are symbolic constructs only made possible by the tendency towards abstraction, hierarchic modes of thought, and the negative. In general, socioanagogic criticism calls for the analysis of everything as social allegory, with the socio-political hierarchy as primary cause, and attempts to show how man has read this hierarchy backwards into the non-verbal natural order and forwards into the meta-verbal supernatural order – in both cases with disastrous results. Since all socio-political hierarchies are verbal constructs, it is at this point that Burke's linguistic and social theories fuse and linguistic analysis becomes a method of social criticism.

According to Burke man is absolutely dominated by the hierarchic motive, which, though manifested in many different ways, is experienced with the greatest immediacy in socio-political terms; that is, in terms of property, possession, social climbing, status and the like. To be sure, the socio-political hierarchic motive is often directly expressed; but most often it is indirectly expressed in some veiled "social allegory," in overt and covert metaphors, in all kinds of seemingly non-hierarchic symbols which turn out to be secretly charged with "judgments of status" through identification with something in the socio-political hierarchy, and through nearly endless analogical extensions of the hierarchic motives of ascent and descent, the hierarchic pattern of experience, and the hierarchic form or structure (RM,219). Socioanagogic criticism culminates in what Burke calls the "range of mountings" and, in its extreme form, in Burke's contention that sexual courtship is in reality but a veiled form of social courtship. Burke lists the following as the seven primary modes of expressing the hierarchic motive, pattern of experience, and form: (1) imagery of height and depth; (2) Alpinism, mountain-climbing in answer to a call; (3) sexual mounting, sexual ambiguities of all kinds; (4) social climbing, improvement of status; (5) ethical mounting; (6) the pyramidal dung heap, transcending of filth, ascent by purification; (7) the dialectic of the Upward Way (RM,301–313; SPCL,107–108). Some of these are spatial representations of the hierarchic motive or form, some are actions, some are biological or psychic processes, and some are what Burke calls linguistic processes. All of them have in common some kind of upward and downward movement – the basic hierarchic motive.

Dramatism

The theory that sexual courtship is really an analogue of social courtship is an extension of the third "range of mountings." In this theory, which is one of the best illustrations of how Burke thinks the language-ridden socio-political hierarchy is read backwards into the non-verbal natural order, Freud is turned upside down by reversing the causal relation between the sexual and socio-political. Burke argues at length in *A Rhetoric of Motives* that sexual courtship, and everything related to it, is not only a poetic means of embodying, but is actually a form of, social courtship — the wooing of one class by another, either higher or lower, for purposes of transcending social estrangement. Burke works out an elaborate analogy between sexual and social relations; he argues that just as male and female are essentially "mysterious" to each other because they are "different" from the other, so every social class is essentially "mysterious" to every other social class because each is different from the other. Division into clearly demarcated ranked classes is inevitable in any socio-political hierarchy; in all cases, the division into classes is accompanied by a corresponding division of property, personal possessions, actions, and the like. The end result is that all persons, places, things, and ideas acquire a "hierarchic charge" and become important in the vast and complex drama of social courtship. Depending upon what class in the hierarchy they represent and depending upon one's position in the hierarchy, the persons, places, things, and ideas acquire "mystery"— what Burke calls the "mysterious glow of status" — and become, as in F. Scott Fitzgerald, both instruments of wooing and that which one hopes to gain by the wooing. By forcing the analogy somewhat, Burke can say that the two most persistent motives in social courtship, as in sexual courtship, are the desire to mount and to be mounted, with the two motives operating both from lower to higher and from higher to lower. Those who are lower most often want to mount higher, but sometimes, out of status awe, they can worship what is higher by being mounted, or, they can actually vicariously rise by being mounted — that is, used in a variety of ways. Those at the top often, out of guilt, desire to be mounted by those below; sometimes they woo those below as a kind of benign granting of favors; and sometimes they woo those below, rather coyly, in order to assert their own position, or in order to tantalize and move higher by rejecting the rejected. The possibilities here are nearly endless; I mention only a few of the more obvious ones to suggest how Burke moves from various kinds of sexual courtship and activities to their social or hierarchic significance. As examples of the relation between sexual and social courtship, Burke cites Castiglioni's *The Courtier*, Plato's *Symposium*, and Kafka's *The Castle*, and in each case tries to show how the social or hierarchic motive, rather than the sexual one, is primary, with the sexual functioning allegorically, or metaphorically and symbolically as a roundabout means of conveying the author's real theme.

Burke's point is that sexual courtship, regardless of what it has now become for man, was originally part of his biological inheritance; as such, it was non-verbal and belonged to the natural order. But now sexual courtship has become a mode of hierarchic action and sex itself one of the most valuable and marketable of hierarchic commodities; consequently, that most natural of urges is no longer ever purely biological, but is most often psychologically and hierarchically motivated: "sheer 'animality' is not possible to the sensory experiences of a symbol-using animal" (QJS,XXXIX,209). For example, the rape of a white woman by a Negro (or vice versa) in the South has very little to do with "sheer animality" and is certainly more satisfactorily explained in hierarchic and psychological rather than sexual terms. Surely the purpose of the rape is only remotely sexual, for the white woman is more symbol than person and the rape more an expression of social frustration, rage, and hate than the satisfying of a biological urge. The recent gang rape of a Negro girl in Florida is again best explained in psychological and hierarchic terms as one of the terrible consequences of the bitter class-color war in the South. Both examples are best understood as "social allegory," as illustrations of the way in which the socio-political hierarchy absorbs and often perverts what is "natural" and non-verbal. The purpose of socioanagogic criticism is to make clear (1) just how this process works, (2) the extent to which this process dominates experience in any socio-political hierarchy, and (3) the extent to which language (symbol-using and the negative) is responsible for (1) and (2).

Language produces hierarchies, hierarchies produce categorical guilt as well as provide man with a means of purging and redeeming himself through the dialectic of transcendence made possible by symbolic action and the verbal hierarchy. Here, then, derived from language, are four of the interlocked moments in the Burkean drama of human relations. This drama, if such a thing is possible, is a secular religious one, very similar in form to the Christian drama of the covenant, temptation, fall, sacrifice, and redemption. According to Burke, no moral action is possible without language (QJS,XXXVIII, 446; RR,187). As he explains it, an act, to be an act, must be willed; the will, to be a will, must be free to choose between alternatives; nature, being governed by law, is not free; so the will must derive its freedom from a realm beyond nature, some ultimate realm of ideas (QJS,XXXVIII,446–447). In other words, only through negation is positive moral action (and hence, freedom of action) possible; it is language that "adds the peculiar possibility of the Negative" to nature (QJS,XXXVIII,252), thus providing man with the "realm of ideas" beyond nature; it is only by means of language and that linguistic marvel, the negative, that moral action is possible. For example: the senses and biological urges — the animal part of man — are what Burke calls natural positives and are part of nature. Among animals, a sexual or biological urge could be frustrated but not consciously negated; among men, however, such an impulse which, if unchecked, would result in a positive act, can be consciously, willfully negated as well as frustrated. From this phenomenon comes all drama, for the essence of drama is moral choice and willed action. The example just given would be the simple negation of a positive. But man, because he can abstract and construct hierarchies of values in which certain persons, places, things, acts, states of mind, and ideas are positive (good) and negative (evil), can consciously negate negatives in order to produce positives. Redemption (for example) must always be preceded by a catharsis or purge; disregarding, for the moment, what might have produced the pollution which makes the purification necessary, there are, according to Burke, two main modes of purification which perfectly illustrate the operation of the negative in the drama of human relations. These are victimage, which Burke defines as "purification by sacrifice, by *vicarious atonement*, unburdening of guilt within by transference to chosen vessels without" (QJS,XXXIX,216); and mortification, which he defines as self-inflicted punishment for one's sins or self-imposed and self-enforced denials and restrictions (QJS,XXXVIII, 264;XXXIX, 216; RR,172ff.).

Victimage is always a mode of purification, whether it moves in the direction of either of its two extreme manifestations: victimage of others (homicide) and victimage of ourselves (suicide). Both are extreme negations in so far as they are willed rather than natural death; that is, they are primarily acts rather than physiological processes. Variations of these two kinds of victimage have been catalogued by Burke under the title "Thanatopsis for Critics: A Brief Thesaurus of Deaths and Dyings" (EIC,II,369–375). In this essay, Burke lists some of the meanings which the negative "idea" of death may have, and various ways in which death functions as a mode of purification. In homicidal victimage, there are two ideal kinds of victims: the polluted agent who is sacrificed because he is polluted, and the unpolluted agent who is sacrificed because he is unpolluted. The first may be called the scapegoat and the second the sacrificial agent. The two kinds appear together in the crucifixion, where Christ, the sacrificial agent, is flanked by two scapegoats. Between the two extremes, combining homicidal-suicidal, polluted-unpolluted, are such mixed victims as Oedipus, Othello, Lear, Hamlet, and Creon. Here mortification and victimage come together for, usually, after making someone else a homicidal victim, the mixed victim turns on himself, negating the negation (pollution) by mortification, often ending by himself becoming a suicidal victim.

The essential difference between victimage and mortification is that the first always directly involves some other person, place, or thing; always calls for a ritualistic transference of pollution to the chosen vessel (whether person, place, or thing); and hence always brings into operation the great paradox of this kind of purification:

in order for A to be cleansed, B must be contaminated, or, if A is to live, B must die. In mortification, however, even in its most extreme form of suicide, or self-victimage, nothing outside of the person involved needs to be polluted or destroyed in order for the purification to take place. If a nun flagellates herself in the privacy of her cell to mortify the flesh (to negate, that is, what her creed tells her is a negative), this is a private affair between herself and God; even if a man does public penitential acts, like the holy man in India who somersaulted fifty miles, this is still essentially self-victimage and does not harm, pollute, or destroy anyone else. Generally, then, to make others suffer for our own sins is victimage; to make ourselves suffer for our own sins is mortification.

Both are modes of purification; both are made possible by the linguistic negative; both are ways by which man can negate negations in order to produce positives; and finally, both may be used for constructive and destructive purposes. As the two primary modes of purification, they are made necessary by all the goads and tensions, by the hierarchic psychosis and the categorical guilt which language and the socio-political hierarchy make part of man's birthright. As is true of almost anything man uses, they are capable of being monstrously perverted, of leading to the unbelievably barbaric carnage of the German concentration camps and the systematic victimization of the Jews. But the two impulses are also capable of producing something as splendid as the drama of Christ and the great tragedies. The study of them leads Burke into so many different areas of human experience and human relations that it is difficult and probably pointless to attempt a systematic presentation of the operation of victimage and mortification in, say, politics, family relations, sexual relations, business, or religion. The principle is everywhere the same and what Burke does is isolate the principle, break it down analytically, and then, following his own four-fold division (grammar, rhetoric, poetics, ethics) apply and reapply it to whatever happens to fall within the range of his knowledge, experience, and dramatistic system.

Language, the negative, victimage, and mortification — with these man builds his moral universe; a study of them touches upon almost every phase of man's moral life, which means, for Burke, almost every kind of experience possible to man, since, thanks to the genius of the negative, man tends to moralize everything. By moralize, Burke generally means "charge with value," with the particular value coming from the over-all social hierarchy in which the person lives. Though Burke preaches his own set of values, he is equally interested in the process of constructing value systems, the origin and operation of which he traces directly to the linguistic negative. The negative is essentially the ability to say "No" to nature's "Yes," and the ability to say "Yes" by saying "No" to "No." For example, every hierarchy is headed by a "godhead" of some kind, the godhead being that which is most valuable in a given value system, whether it happens to be moral excellence, material wealth, physical beauty, athletic prowess, or scholarly excellence. Theoretically, the higher up the hierarchy one is, the closer one comes to the godhead; as one approaches the godhead, one nears perfection and "heaven." Attaining the godhead always calls for the possession of various things and qualities, even if, paradoxically, one is an ascetic Christian and must be nothing in order to be something. Generally, possession is negation, for every value system is built up out of positives and negatives, and in order to attain the godhead, to acquire that self which the hierarchy says is the most valuable, it is necessary to deny oneself certain things in order to affirm the thou-shalt-nots. All negation of this kind is a form of mortification, sometimes self-generated and self-imposed, and sometimes imposed from without. According to Burke, the ideal kind of mortification is free — self-willed and self-imposed. Often, but not always, the negative values of a particular social hierarchy are infused into those things associated with the lower or animal part of man. Though mortification may manifest itself as the denial or negation of almost anything — in some social hierarchies one *must* steal, or rape, or submit sexually, or deny God in order to belong — it most often takes the form of mortification of the flesh: the controlling and denial of the "natural" "animal" impulses. The perfect control of these impulses is set up as an ideal (a high-level abstraction), and one "mortifies the flesh" in order to attain the ideal or, failing that, one mortifies the flesh to expiate the guilt that comes from failing to attain the ideal, for every failure is "sinful." Sins (both of commission and omission) are failures to negate the appropriate negatives; they come from saying "Yes" to too many natural and/or selfish impulses. The sins produce the guilt (or anxiety) which in turn engenders mortification's brother, victimage.

The negative, then, makes for mortification; the two culminate in the Decalogue, most of which is what Burke calls the great thou-shalt-nots. Even the yeas in the decalogue imply a negative, for love thy neighbor means don't infringe upon your neighbor's rights; it means, as Burke points out, respect your neighbor's no-trespassing sign. The two areas of human relations which are probably the most thoroughly infused with moral negatives are the sexual and bodily, and what Burke calls property rights. The sexual and the bodily area is discussed by Burke under two headings, the Demonic Trinity and "No-no imagery" (QJS,XXXIX,216). The Demonic Trinity is so named because all three (urine, feces, semen) are biological, bodily, animalistic positive impulses and processes, and because they represent, generally (for Burke and mankind) the natural, animalistic demons which must be controlled and transcended if any "grace" is to be earned from the Holy Trinity. The urinary and fecal become for Burke the unclean — filth and defilement of any kind; they are the biological counterparts of spiritual and psychic purgation. Aside from the monstrous and unbelievably subtle perversions of which man is capable in his sexual relations, what interests Burke is that the sexual instinct is, like the urinary and fecal, bodily, animalistic, and primarily selfish. Generally, the urinary, fecal, and seminal represent those impulses which, if unchecked (unnegated, unmortified) would return man to the jungles from whence he came. The Demonic Trinity and property rights (possession) come together under the motive of self-aggrandizement, or the opposite of mortification. Unchecked, the drive for possession of property results in the disease of ambition and the pursuit of power for its own sake. Again, if unchecked, this impulse would return man to the jungle law which, through the genius of the negative, he has replaced with the decalogue.

From language, to the essence of language (the negative), to the essence of the negative (the decalogue), to the perfect decalogue (with its ideal of justice), to mortification, to its ideal (the freely willed, self-imposed kind), to the moral positives which will lead to the partial realization of the ideal envisioned in the decalogue — this is the paradigmatic sequence which Burke works out in explaining how man, following the genius of his essence (language and the negative) can move toward perfection. But man does not — in fact, cannot — always move toward perfection; and mortification, whether imposed from within or without, is capable, like everything else human, of being perverted. Since it is one of the great moments in the moral drama of human relations, Burke is interested in all the manifestations of mortification, whether creative or destructive. Since mortification, like victimage, is a process rather than a fixed value, it may remain everywhere the same as a process while at the same time it produces remarkably different results. Everything depends upon what is to be attained through mortification. Sometimes it is the "good life" for which one strives; or sometimes it is eternal life (which calls for the negating of death, or the negating of the monster negative, hell, in order to attain the supreme positive, heaven); sometimes power for its own sake, or money for its own sake is the goal, and these call for the same kind of discipline, austerity, and denial, though the goals are quite different; sometimes the goal is such that mortification takes the form of sacrifice of self — dying for a cause, negating one's own life in order that others may live, be free or happy. Here, mortification and victimage merge in so far as consciously willed self-sacrifice becomes a form of mortification.

As I pointed out above, mortification and victimage are causally related because the first makes the second necessary and because victimage of self and others is often a means of mortification. Though mortification may be perverted, as in the case of fanatical flagellants and misguided idealists (dying for a worthless cause), it is really in victimage that the most terrible perversions occur, for here, masked under the most exalted of motives, some of the most barbaric acts known to man take place. Historical examples come to mind at once: the Spanish Inquisition, the Communist purges, the German extermination of the Jews, and in our own country, the segregationists' victimizing of the Negroes. These happen to be examples of mass victimage, so terrible in themselves that one tends to be stunned by the acts and forgets to examine for causes. What is so terrible about victimage is that, invariably, one man's guilt, or a group's guilt, results in some other person's or persons' injury or death. As Burke has pointed out in his essay on *Mein Kampf* — itself a masterly analysis of Nazi victimage — the motive that results in victimage of various kinds is natural and healthy as a response to the felt need to do something about one's guilt, anxiety, or uneasiness. Where there is some systematic program for peacefully taking care of this profoundly felt need — as in the Roman Catholic church — the guilt that is every man's birthright and the tensions which result from life in any social hierarchy are often taken care of in ways that do not injure others. But there is also a destructive kind of victimage, which is probably best represented by what the Nazis did to the Jews, attributing to them every kind of natural, economic, political, and religious evil, dehumanizing them in order to justify and legalize their extermination for the good of the race and state. The constructive kind of victimage comes to a head in religion and art; the destructive kind comes to a head in war — legalized mass victimage — crime, and various kinds of "justified" homicide.

Whatever the form, the function of victimage is always the same: purification (cleansing, release of any kind) and redemption (rest, stasis of some kind). Like mortification, it is a process and operates in all areas of human experience; it ranges from the simple act of kicking one's dog to the complex collective act of exterminating an entire people. It may take the form of verbal or of physical action; but whichever form it takes, the process is made possible by man's capacity for symbolic manipulation. Every act of victimage must be preceded by a transfer through identification; this is a rhetorical process in which persuasion of the self or others to knowledge, new attitude, or action is effected by means of identification. The transfer is always effected through the manipulation by oneself or others of the negative and positive values within any given hierarchy; and the transfer is always from oneself or some collective self to something else (an actual living person, any symbolic figure created for that purpose, such as Arnold's Empedocles, any group of living people, even an animal or a place), which is then killed (actually or symbolically), driven out or away (as with the actual scapegoat), mocked, spit on, or defiled in various ways (as with the Negroes in Little Rock), or which simply benignly absorbs, absolves, or dissolves the evil that is transferred to it (as with Christ).

Purification by victimage is perhaps best effected, Burke says, in symbolic action generally, and poetic symbolic action specifically, for there actual victims can be replaced by symbolic ones, and actual physical violence can be replaced by verbal violence. This idea is the basis of Burke's theory of art as catharsis, the principal subject of his projected "Symbolic of Motives." But it is also dealt with in *A Rhetoric of Motives* (which is built on the principle of identification), in *A Grammar of Motives* (which is built around substance and the dialectics of transcendence), and is dealt with in *The Rhetoric of Religion* (which is built around the negative, mortification, and victimage). Like the other great moments in the Burkean drama of human relations — hierarchy, the negative, guilt, mortification, catharsis, and redemption — victimage is traced to its linguistic source, related to all the other interlocked moments in the drama, and necessarily, since the drama is the center of the dramatistic system, figures in each of its four major divisions (grammar, rhetoric, poetics, ethics). Though each of the volumes in what Burke now announces will be a "Tetralogy of Motives" concentrates on different linguistic resources, and though each volume concentrates on one of the four major functions of language and the nature of language in fulfilling that particular function, all four volumes will have in common the drama of human relations as well as the dramatistic method (pentad and ratios) developed in the *Grammar of Motives*. The drama is made up of seven interlocked moments; it is developed out of the central tenet of dramatism — man is the typically symbol-using animal — because all seven moments can be traced (or reduced) to a linguistic source and especially to language's two essential characteristics: the tendency to abstraction and to hierarchic modes of thought and action. Another way of putting it would be to say that the drama develops *because* man is the typically symbol-using animal and because there is in him an unremitting tendency to make himself and the world over in the image of his distinctive trait, language. This distinctive trait is man's curse and blessing, for it leads him out of the natural jungle into the jungle of words, and can, if he but learns to use it, lead him out of the second jungle into the symbolic heaven that language makes possible, the benign state (or attitude) which enables him to purify war.

iii

LOGOLOGIC

The drama of human relations with its seven interlocked moments is a constant or set form around which the whole dramatistic system is built. Each of the seven moments is a primary locus of motivation (purpose) for man's verbal and physical actions. The whole tetralogy of motives is a language-oriented study of how and why men do what they do; it is an approach to "the problem of human relations through a study of language" (MPE,267). Burke divides language into four major aspects and devotes a volume to each of them. *A Grammar of Motives* deals with the "logical or indicative" and tries to show what its essence is and how language fulfills its logical or indicative function of teaching and informing, providing one with information as preparation for action. *A Grammar of Motives* is built around a theory of substance (the essence of anything is equal to the sum of its attributes) and develops a "logologic" (the pentad and ratios); the logic is the theory of substance converted into a method (or perhaps vice versa) which always requires the study of one thing (say, agent) in terms of something else (scene, act, agency, purpose). *A Grammar of Motives* is further built around the idea that verbal action is the substance of man and treats the complex relations between all kinds of verbal actions and the non-verbal grounds or scenes out of which they come.

These relations are studied in terms of the various ratios worked out between the five terms of the pentad. Though there are a good many separate ratios, there are really only four general kinds, and of these the last two are more important than the others. The first is the genetic (causal or familial) ratio, which reduces essence (substance) to origins, or that from which a thing comes. It could also be called the evolutionary ratio. The second is the contextual ratio, which reduces a thing to that which surrounds it. The third is the futuristic (the entelechial) ratio, which reduces the indicative to the optative and treats the part as the whole. It could also be called the synecdochic ratio if one remembers that Burke always pushes forward (or upward) until he has isolated what he calls the pure abstract form or paradigm and then works backwards on the assumption that the whole essence is implicit in any part. This might also be called the archetype ratio, for Burke believes that any specific embodiment of an archetype must contain, implicitly, every attribute of the pure archetype. This ratio is developed at length under the name of entelechy or "to the end of the line" thinking. The fourth ratio is the equational one which converts causal sequences, context, and future into a kind of eternal "is-ness." It could also be called the cluster ratio, for a cluster is a set of interrelated terms, any one of which contains all the others. The seven moments of the drama of human relations are such a cluster, for, as Burke has recently (1958) tried to demonstrate, any one of the seven implies the presence of the other six and no matter which of them one starts with or finds evidence of, one always has to talk about all seven in order to get at the substance of any one. (See RR,172–272.)

Burke calls his methodology logologic (a more recent term for his theory of substance and the pentadic logic) because it is the logic which language must follow. The substance of anything turns out to be an equational cluster, a set of interlocked terms all of which imply each other. By using logologic, one can reduce the substance of any act, thing, or place to its equational cluster; one can even reduce narratives to their logological essence, as Burke has done with the first three chapters of Genesis, *Othello*, and every narrative work he has recently analyzed. Burke tries to show in *A Grammar of Motives* that substances vary because the terms tend to cluster around one of the five pivotal terms in the pentad. As a result, one gets the scene cluster (materialism); the agent cluster (idealism); the act cluster (realism); the agency cluster (pragmatism); and the purpose cluster (mysticism). Burke's own system (he says) belongs to the act cluster, for it takes its name, many of its terms, and some of its main principles from drama, the paradigm of action; it stresses moral choice by emphasizing the negative, moral action, linguistic action, purgative and redemptive acts of all kinds, and never, Burke maintains, gets very far away from the creative act.

The theory of substance and the dramatistic method developed in *A Grammar of Motives* are, like the seven interlocked moments in the drama, two more of Burke's constant or set forms; and whether or not he later (after 1945) identifies them as such, he assumes the theory of substance and employs logologic in everything he writes, sometimes with bewildering results. The flat, equational, cluster logic in which everything can be merged and then spun out of itself by the dialectical manipulation of similarities and opposites characterizes *all* of Burke's thinking about grammar, rhetoric, poetics, and ethics. He not only constructs his own vision (the drama) with this logic but subjects everything else to it. The logic is at once flat and equational because it starts always from the assumption that the end result of any analysis is a statement of substance which consists of an interrelated cluster of terms. But the logic is also "entelechial" because it drives always toward the description of the perfect essence (cluster). Burke works in this way because he assumes that, like language with its tendency towards abstraction and the perfecting of itself, everything else has an entelechial motive built into it, and that like man, who tries to make himself over in the image of his distinctive trait, everything else tries to imitate the idea of itself.

Invariably, Burke takes an idea or person or particular kind of act and analytically breaks it down into its perfect cluster; the cluster is logologically complete when its range of possibilities or meanings has been logically exhausted. Burke's works are full of such perfect clusters: he has worked them out for hierarchy, deaths and dyings, the range of mountings, catharsis, "possession," persuasion, the negative, dialectic, and all the terms of the pentad. Once worked out, the perfect cluster becomes the model or paradigm from which he begins in any subsequent specific analysis of one of the terms from the full range of terms in the perfect cluster. According to logologic, any one of the terms contains all the others, and for this reason Burke always seems to be reading a whole book out of a single word. For example, in a recent essay, "The First Three Chapters of Genesis," Burke works out the "cycle of terms implicit in the idea of 'order'" (RR,172–272). He shows how in the "idea" of order there is "implicit" the whole drama of human relations. The essay and the book of which it is now a part — *The Rhetoric of Religion: Studies in Logology* — has a multiple purpose: it describes the drama; it shows that whatever can be said about "god" has its counterpart in something that can be said about language; it is a logological explanation of the creation, temptation, fall, sacrifice, and redemption; and it shows that since the "idea" of God as well as the drama of the covenant, temptation, fall, sacrifice, and redemption is "empirically" derivable from the "logic of language," theology can be replaced by logology (HR,IX,224–225; QJS,XXXIX,209; RR,*passim*). No mere summary could possibly do justice to the thorough spinning out of the cycle of terms implicit in the idea of order; and perhaps only by exposure to the essay can one really grasp the essential nature of the logologic which is so central to Burke.

In the essay Burke reduces the "rectilinear narrative" of Genesis to its logological counterpart, "the 'cycle of terms' . . . found to revolve 'endlessly' about the idea of 'Order.'" The essay makes clear that the cycle or complete cluster of terms is the result of the entelechial actualization of "Order's" potential; the actualization does not follow the laws of organic, but of logological growth, for once actualized as a complete cycle, the cluster is "eternal" and takes its place among other clusters that fill the logological heaven. Starting with the "idea" of order, Burke says that this idea "implies" the idea of an agent (God?) who made the order, and the disorder. In the idea of order is the idea of "covenant," and this in turn implies obedience (maintaining the order) and disobedience (which brings disorder). The order, covenant, disobedience, disorder sequence implies the possibility of a counter-order, or counter-covenant. One sequence of terms, therefore, goes from God to order to covenant to obedience (righteousness, humility) to mortification (the denials necessary to obedience, the "saying yes to thou-shalt-not" of the covenant) to blessing as reward for obedience. The other sequence of terms goes

Dramatism

from God to order to covenant to disobedience to counter-covenant to disorder to sin to pride to punishment for disobedience. Given the terminal point of each sequence — the promise of reward for obedience and the threat of punishment for disobedience — Burke says that order equals "good" and disorder equals "evil." Once the order–obedience–good–reward, and disorder–disobedience–evil–punishment sequences have been set, Burke works out another sequence which he says is implicit in this pair of opposed terms. The order-disorder pair offers the human agent the possibility of alternative courses of action. There is, Burke tells us, "implicit in the idea of act . . . the idea of free will" or "freedom." So act implies will, will implies freedom, freedom implies choice. There is yet one more sequence which Burke works out. If one follows the order–covenant–disobedience–disorder–sin–punishment sequence, one ends with the man of guilt-laden substance; this sets another sequence in motion because implicit in the idea of guilt is the idea of cleansing and rebirth — of mortification, victimage, catharsis, and redemption. Victimage contains the idea of the sacrificial redeemer, the redemption by vicarious atonement which completes the cycle. Though I have omitted a few of the terms in the cluster, the summary should give some idea of what is involved in a logological definition of the substance of "order."

The dramatistic system is built around the "order" cluster (the drama of human relations); it is built with the logological principle of substance-clusters; each of the volumes is in turn built around its own cluster or clusters: *A Grammar of Motives* around substance and dialectic; *A Rhetoric of Motives* around identification and hierarchy; the projected "A Symbolic of Motives" around catharsis; and the projected "Ethics" will certainly be built around the negative. The project as a whole is bound together by a very complex language-cluster, which Burke refers to as linguistic resources and which includes such things as abstraction, merger, division, irony, metonomy, synecdoche, punning, metaphor, dialectic, image, symbol, and oxymoron. These linguistic resources make up the universal principles of discourse which are employed in all verbal acts. Though one tends to think of these "resources" as modes of thought, Burke calls them linguistic resources because they are made possible by language: verbalizing and thinking, words and reason, are interchangeable terms for Burke. These verbal resources constitute the essence of language; they are, like the drama and logologic, another of Burke's constant or set forms around which the whole dramatistic system is built. They are the universal resources which the typically symbol-using animal inherits as part of his equipment for living. He cannot help but use — or misuse — them, for verbal action is not possible without them, and man was born to verbalize. Finally, the whole project is bound together by the division of all verbal acts into four categories corresponding to the two published and two forthcoming volumes of the tetralogy.

The four categories are (1) the logical or indicative, (2) the rhetorical or persuasive, (3) the poetic, and (4) the ethical or "personal." To each of these categories Burke assigns a primary or ideal function, though he repeatedly points out that any verbal act, whatever its ostensible purpose, may function in all four ways at once. The logical or indicative has as its primary purpose to teach and inform, to provide one with information as preparation for action; the rhetorical or persuasive has as its primary purpose to move or persuade the self and others to attitude or action; the poetic has as its primary purpose to please or entertain through the free exercise of the resources of language and the development of an internally consistent symbolic structure; and the ethical or "personal" has as its primary *purposes*, self-expression, "portraiture" (of self and society), and moral action (which includes purgative-redemptive action). Clearly, Burke has divided up the field according to certain universal human drives, all of which are expressed in verbal action: these are the quest for knowledge, the desire for power and change, the need for beauty, the drive for self-expression, the drive for moral excellence, and the need for purification. Though almost any verbal act will have a primary purpose which controls diction, tone, structure, and the like, almost all verbal acts will have grammatical, rhetorical, poetic, and ethical "dimensions," and a complete dramatistic analysis of any verbal act calls for the treatment of that act in terms of the four "dimensions."

Dramatism

The four-fold division of all verbal acts is the final constant or set form around which the whole dramatistic system is built. Such a division calls for the isolation and extended analysis of the substance of each category. This really amounts to answering these questions: what is the essence of a grammatical, rhetorical, poetic, or ethical verbal act, and what is the range of possibilities within each of these categories? At what points do these categories differ, and at what points do they overlap? Though the four-fold division calls for the isolation of the grammar, rhetoric, poetry, and ethic "clusters," the project as a whole calls for the treatment of any verbal act in terms of all four clusters on the assumption that the essence of any verbal act is the sum of its functions and range of meanings. Since all verbal acts employ some or all of the "universal principles of discourse," the analysis of function leads automatically into the analysis of technique and the correlation of means and ends. According to logologic, every individual verbal act must be subjected to a logological analysis in order that the various overt and covert god-terms may be known. The act derives part of its essence from the substance-cluster or clusters to which it is related, and though the given act may employ only one of the meanings within a given cluster, logologically the full range is implicit in the limited use.

For example, a verbal act about mountain-climbing belongs to the "range of mountings" cluster, and this in turn belongs to the larger hierarchy or order cluster — a vast analogically and causally related complex of terms, shapes, structures, motives, and ideas. Applied logologic turns out to be a massive act of reconstruction (or so Burke would have one believe), for it attempts to make explicit everything that is implicit in the verbal act by systematically and intuitively examining the structure of interrelationships within the act and then, in ever broader contexts, the structure of interrelationships between the act and all the parts of the act, and the network of substance-clusters (quasi-platonic Ideas) to which everything must ultimately be related. The over-all movement in applied logologic is always up, for it is derived from the nature of language and perfectly exemplifies that tendency toward abstraction which Burke says is the essence of language. But after one has mounted to the highest level of abstraction, to the level of substance-clusters, one descends to the particular act, image, idea, term, or thing from which one started and examines it *in the light of* the complete substance-cluster to which it belongs. Applied logologic, then, is a hierarchic mode of thought and makes dramatistic analysis a kind of hierarchic experience. In the very act of making a dramatistic analysis, Burke illustrates the central idea of the system.

A dramatistic analysis calls for the placing of the act according to its primary purpose and an examination of it in the light of what is known about that particular category. Then one has to analyze it in terms of the other three categories to complete the four-dimensional approach required by dramatism. The third step is an exhaustive analysis of the "universal principles of discourse" employed in the act; and the fourth step is a logological analysis of the verbal act, which really amounts to placing the specific act in larger and larger contexts of meaning as a way of universalizing it. The final step is an exhaustive analysis of the act in terms of the seven interlocked moments of the drama of human relations — the systematic examination for evidences of guilt, hierarchy and the hierarchic psychosis, the negative, victimage, mortification, catharsis, and redemption.

The "order" cluster constitutes the substance of the human drama; it provides man with the universal motives which produce the verbal and physical action of the drama. A study of this drama as it is enacted, imitated, and reflected in man's symbolic acts is the study of what is basically and fundamentally human, for only man, through the free exercising of moral choice (the negative) can act purposefully. Man actualizes his essential nature in the *drama* of human relations; for this reason the whole *dramatistic* system and method center on a theory of moral (or ritual) drama and a method developed from drama for the analysis of the drama of human relations. The whole system is meant to function as a counter-statement against what Burke calls the decline of realism and the rise of scientism. Scientism (and its variants, such as naturalism, determinism, operationalism) tends to reduce moral (or immoral) action to bodily motion by eliminating the possibility of free moral choice; it tends to

Dramatism

absolve man of responsibility for his "motions" by systematically shifting the cause to the nature of man's nervous system, nature, society, childhood, birth trauma, and the like. It makes man's self entirely the product of outside forces by denying to the self an inherent moral consciousness; man is made like a machine, and runs on the fuel which society provides. But Burke's two dominant images are man as poet and man as actor: the first stresses creativity and purpose; the second freedom, moral choice, and action. It would be a mistake not to see Burke's work in its historical context, not to realize that all of his books are verbal acts upon a historical scene, and that the dramatistic system as a whole is a humanist's counterstatement offered to the public at large as a reaffirmation of *human* purpose and as a means of "purifying war" (man's greatest rational lunacy) so that each person, in his own way, may *peacefully* and intelligently pursue the better life.

Since 1945, Burke has worked with missionary zeal to spread the good word (dramatism) that came to him upon completing the work started in the 1930's when he first began his study of communication and dedicated himself to the attainment of peace through knowledge. Dramatism is dedicated quite literally to "the purification of war"; one of its mottoes —"By and through language, beyond language"— suggests the method of purification. As a theory of language, dramatism attempts to isolate and study the essence of language and, by systematically examining the uses to which man puts it, to isolate and study the essence of man and the drama of human relations. One of the main conclusions reached is that man's views of himself, other men, nature, society, and God are language-ridden—that man necessarily views everything through a "fog of symbols." Dramatism attempts to get men to see that they are looking through this fog, that they tend to make themselves and the world over in the image of their distinctive trait, often with disastrous results. This goal is achieved through what Burke calls "a methodic study of symbolic action." Dramatism attempts not only to get me to look at the symbolic fog and recognize it for what it is, but to adopt a constructive attitude towards it; "dramatism . . . fulfils its purposes," Burke says, when "it makes methodical the attitude of patience" (MPE,

[161]

271). The patience is necessary so that one can contemplate without suicidal despair "the ironic nature of the human species" (MPE, 270), the foibles and quandaries that all men as symbol-using animals have in common. The goal is "By and through language," to move "beyond language." The attitude of patience is one of these beyonds; another is the hope that nourishes this patience, the hope that by going through language one can get "glimpses into the ultimate reality that stretches somehow beyond the fogs of language and its sloganizing" (MPE,300). By "ultimate reality" Burke does not mean a place, such as Heaven; he means ultimate truth, what he has described as "comprehensive, summarizing truth . . . [which] like a spring under the skyscrapers of Manhattan, must somehow still go on — truth, still welling forth, down there in the dark, the brooks still wholesomely flowing, unstoppable, in the dark, down there, somehow" (FAT,372). The truth that would finally set men free would be made up of "the ultimate secrets of man, as the symbol-using animal" (HR,IV,203). Burke himself feels strongly that in dramatism he has moved to some kind of "comprehensive, summarizing truth," to some of the "ultimate secrets of man" the symbol-using animal. In the timeless principles of discourse, in the timeless functions of language, and in the cycle of terms that revolves " 'endlessly' about the ideal of 'Order,' " Burke believes he has found some of those secrets that make up ultimate reality. With these truths and the dramatistic method developed to study them, Burke thinks that he can help to purify war by using both persuasively, curatively, to redirect man's inexhaustible energies toward the pursuit of peace. "Whatever may be the ultimate ground of all possibility," Burke says,

the proper study of mankind is man's tendency to misjudge reality as inspirited by the troublous genius of symbolism. But if we were trained, for generation after generation, from our first emergence out of infancy, and in ways ranging from the simplest to the most complex, depending upon our stage of development, to collaborate in spying upon ourselves with pious yet sportive fearfulness, and thus helping to free one another of the false ambitions that symbolism so readily encourages, we might yet contrive to keep from wholly ruining this handsome planet and its plenitude. (*Poetics*,391.)

·V·

THE
DRAMATISTIC THEORY
OF LITERATURE

i

IMITATION AND INDEXING

SINCE 1950, Burke has been developing within the framework of dramatism a systematic theory of literature which is to be published as the third volume of his tetralogy of motives under the title "A Symbolic of Motives." So far, he has worked out dramatistic theories of imitation, poetic language, catharsis, tragedy, metaphor, symbolism, and form; he has written a number of dramatistic definitions; he has developed a dramatistic method of literary analysis called "indexing"; and he has applied both the theory and method in long, dense, and often brilliant essays on Aeschylus (the *Oresteia*), Goethe (*Faust*, Pt. I), Hawthorne (*Ethan Brand*), Joyce (*The Dead*, *A Portrait of the Artist as a Young Man*), Howard Nemerov (*The Scales of the Eyes*), Theodore Roethke (*Collected Poems*), Shakespeare (*Othello*), and Whitman (*Democratic Vistas*, *Leaves of Grass*). As the list shows, he has been careful to cover the lyric (Nemerov, Roethke, and Whitman; and, in shorter pieces in *A Rhetoric of Motives*, Arnold, Eliot, Hopkins, Milton, and Yeats), the narrative (Hawthorne, Joyce; and, in *A Rhetoric of Motives*, James and Kafka), and the drama (Aeschylus, Goethe, and Shakespeare). Furthermore, whatever else he has done to the works discussed, he has always treated them as poetry before moving on to study them as grammar, rhetoric, or ethics. This is a triumph of sorts, for by his own admission, Burke has always been interested in what is extrinsic to literature while at the same time remaining guiltily conscious of the fact that a poem ought to be treated intrinsically. The dramatistic theory of literature is best understood, I think, if one remembers that, according to it, any literary work should be treated first as literature; *but*, since everything always has implications beyond itself, any literary work can and should be studied in terms of the other three categories, as knowledge, rhetoric, and "portraiture." The consideration of literature in terms of all four categories constitutes a dramatistic analysis.

Dramatism requires the study of literature, for drama provides Burke with "the set forms in conformity with which" he constructs his "terminology." "Since," Burke says,

the real world of action is so confused and complicated as to seem almost formless, and too extended and unstable for orderly observation, we need a more limited material that might be representative of human ways while yet having fixity enough to allow for systematic examination.

In this respect, great dramas would be our equivalents of the laboratory experimenter's "test cases." But this kind of "controlled conditions" would differ from the arbitrary controls of a typical laboratory experiment. The losses are obvious, the gains less so, unless one stops to realize how hard it is to set up laboratory conditions for establishing instances of symbolic action that, while having a form sufficiently stable to be methodically observable, are also sufficiently complex and mature to be representative of human motives. (MPE, 264.)

The system makes the study of literature, and drama in particular, necessary because it is

built . . . about the "indexing" of some specific "symbolic structure," in the attempt to study the nature of a work's internal consistency and of its unfolding. But in contrast with [pure] . . . "literary appreciation," the generalizations at which we aim are not confined to a concern with the work's "beauty." Our quest concerns its linguistic nature in general; and then, beyond that, the insight it may afford into man's ways as symbol-user.

[Dramatism] proceed[s] on the assumption that the "perfect case" for analytic purposes is a definitive literary text. This view, in turn, is doubtless but a variant of the traditional analogy whereby "nature" was likened to a "scripture" which would be legible if one but knew the language it was written in. In this case, the "signs" manifested by a human personality or by a social incident (or social order, or social movement, or cultural trend in general) would be treated as relatively obscure aspects of motivational structures that are least obscure in literary texts. There would thus be no difference "in principle" between textual analysis and social analysis. (MPE,274–275.)

As Burke well knows and a good many sociological and psychological studies well illustrate, it would be shocking to use literature as the paradigm of linguistic action and as a model for the study of human relations in general unless one approached it first of all as what it is. As Burke has pointed out, one has to know what something is before he can know how to "discount" it. Whether a verbal construct which provides us with depth knowledge, or a symbolic journey that purges and redeems us, or a verbal image that portrays the author's self or his society, literature is first of all a particular mode of verbal (symbolic) action, different in kind from other verbal acts and requiring analysis according to the laws of its kind. A system which derives its name and method from drama, and takes as its principal object the study of various kinds of literary texts must somehow make clear how it is possible to move without egregious forcing from poetry as poetry to poetry as grammar (knowledge), as rhetoric (purgative-redemptive symbolic action), and as ethics (self and social portraiture). It cannot be done by fiat and it cannot be done haphazardly for such a procedure would vitiate the whole system; and it cannot be done in such a way as to destroy the nature of literature itself, for in the system literature is a holy object which it would be sacrilegious to defile in any way. The problem is how to preserve literature as an end in itself and still use it as a means to various other ends, notably as the paradigm of all verbal action, as illustrative of the true complexities of "man's ways as symbol-user," and as an imitation of the drama of human relations. It is well to keep this problem in mind when considering the dramatistic theory of literature, for wrenched from the system of which it is the central part and treated or applied in isolation, the theory sometimes seems fantastic. In context, it is powerful, workable, and rewarding.

Burke and the Drama of Human Relations

The poetic is one of the four categories into which Burke divides all verbal acts. Each of these categories has a purpose or purposes proper to it as a distinct kind of verbal act; and though there are certain "universal principles of discourse" which operate in all four categories, in each one there are certain principles which predominate and usually one which is pivotal. The primary purpose of poetry, for example, is to please and entertain. Poetry has (ideally) no end beyond itself, and attempts, through the free exercising of the resources of the medium, and the development of internal consistency (formal beauty), to delight us with the symbolic unfolding of a given structure (ChiR,VIII,88; FAT,367). The poetic category is characterized by sheer love of the medium itself, both for those who create (enact) and those who recreate (re-enact). Burke even suggests that as the typically symbol-using animal man probably derives greater delight from the poetic manipulation of his essential trait for its own sake than from any other thing (MPE,281). Furthermore, the poetic category is characterized by what Burke calls the love of "perfection"—the "freedom" to pursue something "to the end of the line," the entelechial motive (FAT,367). Burke means by this that the poet, motivated in part by a sheer love of the medium, tends to exploit the resources of a given term, form, or subject by freely exploring all the possible variations simply for the sake of the exploration. A poet, for instance, might create a perfect villain because his explorations led him to the perfection of this idea. Burke calls this the "free speculative tinkering with terms" and says that it is "the birthright of man, as the symbol-using species" (FAT,365). Thus, poetry is one of the ways in which man fulfills his nature, for his symbolic fury is appeased by symbolic action itself. In this sense, all poetry is "cathartic"; it provides man with a means of satisfying his word hunger and his desire for "perfection" (the motive that is built into language with its "tendency to abstraction") (MPE,281–282; KR,XXI,364).

Burke's whole poetic theory is built around variations on the term "catharsis." Two of the simplest kinds have already been mentioned: "relief" from word hunger and the satisfying of the desire for perfection. The whole problem of catharsis will be taken up later at some length, but here those kinds of catharsis which result from the poetic act itself ought to be mentioned. "The symbol-using animal," Burke says,

experiences a certain kind of "relief" in the mere act of converting any inarticulate muddle into the orderly terms of a symbol-system. (There would be at least three major critical points in such a process: The poet is in one way "cleansed" of his "extra-poetic materiality" when he hits upon his theme and starts to track down its implications; he is "cleansed" in another way when he becomes so deeply involved in his symbol-system that in effect it takes over, and a new quality or order of motives emerges from it; and he is cleansed in still another way when, the goal having been reached, fulfillment is complete. . . .) (KR,XXI,364.)

Catharsis is the pivotal term because verbalizing in general and poetic action in particular is purgative, and more so as the verbalizing is *free* and leads to the construction of symbol-systems which are characterized by consistency and completeness.

With Aristotle and just about everyone else who has considered the subject, Burke believes that the symbolic structures of poetry are imitations. For him, all poetic acts are imitations of "perfect essences" or "substance-clusters." For example, a work may imitate the perfect essence of an attitude, an idea, an action, a "tension," a motive, a pattern of experience, a scene, or a relationship. To be more specific, Burke says that Goethe's *Faust*, Pt. I, is the dramatic imitation of the perfect essence of "ambition as a disease"; and that *Othello* is the dramatic imitation of the perfect essence of the "possession tension" (the excessive engrossments of possession).

The modifying of essence by "perfect" or "ideal"—Burke uses them interchangeably—is confusing until one realizes what he wishes to indicate by this seeming redundancy. By definition, an essence is an abstraction from experience, made possible by symbol-using. It is perfect or ideal in the sense that it is not "real." Literature is not a representation in the way a photograph is or in the way Zola thought his novels were; it is an embodiment of an abstraction from experience, the abstraction having been arrived at by the poet as a summing-up or distillation of "long or intense personal experience" (ChiR,VIII,97). In creating a poem, the poet translates the abstract

[167]

essence into the equivalent terms of personality; he makes his "policy" "personal" by systematically embodying it in whatever poetic form he chooses, using whatever "body" of material he has at his disposal, and obeying the laws of poetry in general and the given form in particular. In the most general sense, the poet has the "world's body" (nature), the human body, the "body politic" (the socio-political hierarchy, which includes the family), and the "mythic body" to draw on for his images; in all cases, the nature of his selection — the way in which he "personalizes" a particular "policy" or essence — depends upon the extent and quality of his own experience.

The somewhat misleading phrase which Burke often uses to identify the process of embodiment — translation into equivalent terms of personality — is meant to suggest a number of things, but primarily the hierarchic nature of the creative process itself. A poem is the translation of an abstract essence into concrete "worldly" "sensory" images. The abstraction is arrived at through hierarchic modes of thought (the ascent made possible by the dialectic of the Upward Way); once the poet has arrived at the "timeless" essence, either systematically or intuitively, he has something he can translate into poetry. For example, Burke treats the first three chapters of Genesis as the translation into "rectilinear" narrative terms of the essence of "Order." The translation completes the hierarchic process because it is a descent — the perfect hierarchic form is the pyramid — where the poet tries to find appropriate images, characters, and forms in which to embody the essence. In *The Philosophy of Literary Form* Burke called poetry "the dancing of an attitude"; the "attitude" is the "policy," the "perfect essence"; and the "dancing" is the embodiment, the "personalizing." To "translate" an essence "into the equivalent terms of personality" is to "dance an attitude," to give body and movement to the abstract assence. By "personalize" or "equivalent terms of personality," Burke also means to suggest that though all poets have certain common storehouses from which to draw their images and forms, and though all men are biologically and neurologically similar and have certain universals of experience in common, poets, even when they imitate the same essences, personalize them in very different ways because they translate them into the equivalent terms of their own personalities.

This theory of imitation leads to a theory concerning the nature of the creative process itself. When Burke says that a poem is an incarnation, he is being quite literal; he really believes that it is a miraculous bodying forth of some spirit-essence, a process vaguely analogous to the incarnation of some god, and as mysterious. The essence, which is timeless and bodiless and composed of a "cycle of terms," is incarnated by translation into terms of progressive form and concrete images. "Progressive form" is Burke's all-purpose term for movement of any kind, whether narrative, temporal, spatial, or spiritual. Such movement results in a progressive structure of some kind; for this reason he speaks of symbolic *action*, the *dancing* of an attitude, the *temporizing* of an essence, and centers the whole poetic theory on the term catharsis. Not only is the essence translated into progressive form, but the over-all structure which results from the translation is a permanent progressive form in the sense that it forever moves and is forever still as it repeats the same progressions every time it is re-enacted. Once created, the work has a fixed movement which Burke says is absolutely "inevitable" and "irreversible"; unlike the essence, which is made up of "a cycle of terms mutually implying one another" and hence is "without direction," the translation of this essence into poetic symbolic action results in a progressive form with its "own unique progression" which is always "going somewhere" and hence has the "curative effect that comes from a sense of direction in the unfolding of an implicational structure" (KR,XXI,366). In every poetic symbolic act there is always the movement "*from* a beginning *through* a middle *to* an end," whether that movement is in the form of the "dialectic of transcendence" found in Keats's *Ode on a Grecian Urn,* or the narrative progression ("imitating an agent's spiritual adventures") found in Joyce's *Portrait of the Artist as a Young Man,* or in the dramatic progression (tragic rhythm or pattern) found in such works as the *Oresteia, Oedipus Rex,* and *Othello* (*Poetics,*370). The form of a poem, like the hierarchy discussed in Chapter IV (pp. 134–142), is both fixed and moving, or, to use two of Burke's favorite terms, both passive and active, having the properties of both permanence and change. Like the in-carnate God himself, a poem lives in and partakes of two worlds at once; it is both timeless and temporal, the permanent translated into the changing temporal terms of a given personal and historical scene.

Progressive form is almost as abstract as the essence which is being imitated, for though an essence may be translated into terms of journeys, quests, pilgrimages, birth-to-death chronicles, various patterns of experience, rises and falls, falls and rises, all of these are readily reduced by progressive generalization to the recurrent forms discussed in Chapter I (pp. 11–13). A rise and fall is a crescendo–decrescendo; the crescendo–decrescendo is itself a contrast and bal-ance; the pattern of experience might be either the search for the self or the tragic rhythm: if it is the search for the self, it may be re-duced to the recurrent pattern discussed in Chapter II (pp. 42–46); if it is the tragic pattern it may be reduced to the action, suffering, knowledge, change, new act, redemption sequence. The tendency of structural analysis (in Burke, anyway) is always toward such pro-gressive generalization, toward the reduction of a given progressive form to the abstract principles of form.

In Burke's schematization, the creative process starts with experi-ence, moves to the abstracting of essences from experience, thence to the translation of that essence into some kind of progressive form, and then to the bodying forth of that form in concrete images. The last two steps probably occur simultaneously. To be sure, the poet will use his own patterns of experience (both simple and complex), his own spiritual movements, purgative movements, movements of perception, his own search for the self, and his own perceptions of patterns (both natural and human) outside himself when translating the given essence into progressive form. Thus, if he is writing about the search for the self, and if he lives in the twentieth century, the search may have the same abstract progressive form as Chrétien's embodiment of it in *Percival* and *Yvain* simply because the search is a universal pattern of experience; but the search will surely be em-bodied (individuated) in radically different ways, for the creative agent and the personal, historical, and verbal scenes will have changed to such an extent that the stages of the search will be experienced in different ways. A single example will clarify this point: in our own time, it does not seem likely that any thoughtful agent could find himself without somehow confronting and coming to terms with two of the dominant forces in the historical scene — politics and industrial society. The crisis of self which sets the search in motion would be substantially the same though, again, "localized" in very different terms. Whereas Chrétien depicted this crisis in the extraordinary scene where Percival *emerges* from the woods, for someone like Lawrence, the crisis occurs in *Lady Chatterley's Lover* when Constance *enters* the woods. Though the two works deal with substantially the same progressive form, the movement is exactly opposite: Percival starts in the woods and moves out, replacing the natural with a social self and, ultimately, the social with the religious self; but Constance starts in society (a militantly industrial one) and gradually penetrates deeper and deeper into the woods until at the end she leaves society, having found the true natural self. Both works imitate the essence of the search for the self; both translate this essence into narrative terms and into the abstract progressive form appropriate for imitating "an agent's spiritual adventures, in the development of a new attitude, with its corresponding doctrine" (KR, XIII,181).

In the translation of the essence into images and in the individuation of the various abstract progressive forms, each poet makes his policy most personal. "In the depths of his imagery," Burke says, "a poet cannot lie," for every image, whether purely descriptive or whether simile, metaphor, symbol, or myth, is an identification and every identification implies an attitude toward the substantive part of the image. In Joyce's *Portrait*, Stephen is the substantive and Daedalus (the whole myth in fact) is the image part of the complex identification which implies Joyce's attitude. Generally, in any poetic imitation, the complex essence would be the substantive and the whole imitation a mass of identifications reflecting the author's attitudes toward the essence; within the imitation, which is itself a complex whole made up of various parts, there will be other clusters of identifications which express the author's attitude towards a specific part of the essence. Stephen, for example, is a fictional character

(Burke would call him a term or symbol) who represents but part of a larger essence (the artist in the modern world?) which the work as a whole imitates. He is identified with Daedalus and, among other things, with birds, flight generally, priests, communion, blacksmiths, and God. An exhaustive cataloguing and analysis of the images used to depict Stephen and everything related to him would result in an equation in which Stephen equaled the sum of his (Joyce's, really) identifications. These would provide an attitude toward Stephen as a fictional character and toward whatever Stephen represented in the novel as a whole, for they would tell one what (in Joyce's mind) goes with what. In one sense, Stephen as a fictional character is "nothing but" a mass of identifications, for Joyce creates him by giving him a punning name and then, at great length, identifying him with various thoughts, thought processes, bodily processes, places, clothes, actions, people, reactions to him, patterns of experience, mythical events, and characters. By treating Stephen, not as a real person (which he isn't) but as a term or symbol in a poetic symbol-system (which in one sense he literally is), one can shift the emphasis from Stephen as a person to the ways in which Joyce *created* the symbol; that is, to the ways in which Joyce made this part of his "policy" "personal." Stephen then becomes an extension of Joyce (one of his symbolic acts) and a study of the way he is "personalized" becomes a study of the workings of Joyce's mind. The novel as a whole becomes a symbolic replica of Joyce: it is both a poetic imitation of an essence and the self-contained symbolic act of Joyce's. It is *his* symbolic act and in this sense it is forever permeated with the ingredients of his personality. And since every imitation embodies an essence through concrete images, and each image is an identification that implies an attitude, every imitation is not only the dancing of an essence but the dancing of a self; in dancing the essence the poet dances the essence of himself. According to Burke, the expression of self is an inevitable by-product (rather than the primary object) of any poetic imitation, for the poet, in personalizing an essence, cannot help but filter everything through his own personality. The essences and the abstract progressive forms are perhaps common property; but once a poet embodies them in images which he draws out of himself and which are necessarily conditioned by the nature of that self, he makes the essence individual and unique.

At the two extremes, poetry tends towards abstraction and universality, and toward concreteness and solipsism. At its best, poetry mediates between the two extremes, making the abstract concrete and the solipsistic universal. Each self is a unique combination of ingredients, some of which are forever mysterious and hidden, even to the self. But the ingredients out of which selves are made are common to mankind as a whole; the substance (language) out of which poems are made is what Burke calls a "public form or grammar"; and the "bodies of material" from which poets can draw their images are available to all men. From the "common ingredients" come certain universals of psycho-physical experience; from the "public form" come certain "universal principles of discourse"; and from the bodies of material come certain universal principles of image-making, which in turn result in a vast analogical complex (hierarchy) which mediates between the four realms from which the images are always drawn. Taken together, these factors mediate between the two extremes toward which poetry always tends. Even the most solipsistic poem has to use the "public form," has to draw its images from one or more of the available bodies of material, and probably has to deal with an experience which others have undergone, even though never in exactly the same way. And, as Burke points out, even the most "concrete image" has to contain an idea, if only the idea of the thing imaged, or it would not be an image. At its best, poetry makes the abstract concrete, the universal particular, the particular universal, and the concrete abstract; it enables the self to externalize what is private and internal, and in this way to alleviate the solipsism that is natural to man. And for those who re-enact rather than create the poem, it makes possible the same kind of movement outward from solipsistic self to the self in society and in the universe.

Intensive study of these mediating devices led Burke to dramatistic theories of poetic language, form, and imagery, to a dramatistic method (indexing), and to various assumptions about the unity of poetic verbal acts. All of these matters are best seen in Burke's theory of clusters, imagistic and otherwise, which in many ways is the real center of his dramatistic theory of literature. Images, according to Burke, are the second means the poet has at his disposal for embodying an essence. After an essence is translated into progressive form, it is given a body of images and becomes a completed "structure of interrelated terms," which, by its very nature as a poetic verbal construct, is infinitely analyzable in terms of its "internal consistency." Burke assumes an "absolute" unity in the greatest works of art. Everything, down to the last recorded syllable, is a necessary and functional part of the unified structure of terminal interrelationships. Generally, Burke works from a few logological principles of unity. The first deals with the relation between essences (substance-clusters) and poetic imitations. An essence has a cyclical unity in the sense that all of the terms which make up the substance-cluster imply each other. An essence has the unity of a complex idea; all the parts of an essence cohere; they are all related by an "if–then" connective: if guilt, then sin; if sin, then pollution; if pollution, then the need for cleansing; if the need for cleansing, then methods of purification; if purification, then victimage and mortification. Burke calls this unity cyclical because he conceives of an essence or substance-cluster as an eternally actualized potential. By consistently using the expressions "spin out" and "spun out of" Burke suggests an astrological analogy in which the substance term is a sun which spins out of itself a cluster of terms until the solar system is complete — until the substance term's potential cluster of terms has been eternally actualized. Once actualized, the sun with its planetary system is *there*; its unity comes from the fact that each of the terms in the cluster is held within the system by the gravitational pull of the sun; or, if it happened to be a "moon term," by the gravitational pull of one of the terms itself. Some of the terms seem remote indeed, but all revolve "endlessly" about the sun. It is such a logological solar system which a poem imitates, either in part or as a whole. A major work, such as Goethe's *Faust*, Part I, imitates the whole "order" substance-cluster, but a short lyric may imitate only part of the essence, such as guilt or pollution. An imitation, unlike the essence which it embodies, has a rectilinear unity as well which comes from the introduction, development, and completion of a plot, action, or developmental progression of any kind. Burke calls this translation of an essence into rectilinear terms the "temporizing of an essence" to suggest that no matter what rectilinear progression the poet uses, it must always follow a time sequence even if, as in Faulkner, an attempt is made to dissolve chronology in the timelessness of memory and dreaming. Though all poetic imitations have various kinds of rectilinear progression, including the qualitative progression from one kind of imagery to another, and derive some of their unity from such developmental progressions, all poetic imitations have a cyclical unity similar to that found in the substance-clusters being imitated. The cyclical unity comes from the various kinds of clusters which are to be found in all poetic imitations.

Every poetic imitation is analyzable in terms of its formal progressions and in terms of its imagistic, terminological, and phonetic clusters. The clusters are made up of "terminal interrelationships" which result in part from the conscious or unconscious associational logic which characterizes all psychic activity (SAV,289). According to Burke, the three kinds of clusters exist in a given work as factual evidence; the critic establishes the " 'concordantial' connections" between images, terms, or sounds "inductively," "empirically," by means of an analytic method called "indexing" (ChiR,IX,42). Indexing is a method for finding out "what goes with what," "what implies what," and "what equals what" in a given work. The method is simple: the essential meaning of an image, term, or sound is equal to the sum of its generic, contextual, entelechial, and equational relationships. Or, stated another way, the essential meaning of an image, term, or sound is equal to the sum of whatever it is identified or associated with in a given work. Since, Burke argues, the poet personalizes an essence by embodying it in appropriate, and he hopes, effective concrete images, building up as he goes along a veritable labyrinth of identifications made up of significant imagistic, terminological, and phonetic repetitions, sometimes deliberate and conscious, sometimes compulsive and unconscious, the critic can, by analytically unmaking what the poet made, find out not only how he made it but what he meant by it. Thus, indexing is an analytic method for the study of "terminal interrelationships" (with the pun deliberate) in a permanently made verbal act designed to enable the critic to find out how the poet, "within the regular bounds of his methods and terminology," has endowed the poem "with the personal and impersonal *dimensions* that give it scope and resonance" (LOG,101). The three kinds of clusters mentioned above are the three main resources (aside from progressive form) upon which the poet can draw "to endow" his poem — really the essence —"with scope and resonance." In his imagery, the poet exploits the resources of metaphor, analogy, and correspondences generally by making figures of speech (identifications) out of the relationships he perceives between the world's body, the human body, the social body, and the mythic body. In his terminology, the poet exploits the resources of "grammar"; that is, grammar in the usual sense of nouns, verbs, adjectives, syntax, and the like, and grammar in Burke's sense of logic and dialectics. In his sounds, the poet exploits phonetic resources and what Burke calls the resources of "pun logic," both for the sheer delight taken in and derived from the creation of verbal music and because, in exploiting the resources of "pun logic," the poet can add scope and resonance to his work by using words that echo multiple meanings. The very best puns would refer simultaneously to the four main bodies of material from which the poet draws his images: such a pun is found in the *mer, merde, mère, Mère* sequence, which exploits the full range of natural, bodily, familial, and mythic orders of motivation.

Clusters result from the poet's exploitation of the three kinds of resources just discussed; they evolve "naturally," for a variety of reasons. Some grammatical and phonetic clusters are inherent in the verbal medium itself; the poet's free tinkering with terms would make their presence in his work inevitable. Such an inevitable cluster is to be found in Whitman's *Leaves of Grass*; Burke calls it the "leaf motif" and says it is made up of at least the following: leaf, leafy, leaves; leave, leaved, leaving (meaning to put forth leaves); leave, left, leaving (meaning to go away from, to depart); leave (meaning permission to do something); leaving, leavings (meaning that which is left, residue, remains, refuse); and because of their obvious phonetic proximity, such terms as lean, loaf, love, live, and life (LOG, 86–91). Other clusters, sometimes but not always inherent in the

[176]

grammatical and phonetic resources of the verbal medium, result from the poet's conscious and deliberate effort to exploit a term, usually a metaphorical possibility. Such a cluster is to be found in what Burke calls the " 'flower' image, and ramifications" in Goethe's *Faust* (ChiR,IX,53–57). Since there is always the possibility that the poet's exploitation of a term may be partly compulsive and spontaneous rather than wholly deliberate and conscious, this must be added as one of the causes. Burke says in an essay on "Verbal Action in St. Augustine's *Confessions*" that "intimacy with a woman must always argue special intimacy with some word or words like or nearly like the sound of her name," and that if we but had the names of Augustine's unnamed "trifles" or mistresses, we would surely find "roundabout that the names of his mistresses . . . are ambiguously lurking in odd places throughout the text. . . . shining out like unseen stars, ambiguously split perhaps between terms in the constellation of the divine and terms for the problematic body" (RR,83). The compulsive and surely partially spontaneous water imagery in the poetry of Matthew Arnold constitutes such a cluster; in fact such clusters can be found in the work of any poet because no one is ever completely conscious of why he does certain things, writes of certain subjects, uses certain images, sounds, and rhythmical patterns over and over again in different contexts. In such clusters, the poet not only personalizes an essence but portrays himself; the structure of interrelated images, terms, and sounds symbolizes the structure of his psychic and physical self. This is what Burke means when he says that "in the depths of his imagery a poet cannot lie," for even though the resources as such which he exploits are quite impersonal in the sense that grammatical and phonetic resources are inherent in the medium itself and the ability to make metaphors is inherent in the psychic makeup of any poet, each poet puts words together according to impulses generated by his own unique personality. For this reason indexing is an analytic method designed not only for the study of "verbal action" but also for the study of the "personality" of a given verbal act.

A cluster thus derives some of its unity from the self which generated it, some from the verbal medium in which it is expressed, and some from the analogical and hierarchic structure of the universe itself. According to Burke, every act which a self performs is informed by the unity of purpose which motivates that self in all its actions. There are no purposeless acts, only an act the purpose of which is not yet known, or not yet fully understood. There is a total unity of self, much like the total or absolute unity which Burke says is to be found in any great poem. It is the unity derived from a purpose which informs every syllable of the whole work, or every act of the whole self, and is something like the singleness of intent which unifies the myriad details of a Gothic cathedral. This kind of unity is often called unity of design or simply Gothic unity and is opposed to unity of action or classic unity. The former is like Burke's cyclical unity and the latter is like his rectilinear unity. However, he does not oppose them to each other, but maintains, more sensibly, that all works have both kinds and that the combination of the two gives the work its absolute unity. The unity which a self has comes from the fact that many different acts are expressions of the same underlying motive; one perceives the unity by making the connections between seemingly contradictory acts and realizing that what one originally saw as diversity was really a very subtle and complex pattern of significant repetition, the unity coming from the conscious or unconscious master motive. It is possible to say that every cluster is unified by the presence of such a conscious or unconscious master motive, some complex idea which, like the master motive in a chess game, explains all the moves. Though the motive leads to the activity which results in the clusters, once embodied in a finished poem, the structure of "terminal interrelationships" which constitutes a cluster is static and timeless in the sense that all the terms, images, or sounds which make up a cluster can be said to "revolve endlessly" about the now fixed master motive which generated them.

According to Burke, clusters are spontaneously generated and/or deliberately contrived as a result of a process of identification or association which operates under all conditions and in every human activity. In verbal acts, especially poetic ones, the process operates to produce phonetic and semantic clusters; these, in the form of repeated or similar clusters of sound, and groups of words with related or overlapping meanings, provide the poet with two ways of embodying and personalizing the essence he is imitating. When the sounds and meanings form a meaningful pattern, they contribute to what Burke calls the "labyrinthine internal consistency" of the poetic verbal act and can, if properly interpreted, provide one with a good many clues to the unity and meaning of the work (SAV,306). More importantly, however, the process of identification or association operates in poetic verbal acts to produce what Burke rather loosely calls image clusters; and it is really through his imagery that the poet makes most of his identifications and embodies and personalizes the essence he is imitating. Furthermore, it is the image clusters which finally give the work its real "labyrinthine internal consistency." Every image identifies or associates some fixed subject with one or more persons, places, things, ideas, qualities, attitudes, smells, colors, and the like (RM,17–20). Or, one can turn the statement around and say that any group of words in which two or more things are identified with each other, are linked or associated in any way, may be regarded as an image. At best this is a rather loose definition of an image; so loose, in fact, that it makes any complete sentence and phrase in which there is a noun and at least one modifier an image. The definition is so loose that, theoretically, a study of the "image" clusters or, more accurately, the clusters of identifications in anything but a relatively short work, would be an almost impossible undertaking. One would have to treat the whole work as if it were an enormous sentence and completely diagram it to show exactly what goes with what. Although Burke believes that this is theoretically possible, he admits that such an attempt on anything but a short lyric is not feasible. At best one can only try for a partial analysis of the clusters in longer individual works or in the complete works of a single author.

To avoid what he calls the "methodic demoralization" and the large amount of "waste motion" which would inevitably result from any attempt to index completely a work of considerable length and complexity — say, *Howards End* — Burke limits the number and kinds of "terms" which must be indexed if the critic is to "characterize, in

as well rounded a way as he can, the salient traits of a given work
. . . [and] give an over-all interpretation of it as a unified symbolic
act" (SAV,288). The word "term" is somewhat misleading until one
realizes that in a *symbolic* act, everything may be regarded as a
"term"; in *Howards End*, for example, Margaret Schlegel, Henry
Wilcox, Leonard Bast, London, Howards End, wych-elm, and love
would be treated as terms by Burke, though some are characters,
some places, one a natural object, and the last an abstraction. One
cannot really say beforehand what the key terms of a work are going
to be; they emerge as the work unfolds; sometimes they are persons,
places, or things; sometimes they are ideas, acts, attitudes, or relations; and sometimes they are qualities or processes — it does not
really matter, for they can be anything which is important and significant. Every symbolic act is a permanent structure of terminal identifications which unfolds in a particular way; as it unfolds various
terms are linked with and opposed to each other by a variety of
means, and some terms, because they appear in different contexts
at different points in a work, undergo transformations as the work
progresses. Burke regards these identifications, oppositions, transformations, and progressions as the empirical facts which one gath-
ers in the course of indexing a work; from these facts inferences can
be made about the work's unity and meaning.

In *Howards End*, for example, the following empirical facts are
known about the wych-elm. (It is well to remember while going
through this list of facts about the wych-elm that Burke regards all
poetic verbal acts as deliberately contrived symbolic acts which imitate an essence rather than reproduce an actually existing reality.
They are verbal acts spun out of the author's mind and body and are
governed by laws of symbolic action. If, as in *Howards End*, there
is a wych-elm located at Howards End, it is because Forster put it
there, quite deliberately, so that it could be identified with Howards
End.) This, then, is the first fact about the wych-elm and it appears
on the first page of the novel (Vintage edition): "Then there's a very
big wych-elm — to the left as you look up — leaning a little over the
house, and standing on the boundary between the garden and
meadow. I [Helen Schlegel] quite love that tree already." The second

fact, aside from details of the tree's size, location, and attitude, is the identification with Helen, who perceives and responds to it. The wych-elm is next mentioned on page 22 where Forster says that Ruth Wilcox "seemed to belong not to the young people and their motor, but to the house, and to the tree that overshadowed it." In Burke's terms, this constitutes an identification between the tree and Ruth Wilcox and has the effect of transferring those terms associated with Ruth Wilcox to the tree and vice versa. On the same page, for example, Forster says of Mrs. Wilcox: "one knew that she worshipped the past, and that the instinctive wisdom the past can alone bestow had descended upon her — the wisdom to which we give the clumsy name of aristocracy." "Instinctive wisdom" and the "past," then, are part of the symbolic meaning of the tree. The wych-elm is next mentioned on page 25 where we learn that one of these seemingly minor and trivial episodes which turn out to be so important in Forster's novels took place under the wych-elm; it is under the tree that Helen receives the first of her romantic "wounds" when, caught up in the whole atmosphere of Howards End, and "desiring love," Paul kisses her and whispers "I love you." The effect of this "wound" on Helen is "panic and emptiness."

The wych-elm is next identified with Margaret Schlegel (the third major female character in this woman-dominated novel) when she says "the wych-elm I remember. Helen spoke of it as a very splendid tree." Ruth Wilcox then says, "It is the finest wych-elm in Hertford-shire. . . . There are pigs' teeth stuck into the trunk, about four feet from the ground. The country people put them in long ago, and they think that if they chew a piece of the bark, it will cure the tooth-ache. The teeth are almost grown over now, and no one comes to the tree." Margaret answers that she would like to see the tree for she "love[s] folklore and all festering superstitions," and asks Ruth Wil-cox if she thinks "that the tree really did cure toothache, if one be-lieved in it?" Ruth Wilcox answers: "Of course it did. It would cure anything—once. . . . Certainly I remember cases—you see, I lived at Howards End long, long before Mr. Wilcox knew it. I was born there." (71–72.) Here, in this brief interchange between the first and second Mrs. Wilcox, the wych-elm is identified with both women, with superstition and folklore, with miraculous curative powers, with pigs' teeth, with an outdated or discredited belief in the curative powers of magic and nature. At this point, if it has not already occurred to the reader, we are reminded that this is not an ordinary elm, but a wych- or witch-elm and that it was deliberately identified by its very name with superstition and magic, with women generally, and with organic growth.

Then for many pages the wych-elm is mentioned only twice, briefly on page 85 and at length on page 99 where the Wilcoxes are trying to decide whether to honor Ruth Wilcox's death-bed wish that Howards End go to Margaret Schlegel. Here, the wych-elm is identified with the spiritual, the soul, the passions, "blood" bonds, the personal, friendship, and, of course, Ruth Wilcox, Margaret Schlegel, and Howards End. Here, also, it is dissociated from and finally opposed to Henry, Charles, Evie, and Dolly Wilcox because none of these Wilcoxes ever really perceives the tree; each sees Howards End as just a house and the wych-elm as just something sticking up out of the ground. But to the three women identified with it, the wych-elm, Howards End, and such natural, growing things as "a vine, [and] a wisp of hay with dew on it" are possessions of the spirit. Not only are Henry, Charles, Paul (by implication), Evie, and Dolly Wilcox dissociated from the wych-elm by failing to notice it, respond to it, or be attached to it in any way, but they are all carefully opposed to the wych-elm by being identified with a set of opposed terms. For example, whereas the wych-elm is here identified with the spiritual, the soul, the passions, "blood" bonds, the personal, and friendship, the Wilcoxes are identified with the rational, the legal, the methodical, the unemotional, and the impersonal (98–99).

The wych-elm is mentioned briefly on page 135 where we learn that Henry Wilcox "messed away with a garage all among the wych-elm roots." The passage is significant because it continues the dissociation between Henry and the wych-elm and between the wych-elm and its principal counter-symbol, the motor car. There is an indirect reference to the wych-elm on pages 149 and 150 which, if one remembers Henry "messing" "all among the wych-elm roots" building a garage for his car, takes on added meaning. Forster says,

The Dramatistic Theory of Literature

"The feudal ownership of land did bring dignity, whereas the modern ownership of movables is reducing us again to a nomadic horde. We are reverting to the civilization of luggage, and historians of the future will note how the middle classes accreted possessions without taking root in the earth, and may find in this the secret of their imaginative poverty." On pages 189 and 190 there are other references to the wych-elm which, again, continue the dissociation between Henry and the tree. In thinking about the subletting of Howards End, Henry says he "shouldn't want that fine wych-elm spoilt. It hangs —" and that is as far as he gets. Henry is conscious of the tree's presence but he has never really "seen" it and it has no meaning for him. When, immediately after this remark, Margaret asks Henry, "Aren't there pigs' teeth in the wych-elm?" all Henry can say is *"Pigs' teeth?"* And when Margaret tells him that you can "chew the bark for toothache," Henry says "What a rum notion! Of course not!" The next reference to the wych-elm occurs on page 200 where Margaret Schlegel is again identified with the tree simply by being conscious of it and where the wych-elm is again identified with natural beauty, fertility, and organic growth. The tree is next mentioned twice on page 206. The second reference again dissociates Henry Wilcox from the wych-elm for it makes clear that in all his years at Howards End he had never really noticed the tree, had never got close enough to notice the pigs' teeth imbedded in it. Margaret points out the teeth to Henry, who responds, "extraordinary . . . who told you?" (206).

The other passage in which the tree is mentioned is a rather long one which quite unexpectedly identifies it with a whole new set of terms. If the other passages have not already done so, this one makes it perfectly clear that the wych-elm and Howards End, where it has its being, are two of the novel's major symbols, related in such a way that what is said of one can be applied to the other. The passage is as follows:

it [Howards End] was English, and the wych-elm that she [Margaret] saw from the window was an English tree. No report had prepared her for its peculiar glory. It was neither warrior, nor lover, nor god; in none of these rôles do the English excel. It was a comrade, bending over the house, strength and adventure in its roots, but in its utmost fingers tenderness, and the girth, that a dozen men could not have spanned, became in the end evanescent, till pale bud clusters seemed to float in the air. It was a comrade. House and tree transcended any similies of sex. Margaret thought of them now, and was to think of them through many a windy night and London day, but to compare either to man, to woman, always dwarfed the vision. Yet they kept within limits of the human. Their message was not of eternity, but of hope on this side of the grave. As she stood in the one, gazing at the other, truer relationship had gleamed. (206.)

The passage may first of all be examined for its negative identifications, for those terms which are dissociated from and opposed to the wych-elm: warrior, lover, god, London, and eternity. By warrior Forster seems to mean both the kind of person and the activity he stands for; by lover he seems to mean sexual passion and sexual attachments between men and women; by god, he seems to mean the supernatural rather than organized religion; by London (which he elsewhere calls a "symbol of infinity") he seems to mean the urbanization which results from industrialization; and by eternity he seems to mean some concern with an afterlife. Looking at the positive identifications, one finds that most of them, with the exception of England, are directly opposed to the negative ones. Protection, tenderness, growth, evanescence, and personal relationships are opposed to war; comradeship, asexuality, and truer relationships are opposed to lover; the whole tree, with its enormous girth, its roots, its buds, its physical beauty, its organic natural growth, is opposed to the supernatural; Howards End as place and the tree as a natural phenomenon, as natural outgrowth, are opposed to the impersonal, artificially constructed city; and finally the identification of the tree with the human, the physical, the here and now, with "hope on this side of the grave," is opposed to eternity. The whole passage, since it depicts Margaret's intense personal-emotional response to the beauty of the tree and the place again identifies the tree with the personal, with spiritual possessions and blood bonds, with direct and powerful response to what Forster calls "the appearance of the earth" (199).

Here, as in previous passages, Forster is careful to identify the tree with various key terms which clearly have a positive, affirmative value; and he is equally careful to oppose the tree, and the identifications which cluster around it, to other key terms which have a negative value. As the work progresses and the identifications multiply, the wych-elm as a term undergoes certain transformations by having its symbolic meaning amplified and continuously modified with each new identification and each new opposition. As the novel progresses or unfolds, there is an almost continuous process of amplification, opposition, and transformation; yet by the time the novel ends one can say that there are clustered around the wych-elm statically interrelated identifications which will forever unfold in a particular order and forever remain statically interrelated in a fixed way. These are the facts which can be objectively cited about any work; they are facts having to do with various identifications, oppositions, progressions, and transformations within a given symbolic act.

It is a fact — and a very puzzling one — that the wych-elm is explicitly identified with England in such a way as to make it clear that the wych-elm is a symbol of England, or, at least, of what is best about England and the English. Since the wych-elm is also explicitly identified with Helen and Margaret Schlegel, with Ruth Wilcox and, on page 274, with the witch-like (or is it bird-like?) prophetess, Miss Avery, by the roundabout route that is characteristic of clusters of identifications, one can say that England is also identified with these four women in such a way as to make them symbolic of what is best about the English; or one can say that those things identified with the wych-elm on page 206 are also identified with the four women; or, finally, that what is identified with the four women is also identified with the wych-elm, Howards End, and "the best of England." Burke thinks of clusters as substance-clusters, and of all the terms within a cluster as consubstantial because they are all parts of the same larger complex essence. The various identifications link the terms, radiating out until all the key terms within a cluster have been linked to each other to form a statically interrelated cluster of terms which embodies and defines an essence.

At one point or another in the novel, every major character is either identified with, opposed to, or excluded from the wych-elm.

Burke and the Drama of Human Relations

Up to the point where he refuses to ride in a motor car (328), Henry Wilcox is explicitly opposed to the wych-elm and what it represents; he belongs to the "city" cluster, the main symbol of which is London. But Leonard Bast, in one of Forster's seemingly casual phrases which can be read either literally or symbolically, is excluded from rather than opposed to the wych-elm and what it represents. Henry, Charles, Paul, and Evie Wilcox simply never noticed the tree or the teeth imbedded in it; but on page 311 Forster tells us that Leonard Bast could not see the foot of the tree because it was hidden by the shadow of the house; in effect, then, he cannot see the pigs' teeth. This seems to be Forster's way of saying that because of some defect in him, or because of some unfortunate combination of circumstances, Leonard Bast is partially excluded from whatever it is the elm represents. It is, after all, a wych-elm rather than a wizard-elm; and what it represents seems peculiarly tied up with women. A few pages later there is a scene involving two of these "witches," Margaret and Helen, part of which takes place beside the wych-elm and part of which takes place inside the house. After telling Margaret of the extraordinary way in which she came to seduce Leonard Bast, Helen "laid her face against the tree," and said "the little, too, that is known about growth! Both times it was loneliness, and the night, and panic afterwards. Did Leonard grow out of Paul?" (313.) The first of these identifications is the more puzzling one, for it is not clear whether the tree is here identified with Helen's lovers or whether it is opposed to them as a kind of asexual object of affection. Since Forster has explicitly said that the tree transcends any similes of sex, it is probably the latter. The second identification is clear enough, for previous and later identifications spell it out. The wych-elm knows about "growth"; it is a living symbol of natural, organic growth and suggests the principle to be followed by humans. Then, in a passage that seems curiously irrelevant, Forster says, "Margaret did not speak for a moment. So tired was she that her attention had actually wandered to the teeth — the teeth that had been thrust into the tree's bark to medicate it. From where she sat she could see them gleam. She had been trying to count them." Margaret then says to Helen: "Leonard is a better growth than madness. . . . I was afraid that you would react against Paul until you went over the verge." (313.) In the four passages quoted, the sequence is from seduction to leaning against the tree to loneliness, darkness, and panic, to growth, to teeth "thrust into the tree's bark to medicate it," to growth to possible madness. If it were not for the phrase "thrust into . . . to medicate" following closely on talk of two sexual encounters (one under this very tree) which came about at night because of loneliness and resulted in panic, a kind of madness, and finally in the death of Leonard Bast, I do not suppose one would pay much attention to the "thrust . . . medicate . . . growth" sequence. But it seems fairly obvious that Forster here means us to take the parallel seriously; the teeth were thrust into the tree to medicate it; but the tree, which was once smaller than the house, grew around them until, so big that "a dozen men could not have spanned its girth," it "leaned" over the house in an attitude of protection, and "rustled" in the wind, as it had rustled before they were born and would rustle after they were dead, its "rustle" the "song of the moment" (315). It is from the tree, then, that one is to learn of growth, of living in the present and for the moment; like the tree, one must grow around one's wounds; and in a sense, one must have wounds to grow. One must also have a sense of "adventure," "strength," and "tenderness." And one must have a sense of comradeship; one must be related (connected) as intimately and "naturally" to another person as the wych-elm is to the earth and the house it shades. Finally, one must have all of the things the tree has: deep, strong roots in the earth; the strength to continue growth; and room to grow so that one can naturally become what one is.

The final references to the wych-elm complete the cluster of identifications and give one the statically interrelated set of terms for that key term only. Most of these references occur in the same scene between Helen and Margaret at Howards End. Still discussing Helen's "wounds," her two encounters with Paul and Leonard, Margaret says, "Except [for] Mrs. Wilcox . . . no one understands our little movements. . . . I feel that you and I and Henry are only fragments of that woman's mind. She knows everything. She is everything. She is the house, and the tree that leans over it. . . . She knew about realities. She knew when people were in love, though she was not in the room. I don't doubt that she knew when Henry deceived her." (313–314.) Here, the equational logic characteristic of clusters is evident, for the wych-elm, Howards End, and Ruth Wilcox, as well as Helen, Margaret, and Henry — the three main characters who end up at Howards End — are all collapsed and, in a sense, made interchangeable. That is, they all stand for the same thing; by the end of the novel Helen, Margaret, and Henry become what the wych-elm represents: the principal people, the main place, the main thing — *the* key terms in the Howards End substance-cluster — all connect and merge to form one large complex statically interrelated set of terms which embodies and defines the essence of Forster's ideal way of life. In the next reference, Helen says "sitting under this tree, one forgets" (314); and in the next references to the wych-elm, Forster and Margaret say:

The present flowed by them like a stream. The tree rustled. It had made music before they were born, and would continue after their deaths, but its song was of the moment. The moment had passed. The tree rustled again. Their senses were sharpened, and they seemed to apprehend life. Life passed. The tree rustled again.

"Sleep now," said Margaret.

The peace of the country was entering into her. It has no commerce with memory, and little with hope. Least of all is it concerned with the hopes of the next five minutes. It is the peace of the present, which passes understanding. Its murmur came "now," and "now" once more as they trod the gravel, and "now," as the moonlight fell upon their father's sword. They passed upstairs, kissed, and amidst the endless iterations fell asleep. The house had enshadowed the tree at first, but as the moon rose higher the two disentangled, and were clear for a few moments at midnight. Margaret awoke and looked into the garden. How incomprehensible that Leonard Bast should have won her this night of peace! Was he also a part of Mrs. Wilcox's mind? (315.)

In these passages, Forster makes few new identifications; he mostly repeats the old ones in a new way and in a new context, as he gives us a final statement about the wych-elm. In Helen's remark, forgetfulness is identified with the tree — specifically, forgetfulness of old wounds, of old hates, of old panics. Properly read, the remarks of

Margaret and Forster repeat this idea and amplify it; all the remarks take one back to the thrust-medicate-growth sequence discussed earlier. A certain kind of continuity, the kind that comes from steady spiritual growth through time, is identified with the tree. This is what the tree tells them: that continuity and growth are the important things. It also tells them how to achieve them, for in responding to the tree their "senses were sharpened"; thus opened to experience, they "apprehended" the moment and in so doing apprehended "life."

The next paragraph is dominated by the two words "peace" and "now." Forster seems to suggest that it is the country which makes or enables one to be conscious of the moment, the now, as Helen and Margaret are conscious of Howards End, the moon on house and tree, the rustle of leaves, the moon on their father's sword, and last, of the "true" relationships between them and of the great pleasure they derive from it. As Helen says, the tree makes one forget both the memories (the past) and the hopes (the future); this permits an extraordinary concentration on and enjoyment of the present moment — depicted in the last scene of the novel — which brings the "peace of the present which passes understanding." Earlier in the novel Ruth Wilcox said that the wych-elm would cure anything if one but went to it. The cure is explained by means of the identifications of pages 312–315 and is illustrated in the final chapter of the novel. There, Forster first gets rid of all the unwoundable and hence incurable people, those Wilcoxes whose senses are so blunted that they are not open to experience (the now) and hence cannot be wounded, cannot apprehend life, cannot grow. Their symbols are the motor car and the city, but especially the motor car. After this Forster shows us all the once wounded but now cured and growing people gathered at Howards End under the aegis of the wych-elm. Each has had his own particular wound or wounds, and all have experienced the terrible trauma of Leonard Bast's death. In the final scene of the novel, Forster first presents a "true" husband-wife, man-woman relationship: "Margaret saw their visitors to the gate. Then she returned to her husband and laid her head in his hands." (342.) Then, very quickly, he brings the other cured and growing people in to leave us with an image of the wych-elm made flesh: "From the garden came laughter. 'Here they are at last!' exclaimed Henry, dis-engaging himself with a smile. Helen rushed into the gloom, holding Tom by one hand and carrying her baby on the other. There were shouts of infectious joy. 'The field's cut!' Helen cried excitedly — 'the big meadow! We've seen to the very end, and it'll be such a crop of hay as never!' " Portrait-like, the scene presents certain "true" rela-tionships — man-wife, sister-sister, friend-friend, mother-child, child-friend, adult-child — as well as the attitude of joy, the sharpened senses, the absorption in the now.

Certain inferences, then, can be made about the symbolic meaning and function of the wych-elm in *Howards End* from a careful index-ing of the term. As the novel progresses the term is gradually trans-formed from a word standing for a natural object to a word having subtle and complex meanings peculiar to it in a given symbolic struc-ture. No dictionary definition of wych-elm could possibly provide the meaning of this term in *Howards End,* for it accrues as the term appears in different contexts and is identified with or opposed to other terms in the course of the novel. Only when one has finished the novel, and sometimes, only when one has read all the works by the same author in which the term under discussion (or a closely related term) appears, can one say with any kind of assurance and finality that this *is* what the term really means. Though every term belongs to phonetic, grammatical, and semantic clusters over which the author has no control, and usually belongs to a substance-cluster over which the author also has no control, all key terms in a given symbolic structure also belong to a cluster of identifications of the author's own making, one that he creates out of himself, out of the deepest and most secret resources of his being. Since no two people could have exactly the same range and quality of experience, exactly the same body and mind, no two authors could ever embody and personalize an essence in exactly the same way. This being so, the only way in which one can ever find out what a key term and a set of interrelated key terms (a completed symbolic structure) really means is to index the work so that one can find out how the private grammar the author creates deviates from the public grammar which all authors use.

The Dramatistic Theory of Literature

Every work has its own inner logic, and all the works by one author will have the same kind of inner logic because every life and every self has a grammar or logic of its own. There are no "anonymous" poems. An author could not, even if he wished, depersonalize a poem; it is out of his own mind and body, out of that mind-and-body's perceptions of the relationships between the "world's body," the "body politic," the "mystical spiritual body," and the "mythic body" that he creates. As Burke uses the terms, to embody an essence *is* to personalize in the image of the self, for the essence is the mind's and the images are the body's counterparts. And as the artist's self sees the world so will it be reflected (or deflected) in the symbolic structure which he creates. This does not mean that the poem has to be read as a self-portrait, although it can be; it is just that this is the way in which Burke thinks poems get made and this is the kind of relation he thinks exists between the essence being imitated, the self doing the imitating, the medium in which it is imitated, and the completed symbolic structure.

ii

POETRY AND BEYOND

Though every poet imitates an essence by embodying and personalizing it, all poets have open to them different specific ways of imitating: they can write poetry or prose, can write lyrics, narratives or dramas, and can use conventional forms or create partially unique ones. Realizing this and bent, as he says, on "carving out a poetics," Burke, since 1950, has been in the process of defining as many of these differentiae as possible within the context of dramatism and in terms of his own theory of imitation. It is not necessary to study in detail all of Burke's dramatistic definitions — they include the lyric, the short story, the lyric novel, the platonic dialogue, tragedy, the narrative, and drama in general. But it is useful to examine representative definitions and see how he moves from general to specific propositions about literature and how he applies both to individual poetic imitations.

Burke defines the lyric as

Burke and the Drama of Human Relations

A short complete poem, elevated or intense in thought and senti-
ment, expressing and evoking [the essence of] a unified attitude towards a momentous situation more or less explicitly implied — in diction harmonious and rhythmical, often but not necessarily rhymed
— the structure lending itself readily to a musical accompaniment
strongly repetitive in quality; the gratification of the whole residing
in the nature of the work as an ordered summation of emotional experience otherwise fragmentary, inarticulate, and unsimplified. (KR,
XIII,174.)

As one would expect, the lyric attitude or lyric arrest is contrasted
to the dramatic act or dramatic action. An attitude is an "incipient
act," a "gesture" or "posture," a "summing-up." And lyrics are "moments" because they "pause to sum up a motive." "In one's moments," Burke says, "one is absolute. Though there may not be current names for some of them, all moments are as though capitalized:
Delight, Promise, Victory, Regret, Apprehension, Arrival, Crossing,
Departure, Loneliness, Sorrow, Despair, etc. In summing up a past,
they ambiguously contain a not yet unfolded future" (BOM,ix).
What is imitated, then, is the essence of an attitude (presumably the
poet's) towards a "momentous situation" (Burke's rather loosely
used term meaning just about anything of importance to the poet).
From the examples he gives, it is clear that Burke means *both* an
attitude or posture of prayer, lamentation, meditation, joy, admo-
nition, invective, or self-expression, *and* the attitude which is expressed in the poem toward the "momentous situation." A lyric
imitates *both* the body *and* the mind of the attitude, for it shows the
poet in a particular posture, a particular moment of arrest, and it
presents the attitude through the imagery, prosody, and structure.

Burke says very little in his definition about the means used to
imitate the attitude save that it is verbal, should be "harmonious and
rhythmical" in diction, and have a repetitive structure. One can con-
clude from this that the chief defining characteristic of the lyric is
to be found in the essence being imitated. Lyrics do not imitate the
development of an attitude, although a sequence of lyrics might
trace such a development, but the attitude itself; consequently, they
are usually plotless and do not follow the logic of events or even a
pattern of experience but the logic of such things as argument, medi-

tation, reverie, and metaphor — a kind of associational and emotional logic which is complete or unified when the particular attitude being imitated has been adequately presented. Only the poet really knows how much is enough, for the principal unifying device is the attitude being imitated and everything in the poem is a manifestation of this single attitude, a means of embodying and personalizing it (KR,XIII,176).

In Keats's *Ode to a Nightingale*, for example, there are only two external events: the nightingale sings and then leaves; the rest of the poem is made up of Keats's reveries and meditation, and follows the subjective, associational logic that characterizes them. The poem may be said to imitate the poet's ambiguous attitude toward his own ambiguous situation, the song of the nightingale having set in motion the reverie and meditation which crystallize the ambiguous attitude stated in the last half line of the poem: "Do I wake or sleep?" "Strictly speaking," Burke says, "an attitude is by its very nature 'unified.' Even an attitude of hesitancy or internal division [as in Keats's poem] is 'unified' in the formal sense, if the work in its entirety rounds out precisely that." (KR,XIII,175.) Thus, though Keats is unresolved, the poem is complete, for its object was to present the attitude of irresolution and it does this by showing the poet actually in a posture of irresolution and by stating the attitude itself. Here, quite literally, the poet personalizes the essence by using himself as an embodiment of it, presenting it in terms of himself in a moment of lyric arrest. In that moment, "one is absolute," for, to paraphrase Coleridge, the poet fills all things with himself and makes all sounds tell back the tale of his own sorrow or joy (*The Nightingale*, lines 19–21). Whatever is outside is internalized and transformed by the symbol-making imagination into images which will embody the attitude. For this reason, the lyric attitude unifies the poem by making all the images "manifestations of a single *attitude*," so that all the images imply an "attitude towards the thing imaged" (KR,XIII,176).

This, in general and rather briefly, is the lyric mode; it operates to produce not only the short lyric poem which Burke defined but, often, as Burke's comments make clear, the short story (the prose fiction variant of the lyric poem), lyric passages in longer narrative and dramatic works, such as the soliloquies in Shakespeare's tragedies and the choral odes in Greek tragedy, and, sometimes, lyric dramas, such as Byron's *Manfred*, and lyric narratives, such as *The Rime of the Ancient Mariner*. The lyric posture is a universal human stance, primarily private, always subjective, and usually characterized by great intensity and brevity. In this stance, the self tends to internalize the external and view all things from its perspective. A particular lyric world always recedes inward toward the self which created it and the set of values which informs and unifies it. In the lyric posture, the self tends to experience everything as internal drama (the self confronting the self). Sometimes, as in Yeats's *A Dialogue of Self and Soul*, the poet splits himself in two, projecting or embodying the internal conflict in this way. Sometimes, he assumes a self to present the attitude, as in Yeats's "Crazy Jane" poems; but most often the internal conflict is embodied in opposed images, as in Yeats's *Sailing to Byzantium*, and the "unified attitude" emerges from the opposition.

By way of illustration, consider Hopkins' poem *God's Grandeur*, a conventional Italian sonnet which has, aside from the absolute unity that comes from Hopkins, the purely formal unity of a well-made Italian sonnet having four rhymes and an 8/6 sense division.

> The world is charged with the grandeur of God.
>   It will flame out, like shining from shook foil;
>   It gathers to a greatness, like the ooze of oil
> Crushed. Why do men then now not reck his rod?
> Generations have trod, have trod, have trod;
>   And all is seared with trade; bleared, smeared with toil;
>   And wears man's smudge and shares man's smell:
>   the soil
> Is bare now, nor can foot feel, being shod.
>
> And for all this, nature is never spent;
>   There lives the dearest freshness deep down things;
> And though the last lights off the black West went
>   Oh, morning, at the brown brink eastward, springs —
> Because the Holy Ghost over the bent
>   World broods with warm breast and with ah!
>   bright wings.

The Dramatistic Theory of Literature

The essence imitated is an attitude toward God which is summarized imagistically in the final lines of the poem. The "momentous situation" which gave rise to the poem is presented imagistically through two opposed sets of images in lines 1–8: the first establishes a relationship between nature and God, and the second describes man's continued abuse of nature (really God or God's Grandeur). After the explicit imagistic embodiment of the situation, Hopkins moves to the embodiment of the attitude, or to God's true grandeur, which is His mother-like love and compassion for both man and the world man abuses. Actually, the last two lines metaphorically present God (the Holy Ghost) in an attitude of love, and of protective, patient waiting; but the metaphor itself presents or embodies Hopkins' attitude both toward God and the momentous situation. The whole poem presents the poet in an attitude of meditation, progressing from an ecstatic affirmative outburst of joy to a violently negative lamentation to a quiet, almost breathless affirmative joy. In a sense, the poem ends where it began, with God's grandeur, but even in so short a poem as this, the words "God's Grandeur" have undergone a transformation (or perhaps an expansion), for by the end of the poet's meditation they have a different meaning than they had at the beginning. The poem begins as an outburst and ends as a persuasion and thus imitates the lyric process of creation in the same way George Herbert's *The Collar* does. The transformation of the key words, "God's Grandeur," corresponds to this progression from outburst to persuasion. Actually the progression is in three stages, for the outburst has two parts, one of joy and the other of sorrow. The two violently conflicting outbursts, which are opposites in the sense that the coexistence of the two conditions which gave rise to them is both emotionally and rationally intolerable to the poet, are transcended by the attitude embodied imagistically in the last four lines of the poem. The poet is persuaded to "accept" the situation by taking the attitude towards it embodied in the last four lines. The situation is only apparently intolerable (the two-part outburst stage of the poem), for the knowledge (intuited or affirmed rather than logically demonstrated) that the mysterious, inexhaustible "grandeur" of God will endlessly recharge a "seared," "bleared," "smeared," smudged, stripped, "spent," and "bent" world, though it may not alter or remove the situation, permits the poet to "accept" or, to use one of Burke's favorite words, "resign" himself to it. This is the "persuasion" stage, which completes the poem by "resolving" the dilemma with which the poem began.

The lyric, Burke says, tends to be "first an outcry," an expression of self, and "second a persuasion," an evocation of the "unified attitude" which the self expressed. As an "outcry," it performs an obvious cathartic function for the poet; but what starts as an outcry ends as "an ordered summation of emotional experience otherwise fragmentary, inarticulate, and unsimplified." Paraphrasing Croce, Burke calls this progression the "transcending of emotional matter by artistic form, or 'expression,'" and says that it, too, is cathartic for the poet because it imposes "order" on experience otherwise "unsimplified." As an "ordered summation" the lyric is a persuasion in two senses: it acts rhetorically on the poet, persuading or moving him from "chaos" (outcry) to "order" (evocation). Or, as Burke has often expressed it, the poem persuades the poet to make himself over in the image of his own imagery. Once the outcry has been transformed into an "ordered summation" "wherein things fall together felicitously," and as such has become a completed symbolic structure which can evoke a unified response in the reader, the poem can act rhetorically on the reader either in the same way it does for the poet, persuading him to make himself over in the image of the imagery, or simply by arousing certain emotions and gratifying the emotions it arouses. Either kind of "'gratification' (or 'lyric pleasure')° would correspond," Burke says, "to the 'catharsis' of 'pity, fear, and like emotions' (named by Aristotle as the tragic pleasure)" (KR,XIII, 177).

Like any other kind of poetic verbal act, the lyric can perform a number of different functions for the poet and the reader. The poem can serve as the symbolic act of the poet, as a verbal act which performs a purgative-redemptive function for him, as self-portraiture, as a "portrait" of the character of a particular social hierarchy, and as a verbal structure which communicates depth knowledge. In treating literature as literature, Burke arranges things so that he can move effortlessly from the poetic to the grammatical, rhetorical, and ethical-personal categories; and once he has indexed a work, he can use the results not only for an analysis of the work as poetry, but as grammar, rhetoric, and portraiture.

This distinguishing characteristic of Burke's dramatistic theory of literature is well illustrated in what he says of the lyric novel and tragedy. Burke defines the lyric novel as

a serious prose narrative, imitating an agent's spiritual adventures, in the development of a new attitude, with its corresponding doctrine; it employs an intense, elevated, or otherwise exceptional diction (involving a principle of selectivity that makes it representative in the *culminative* sense rather than as tested by *statistical averages*); the unity of action centers in the unity of the main character, whose transformations coincide with the stages of the plot; like the lyric proper, it places great reliance upon sensory images, not merely for purposes of vividness (*enargeia*) but to serve structural ends (the images thus taking on "mythic" dimensions that transcend their specifically sensory significance); the seriousness of the agent and the magnitude of his trials serve to dignify the development towards which the work is directed. (KR,XIII, 181.)

The definition is actually based on Joyce's *Portrait*, which Burke analyzes briefly in his comments on the definition, and at greater length in his essay on "indexing" (SAV,283–306). However, the lyric novel seems to have developed out of the romance, or lyric narrative, and what Burke says about the *Portrait* applies to most lyric novels, such as Alain-Fournier's *Le Grand Meaulnes*, Salinger's *The Catcher in the Rye*, Waldo Frank's *The Death and Birth of David Markand*, and Glenway Wescott's *The Grandmothers*.

The lyric novel always tends toward symbolic narrative, with the events of the plot — the agent's movement through time and space — symbolizing a "spiritual movement," a completed pattern of experience. In the lyric novel, the essence being imitated would always be embodied in a plot of some kind, which is an extended *double-entendre*. If there is a plot, there must be a scene or scenes in which the events take place; and like the plot, these are usually symbolic, for where the agent is usually corresponds to what he is (the scene-agent ratio) and where he goes or wishes to go usually corresponds to what he will become or wishes to become. Neither the plot nor the settings can be taken at face value in a lyric novel, for the first is a progressive form symbolizing the agent's pattern of experience and the second are static symbols which embody in details of place stages in that pattern of experience. Many lyric novels end with departures, often for unknown or unspecified places, for often the new attitude arrived at by the end of the novel makes it necessary for the agent to leave the place where he is to go in search of a setting in which an agent with that attitude can live. Stephen Dedalus, for example, like the birds which he is always noticing, simply takes off at the end of the novel for places unknown "to encounter for the millionth time the reality of experience." At the end of *The Grandmothers*, Alwyn Tower, like Dedalus, departs because the new attitude he has developed makes it impossible for him to stay where he is. Sometimes, as in *The Death and Birth of David Markand*, the lyric novel ends with a return, having begun with a departure and dealt primarily with a journey wherein the new attitude was developed which made the return possible.

Lyric novels deal primarily with the process of growth and change, both physical and spiritual, usually in a single central agent, but sometimes, as in multiple quest novels or romances, in a number of agents. Whether they deal with one or more central agents, the unity of action in a lyric novel always "centers in the unity of the main character" for it is his development which controls the selection and arrangement of detail in the novel as a whole. Everything in the novel serves what Burke calls "structural ends"; everything derives its meaning and significance from its relationship to the central agent — the lyric self which unifies by absorbing everything in a self-contained universe. As with the lyric moment when the self is "absolute," viewing everything from the perspective of itself as long as the moment lasts, in the lyric novel — which is really a collection of moments of varying lengths in a narrative framework which works out a completed pattern of experience — the self is absolute in the same way only for a much longer period of time. This is what gives many lyric novels their peculiar intensity.

The Dramatistic Theory of Literature

As a description of a particular type of novel, Burke's definition is useful because it describes the type and, when applied, using the methodological approach Burke calls "indexing," illuminates the formal qualities of the work. Though one need never move beyond the formal qualities of the novel, the definition is set up so that such a movement is effortless, especially within the context of Burke's dramatistic theory of literature. An aesthetic analysis of the work would make explicit the main coordinates of the completed symbolic structure — the main identifications, oppositions, progressions, and transformations within that particular symbolic act. Presumably, the formal analysis of the work should be made first, for the novel is primarily a poetic verbal act; but, Burke says, it would be foolish to claim that the novel is only a poetic verbal act and once analyzed as such must be thrown in the bin reserved for such verbal acts. The work can also be examined for various kinds of knowledge. For example, it can be analyzed for its verbal action and from it we can learn something about language itself. This knowledge could be useful in a number of ways, for man is essentially the symbol- or language-using animal, and whatever we can learn about language will tell us something about both the essence of man and symbol-using itself. According to the definition the novel also embodies an essence in narrative and lyric terms. In this instance, the "essence" would be complex and have a number of interrelated parts: the largest essence would be the pattern of experience itself, but also included would be the rejected attitude, the new attitude, and the doctrines which go with both. The way in which the essence is embodied and personalized can be studied; but the essence being imitated can also be abstracted from the work and treated as knowledge which can serve as "a preparation for action." In Joyce's *Portrait*, Burke says, "Stephen is not 'representative' in the 'statistical' sense. He is a rarity. But many modern writers have in one way or another adapted religious coordinates to aesthetic ends. And Joyce imagines such a course 'to perfection'" (KR,XIII,182). The novel, then, may be studied for whatever knowledge it yields about the search for the self in general, and Stephen's particular kind of search. To examine the work for whatever knowledge it may give us of verbal action,

[199]

patterns of experience, and attitudes is to treat the novel as a poetic verbal act which quite naturally functions also as a grammatical verbal act. The poetic verbal act uses essences — the universals of experience — as the basis for the imitation; and this implies a certain knowledge of them on the part of the poet. For this reason, every imitation is a definition in lyric, narrative, or dramatic terms. And though the poet may not deliberately attempt to teach and inform, to provide us with information and knowledge as a preparation for action, it is inevitable that he *will* do this, for in imitating the essence the poet cannot help but define that essence when he embodies and personalizes it.

As definitions, poetic imitations provide us with depth knowledge. The knowledge may be of almost anything, for poets write of whatever compels them and this includes just about everything. One of the central tenets of the dramatistic theory of literature is that poetic verbal acts also function as grammatical, rhetorical, and ethical-personal verbal acts; every imitation is also a definition, a persuasion, an expression of self, a piece of portraiture, and a moral act. So the movement or progression in a dramatistic analysis is always from imitation to something else: from imitation to persuasion, from imitation to self-expression, from imitation to portraiture. And generally, though a dramatistic analysis first deals with the work as poetry, it goes through the work, away from it and beyond it toward what it symbolizes or what it does for the reader.

Burke says that all poetic verbal acts function rhetorically "to move or persuade to attitude or action." As rhetoric, the poem can work persuasively either upon the agent enacting it or on the agents re-enacting it, or on both, and either in the same way toward the same end or in different ways toward different ends. As rhetoric, the poem functions primarily as private and public purgative-redemptive symbolic action by persuading the poet and reader to make themselves over in the image of the poem's imagery. The whole theory of symbolic action discussed in Chapter III is simply absorbed into dramatism as *one* of the functions which verbal acts perform. The coordinates of dramatism — hierarchy, the negative, victimage, mortification, catharsis, redemption, and categorical guilt — are now used in the analysis of poetry as either private or public symbolic action, but what this amounts to is a use of some new terms rather than a whole set of new ideas. The primary emphasis is the same — upon the cathartic function which poetry performs for the poet and reader alike.

To the traditional three-fold division of language into grammar, rhetoric, and poetics, Burke adds a fourth division or "office": the ethical-personal (see ChiR,VIII,88–102). Actually, there is a certain margin of overlap between this fourth office and at least two of the others, for Burke says that ethical-personal verbal acts function primarily as self-expression, portraiture, and moral action. For example, as self-expression (outcry) poetry is obviously cathartic; it functions as a release through an outpouring of words. As such, it would be covered under rhetoric for it moves the poet from one state to another, from one attitude to another through verbal unclogging. And since purgative-redemptive symbolic action, whether public or private, is moral action which moves the poet or reader from unclean to clean by means of symbolic cleansing, poetry as moral action could also be covered under rhetoric. By portraiture, Burke means two things: self-portraiture and social portraiture. Poetry as self-portraiture was discussed as representative symbolic action in Chapter III (pp. 68–71) and little more need be said about it here. If the poet portrays himself in his poems, then obviously the poems may be studied as symbolic autobiography and such a study will yield knowledge — of the self in general, of a particular self, and of the self in quest. The study of poetry as knowledge comes under grammar, for the primary purpose of a grammatical study is to provide one with knowledge as a preparation for action. As was pointed out in Chapters II and III, the self is moral and the self in quest is engaged in moral action. For this reason, Burke places self-portraiture and moral action in the ethical-personal category; but to study poetry as either of these is to treat it as knowledge (grammar) and persuasion (rhetoric), or as both, which is what Burke does when he analyzes a poem as symbolic action.

Finally, Burke includes one other function which poetic verbal acts can perform in the ethical-personal category: poems not only portray the self but the character or personality of the society in which that self had its being and the kind of drama which results from the interaction between a given social-political hierarchy and a particular self. A social-political hierarchy constitutes the scene in which agents are formed, in which they act, and against which they react. To alter the scene is to change the formation, action, and re-action of the agents, even though all agents are born into any scene with certain fundamental characteristics which are not ultimately de-rivable from the social-political scene but are part of a biological-neurological inheritance. Though there are natural and supernatural as well as social-political scenes, it is the latter in which Burke is primarily interested, for so overwhelming is its effect that everything else tends to be seen in terms of the socio-political hierarchy as "so-cial pageantry." Kafka's *The Castle*, Burke implies, is not fiction, but brutal fact — a true if somewhat grotesque image of the ways in which every kind of experience possible to man is permeated and distorted by the socio-political hierarchy to the point where man either loses his sense of what is real or takes the socio-political hierarchy as the only reality, ultimately conceiving it as god in the way Orwell imag-ined it in *1984*. Therefore, when Burke says that poems also portray the character or personality of a given society, what he means is that in major works — he mentions *Venus and Adonis, The Castle, Othel-lo,* and *Faust,* Part I — not only is the value-structure of a given socio-political hierarchy portrayed but so is the role it plays in the drama of human relations. A poem can be studied, Burke says, as a sceneless act, but in reality, no act is without a scene or scenes: a par-ticular agent enacted it in or upon a particular social scene and, to use Burke's own play on words, the "personality" of that society helped form the "personality" of that agent and the two together are largely responsible for the "personality" of the poem. To focus on the personality of the poem — the self-contained verbal act — is to treat the work as poetry, according to the laws of its kind and in the way discussed earlier. One discovers this personality by indexing; the other two personalities are discovered by a variety of means, all of which turn on the questionable assumption that everything in the "personality" of the work is a deception, deflection, *double-entendre*, or pun of some kind. To focus on the work as self-portraiture — representative symbolic action — one takes the self as the basis of the symbolism and by tinkering attempts to move from the personality of the work to the personality of the author, treating the work, finally, as pure symbolic autobiography. To focus on the work as a portrait of the personality of a given society, one takes the socio-political hierarchy as the basis of the symbolism and attempts to move from the personality of the work to the personality of the society, treating the work, finally, as social or hierarchic allegory.

For this purpose, Burke devised what he calls socioanagogic criticism, the basic assumption of which is that hierarchy, and particularly the socio-political hierarchy which man creates *because* he is the language-using animal, is the most immediate of all man's concerns, and that the presentation of socio-political or hierarchic themes and conflicts is the actual end toward which most works tend. The socio-political hierarchy is the anagoge; or, more accurately, the "order-cluster," and the drama of human relations implicit in it, is the anagoge, the "analogical matrix"; all other hierarchic images (images drawn from what Burke calls the "range of mountings" or "bodies of imagery") are but symbols of some part of the total anagoge. A socioanagogic approach reduces all problems, finally, to social rather than, say, sexual or religious causes. In Burke there seem to be two primary linguistic-social motives or causes from which all others come: the hierarchic motive itself, which is simply the desire to mount and comes from the tendency towards abstraction which is part of the birthright of the symbol-using animal; and the hierarchic psychosis, the "categorical guilt" and "tension" which are natural to existence in the various social orders which man builds with language. From these develop naturally the other moments in the Burkean drama of human relations: the negative, victimage, mortification, catharsis, and redemption. Altogether, they make up the anagoge, which, as Burke tries to make clear, is universal and timeless; given man, the drama is inevitable and it is simply a matter of how, with all the variables, the drama will unfold in a specific historical period, in a particular society, in the works of a single author. There will, for example, always be a socio-political hierarchy, but change the value-structure of the hierarchy (what one strives for), and the kinds of categorical guilt and tensions produced will change; so will the kinds of victims, the modes of victimage, the ways of mortification, and the methods of catharsis and redemption. The general purpose of socio-anagogic criticism, then, is to study this drama as it is variously embodied in poetic verbal acts of sufficient length and complexity to make depth analysis possible.

To take an obvious example: according to Burke, man's experience is so dominated and his consciousness so permeated by the socio-political hierarchy that it tends to "shape" his ideas of everything else: he sees nature, super-nature, and himself through a socio-political fog in the sense that everything derives meaning and value from its relation to the value-structure of the socio-political hierarchy. For his text, Burke takes Kafka's *The Castle*, the theme of which he says is "bureaucracy, communication between higher and lower orders, involving the mysteries of 'reverence'" (RM,234). Among other things, Burke tries to show how sexual, vocational, educational, personal, familial, natural, and divine terms (or motives) become interwoven and finally fused (or confused) with social terms in this grotesque novel about a nameless dislocated self which is all but destroyed by the hierarchic motive and psychosis. To take a less obvious example: one of Burke's notions amounts to an inversion of Freud. Burke maintains that most problems are socially rather than sexually caused and that many such problems are presented roundabout in literature through sexual symbols. Burke arrives at this notion by a way as roundabout as some of his applications of it. Briefly, the matter turns upon an elaborately worked out analogy between sexual courtship and social relations. Burke argues, for example, that Shakespeare's *Venus and Adonis* is not really an erotic poem, for it "is not primarily [about] sexual lewdness at all, but [about] 'social lewdness' mythically expressed in sexual terms" (RM, 208). Burke tries to show how the poem, ostensibly a story of sexual courtship, is really about social courtship and the social hierarchy. The poem, in other words, is a "social allegory" (RM,219). Briefly, this is Burke's interpretation: Venus, Adonis, and the Boar represent, respectively, the upper, middle, and lower classes; the horses represent the "potent aspect of the middle class." The poem was written, Burke maintains, at a time when the old way of life (the courtly way) was breaking down and the upper class was being challenged by the middle and lower classes. Viewed socioanagogically, what the poem enigmatically prefigures is the great social upheaval which culminated in the French Revolution when the upper class was forced to woo the middle class to stay in power; but the middle class finally revolted and caused great bloodshed among all classes. The poem deals with the passing of the old order, the coming of the new one, and the rise of the middle class with its "cult of acquisition"—Adonis as huntsman. The poem ends with a whole series of images depicting the "topsy-turvy" state of the world which will result from the breaking down of the old order. Burke does not maintain that the "social allegory" was deliberately contrived; the "identifications" or symbolic meanings "can be implicit, and 'unconscious' " (RM,219). In fact, Burke's real argument turns on the assertion that "the vocabularies of social and sexual courtship are so readily interchangeable, not because one is a mere 'substitute' for the other, but because sexual courtship is intrinsically fused with the motives of social hierarchy." "Thus," Burke says, "when this poem is viewed 'socioanagogically,' it will be seen to disclose, in enigmatically roundabout form, a variant of revolutionary challenge. By proxy it demeans the old order, saying remotely, in sexual imagery, what no courtly poet could have wanted to say, or even have thought of saying, in social or political terms" (RM,217).

Socioanagogic criticism works on the assumption that, in Burke's rather charged language, "a poetic observation involves no naked relation between an observed object and the observer's eye. The topics that the poet uses are 'charismatic.' They glow." What they glow with are the "mysteries," not as the medievalists thought, of the "celestial hierarchy," but of the "social hierarchy." "Even the world of natural objects," Burke says, "as they figure in poetry, must have secret 'identification' with the judgments of status." "The veil of Maya is woven of the strands of hierarchy — and the poet's topics glow through that mist." (RM,219.) Actually, Burke's socioanagogic interpretations take many directions. Sometimes it is a matter of illustrating from a poetic text the degree to which various natural and man-made objects become "status symbols" and glow with a particular hierarchic charge; sometimes it is a matter of showing how, in a poetic text, the idea of God is shaped by the socio-political hierarchy or how communication with God is conceived after the analogy of social relations; sometimes it is a matter of working out the whole hierarchic drama as it appears in a particular text; and sometimes it is a matter of allegorically interpreting a work which seems to have nothing whatsoever to do with the hierarchic motive, the hierarchic psychosis, and all the other moments in the drama.

All of Burke's socioanagogic interpretations are radiations from a single center, variations on a single theme, documentations of what Burke takes to be a universal phenomenon: the drama of human relations as he conceives it — a drama which is initiated by language, complicated at every point by language, reflected in linguistic acts, sometimes enacted and resolved in symbolic acts, and finally studied analytically in dramatistic criticism. The essence of this drama is embodied in dramatic form in the first part of Goethe's *Faust*, which he analyzes in order to describe the drama, to show how it is embodied, and to illustrate the socioanagogic method. The play, Burke says, is about the very essence of the hierarchic motive (striving) and categorical guilt (erring); it really deals with socio-political striving and erring (the desire for "power," ambition as a disease), with the tendency toward socio-political riot (revolution) and its disastrous results, particularly the violation of Gretchen, the victimage of both Gretchen and her brother, and the "riot" — imagistically presented in the Walpurgis Night episode and in other set pieces throughout the play — which follow the violation of the socio-political negatives (Faust saying "No" to the thou-shalt-nots or, as Burke would have it, Faust violating the "sanctities of private property" which the thou-shalt-nots are specifically designed to protect). As in the essay on *Venus and Adonis*, Burke's socioanagogic analysis turns upon the idea that an essentially socio-political theme is expressed in terms of its sexual analogues. In the essay Burke studies at great length all of the moments in the drama of human relations, but especially victimage; and near the end of it he says,

The Dramatistic Theory of Literature

Frankly, we don't know what all this adds up to. . . . But we do believe that when in quest of basic human symbolism one should risk even many blind and pointless tentatives, in the attempt to understand what ideal types of human victimage there may be, and how they are related to whatever system of property and propriety, public and private, goes with any given social order. For human relations are dogged at every turn by victimage, and the freedom with which poetry can concern itself with these matters prompts us to inspect poetic symbolizations above all for their ability to express all variants of victimage. (ChiR,IX,67–68.)

At the very end of his essay, Burke says, "We believe that the analysis of poetic forms, when approached from this [socioanagogic, dramatistic] attitude, points both to the essential motives of poetry in particular and of human relations in general" (ChiR,IX,72).

Approached socioanagogically, a work is treated as a verbal construct which has a unique poetic "personality"; at the same time it portrays both the "personality" of the author and the "personality" of a given social order. By using the Burkean drama as anagoge, the work can be treated as a completed symbolic structure in which man's ways as symbol-user and the drama of human relations can be studied. The end toward which all of Burke's criticism is directed is a study of the drama of human relations as it is reflected in man's verbal acts. Having defined man as essentially a symbol-using animal, and having selected the poetic verbal act, particularly drama, as the ideal or perfect verbal act, it is not surprising that Burke should derive a whole system from the contemplation of drama, that he should take literary texts as representative human acts, that his applied criticism, ostensibly literary, should follow the same pattern, starting always with the text, with the work as a poetic verbal act, moving always through the text, beyond the text, from verbal action to symbolism, from imitation to essence, from embodiment to attitude, from the verbal to the meta-verbal, beyonding, always beyonding. "By and through language, beyond language"; this is the motto of dramatism as a whole: "By and through poetry, beyond poetry"; this is the motto of the dramatistic theory of literature. Though Burke acknowledges that poetry is or should be an end in itself, the theory calls for a variety of beyondings: through the poem to the poet (symbolic autobiography); through the poem to its purgative-redemptive function for the poet (symbolic action); through the poem to the essence it imitates (the poem as definition, as depth knowledge); through the poem to the society it portrays (socioanagogic analysis); through the poem to the drama of human relations (the pure dramatistic approach).

···
iii

TRAGEDY AS THE REPRESENTATIVE ANECDOTE

Probably nowhere in Burke are all of these ideas and methods so clearly seen and brilliantly applied as in the theories of tragedy and catharsis developed since the early forties. All of Burke's thinking about literature as poetic, grammatical, rhetorical, and ethical-personal verbal action culminates in the theories of tragedy and catharsis and the method developed to apply them. This is so because Burke considers tragedy the "ideal" or "perfect" poetic verbal act, the paradigmatic form; he makes tragedy the "essence" of poetry and approaches "poetics" in terms of tragedy. His procedure is to isolate the essential characteristics of tragedy and then, having established the "paradigm" or "pure" form, to look at other poetic verbal acts in terms of or under the aegis of tragedy and to find in other poetic verbal acts what he found in tragedy. The essence of tragedy, Burke says, is the cathartic function which it performs, the purging of the audience's bodily, personal, civic, and religious irresolutions. By this route, Burke goes from poetry to drama to tragedy to catharsis (the term around which the dramatistic theory of literature is built) and back to poetry. Catharsis is also one of the key terms around which his whole system is built, for though it belongs to the poetry-drama-tragedy cluster, it also belongs to the order-cluster discussed in Chapter IV (pp. 155–157). This means that in any discussion of catharsis Burke will logologically "radiate out" and consider the negative, victimage, mortification, hierarchy, redemption, and categorical guilt. By his logic, all are implicit in the term "catharsis" and, by implication, in the terms "poetry," "drama," and "tragedy," since catharsis links the two clusters.

The Dramatistic Theory of Literature

A great lover of paradigms, of "pure" or "ideal" forms arrived at through dialectical ascent to ever higher levels of abstraction, and an equally great lover of the paradigmatic embodiment of the "pure" or "ideal" form — the "representative anecdote," the archetypal myth, the perfect imitation of the pure essence — Burke attempts to read into (or is it out of?) tragedy a whole poetics as well as a whole system. One might say that tragedy is Burke's representative anecdote, if one remembers that he selects the *Oresteia* as the ideal tragedy and that this trilogy, in spite of the many differences, is similar in many respects to Dante's *Divine Comedy* in so far as the progression in both is from "hell" through "purgatory" to "heaven." Both follow the purgative-redemptive form discussed in Chapter III (pp. 96–111) and both embody the paradigm of catharsis, though one is called a tragedy and the other a comedy. "The paradigm of catharsis," Burke says, "must contain ideas and images for at least these major elements: unclean, clean, cleansing, cleanser (personal or impersonal), cleansed." As Burke points out, "the cleansing process" does not always "go simply from unclean to cleansed, since the cleanser in some way takes over the uncleanness, which in turn must be disposed of" (KR,XXI,367). Like the two works mentioned above, the Burkean drama of human relations and the "myth" he selects to illustrate the drama — the Eden-Christ "myth" — also embody the paradigm of catharsis. If one takes this paradigm as Burke describes it, one can move effortlessly back and forth from it to the seven moments in the Burkean drama: one might be "unclean" because of categorical guilt, the hierarchic psychosis, or the violation of any moral negative; one gets clean through mortification or victimage of some kind, or the clean person may be used as sacrificial victim; cleansing is got by purgation (catharsis) or mortification; the cleanser may be either a sacrificial victim or various acts of mortification; the cleansed is the redeemed person. In other words, all those things discussed in Chapter IV (pp. 134–153) in relation to the order-cluster and the drama of human relations figure in any discussion of catharsis and tragedy. The better one knows Burke the more obvious it becomes that his theory of tragedy and catharsis, ostensibly a theory of poetry — a poetics, as he calls it — is really a theory of human relations as a moral drama in which the "fall" is inevitable and the driving need purgative-redemptive. Unclean, clean, cleansing, cleanser, cleansed; hierarchy, categorical guilt, negative, victimage, mortification, catharsis, redemption; symbols, form, symbolic action, symbol systems: over these terms and their relationships Burke has brooded all his life. In the poetry, drama, tragedy, catharsis, drama of human relations cluster Burke achieves a masterful synthesis in which key concepts from every phase of his long and productive career come together to form a final, coherent system.

Within the framework of his dramatistic theory of literature Burke develops his theories of tragedy and catharsis. This means that tragedy will be defined as the imitation of some essence and will be characterized by identifications (images), oppositions (an agon, or its analogue), progressions (plot, or its analogue), and transformations (dialectic, or its analogue). According to Burke, tragedy is the imitation (or exploitation) of the perfect essence of a tension (or psychosis) in dramatic form where the action (or "plot") of the play as a whole follows, and the tragic protagonist undergoes the tragic rhythm (the progression from action through suffering to knowledge and redemption); the tragic imitation having as its purpose the purging and resolving of the audience's bodily, personal, civic, and religious irresolutions (or tensions). This brief definition is a concocted one because, though Burke has written more about tragedy than any other form, he has never bothered to write a formal definition. I mention this because there is a certain amount of confusion as to exactly what Burke means by a number of crucial terms. Take tension, for example: in writing about tragedy, Burke speaks most often about the particular tension which a given tragedy imitates; but, as is his practice, he usually uses tension in combination with a number of other terms, all of which seem to be synonyms: the most important of these are psychosis, pollution, civic disorders, civic pollutions, disorders within the polis, civic guilt, class conflicts, temporal tensions, and mysteries. The more one studies these terms the more apparent it becomes that by tension Burke means any kind of hierarchic psychosis. As I pointed out, the hierarchic psychosis is produced by the

The Dramatistic Theory of Literature

hierarchic motive and causes all kinds of "categorical guilt." So by tension, Burke seems to mean this cluster of hierarchic terms; and in his remarks on tragedy, he seems to suggest that this is what tragic playwrights imitate. There is also a certain amount of confusion as to what Burke means by imitate, for again he uses this term in combination with a number of others, all of which seem to be synonyms. The two most frequently used are symbolize and exploit; the second is probably the most revealing for Burke suggests that tragic playwrights deliberately exploit a tension through complex symbolic manipulations for cathartic purposes. That is, they use (or exploit) the resources of the tension (the perfect essence of which they have come to know either through intensive or extensive experience and study) as well as the resources of their medium (symbolic action) in order deliberately to contrive a cathartic drama which releases the specific civic tensions, as well as various other bodily, personal, and religious tensions which the playwrights have exploited.

Burke establishes as a pre-existing and permanent condition what he calls the extra-aesthetic tensions which a tragedy imitates; the "civic 'pollution'" which tragedies "are designed to ritually cleanse" is "intrinsic to the nature of the state" (*Poetics*,225). "A state of social tension," Burke says, "just *is*" (*Poetics*,273); it is "static and ineradicable to human societies in the large" (*Poetics*,226) and is like a "stagnant miasmatic" swamp, "trackless" and "aimless" (*Poetics*,273). Tragedy, or any poetic verbal act, does not, could not, bring either permanent relief or permanently remove the ineradicable cause of the tensions, but it can bring temporary relief — to use Burke's own metaphor — by leading one out of the miasmatic swamp for a while. According to Burke, tragedies are purgative journeys which lead one "*from* there [the swamp], *through* here [the work], *to* that place yonder [the state beyond catharsis]" (*Poetics*,226). It is well to remember that a good deal — most of — what Burke writes about poetry starts from this belief in the pre-existing and permanent state of trackless, aimless, miasmatic tension-pollution-guilt which is man's "natural" condition as symbol-user; since all men are in this state most of the time, purgation is a permanent need which can be partly satisfied through symbolic action.

Burke and the Drama of Human Relations

When Burke says that tragedy imitates and exploits the perfect essence of a tension or psychosis he means two things: that every tension has a particular character or personality which constitutes its essential nature; and that there exists in every tension the entelechial possibility of perfect actualization. Tragedy, then, imitates not just the essence of a tension, but the perfect essence, which is Burke's way of saying that tragedy deals with "excessive engrossment," the conditions under which the potential completely actualizes itself. Burke says, for example, that Shakespeare's *Othello* imitates the perfect essence of the "possession" or "ownership" tension. This particular tension is a "triune" one, having as its essential characteristics the three abstract principles of possession: the possessor, possession and what is possessed, and estrangement or threat of loss. The essence of the tension is a paradoxical dialectic; the perfect essence of the tension is a tragic dialectic in which the threat of loss inherent in any ownership situation actualizes itself and becomes partial or total estrangement. Usually it is the latter, for the excessive engrossment, the attempt at absolute possession, leads to the opposite reflexive state of absolute loneliness. Furthermore, the route from absolute possession to absolute loneliness is littered with the victims of the possessor's excessive engrossment; and by the time the possessor has traveled that route, he has himself become the guilt-laden victim of his own excessive engrossment.

It is this tragic dialectic of the possession tension which Shakespeare imitates in *Othello*. The tension, one of Burke's timeless universal clusters that just is, can obviously manifest itself in many ways; in as many ways, in fact, as one can possess a person, place, idea, thing, or means; and in as many ways as there are motives for ownership. In literature the following works imitate some particular manifestation of this always potentially tragic tension, though not all are tragedies and some are not even tragic: *Antigone, The Jew of Malta, Macbeth, Manfred,* Goethe's *Faust, The Spoils of Poynton, 1984,* and *All the King's Men.* The particular manifestation of the tension which Shakespeare imitates and exploits in *Othello* is "the disequilibrium of monogamistic [romantic] love," or, as Burke variously describes it in his essay on *Othello*: "property in human affections";

[212]

"sexual love as property and ennoblement"; "the analogue, in the realm of human affinity," to "the enclosure acts, whereby the common lands were made private"; "an act of spiritual enclosure," whereby "love, universal love," is "made private"; and sexual and spiritual ownership, as they are fused in romantic love and marriage. (HR,IV,166–170.) Here, then, is the particular tension which Shakespeare imitates and exploits. Whatever the actual steps in the creative process, Burke says that ideally the dramatic poet imitates by first "translating" the tension into progressive form, which in a play would be "plot" or "action"; and then by "translating" the tension into the "equivalent terms of personality" by "dramatic dissociation into interrelated roles." Characters, or, as Burke likes to call them, "character recipes," are contrived or built "in accord with the demands of the action"; and the "logic of the action as a whole" is contrived or built in accord with the demands of the tension being imitated; and the play as a whole is contrived or built in accord with the demands of the specific purpose of tragedy, which is to release or purge tensions through symbolic action.

Given the tension and its dialectic, a particular kind of plot progression immediately suggests itself, for the initial and terminal events (possession, estrangement) are themselves part of the triune tension. The specific details of the "intrigue" (another of Burke's words for plot) will connect these two principal events by leading up to and away from the act of possession; from the act through the various complications that result from any attempt at absolute possession (the excessive engrossment necessary for tragedy); to the estrangement (psychic and physical, and usually total) which is the tragic consequence of the excessive engrossment. Often the plot will end here (with total aloneness), but more often, for cathartic purposes, the intrigue will lead away from this state toward some unifying event. The translation of the tension into narrative terms gives the imitation its "rational" structure or form; but, Burke says, all tragedies have a double structure, for "there is a kind of ritualistic form lurking behind" the "intrigue"; "the mythic or ritual pattern (with the work as a viaticum for guiding us through a dark and dangerous passage) lurks behind the 'rational' intrigue." Aside from the ra-

[213]

tional structure which presents "the natural development in terms of probability and necessity," there is a mythic or ritual structure which follows the form of a cathartic journey. (HR,IV,175–176.) This cathartic journey is actually the tragic rhythm or progression which the play as a whole follows, the progression from initial act through suffering to knowledge and redemption. Sometimes Burke calls this mythic or ritual structure a "persecutional" form because the playwright persecutes the audience in order that it may be purged; due to the marvelous illusions of art and the wonderful skill of the playwright, the audience re-enacts the persecutional and purgative "ritual of riddance."

The mythic or ritual structure is as much a part of the imitation as the rational intrigue for both are ways of translating the tension into progressive form; the mythic pattern is not, Burke says, what is being imitated, but a method of imitation — one of the playwright's resources — and one of the principal means of effecting the catharsis that is the purpose of the play. Considered as a "viaticum" the first part of a tragedy is the "way in"; "it states the primary conditions in terms of which the journey is to be localized or specified this time." And "though the ritual must always follow the same general succession of stages regardless of the intrigue, this course is repeated each time in the details proper to a particular intrigue." This, then, is what gives the play its double structure. In terms of the cathartic journey, the first part of the play is really preparation for that journey; the next part, within the journey metaphor, is "the definite pushing-off from shore" and the certainty of being "under way" on a particular journey. Depending upon the play and the specific rational intrigue, one can be "under way" for varying lengths of time; eventually, however, one has to arrive at "the withinness-of-withinness," "the principle of internality" where, quoting Plato, Burke says "there abides the very being with which true knowledge is concerned; the colorless, formless, intangible essence, visible only to mind, the pilot of the soul." In less abstract terms, one arrives at knowledge of the perfect essence of the tension being imitated. In *Othello* this is the moment of reversal, the peripety, when absolute possession becomes estrangement. "From this point on," wherever it happens to occur in the play, "we are returning. We shall get back to the starting point, though with a difference" for "there is presumably to be some kind of splitting, a 'separating out.' Something is to be dropped away, something retained, the whole [journey] thereby becoming a purification of a sort." The last part of the play would complete the journey and the "separating out" process. "All told, the rite is complete when one has become willing to abandon the figures who vicariously represent his own tension," and when the passion (persecution and suffering) has been transformed into an assertion. (HR,IV,176–178.) In *Othello*, for example, the passion is transformed into an assertion when Othello, after coming to knowledge, reaffirms the values he denied in murdering Desdemona, and redeems himself (and those values) by sacrificial suicide. The final event in the rational intrigue both completes the cathartic journey (mythic structure) and resolves the tension by completing it. The tragic dialectic inherent in any attempt at absolute possession has been worked out when we arrive at Othello's absolute estrangement, epitomized in his reflexive act of suicide.

When Burke says that the characters or "character recipes" are built in accord with the demands of the logic of the action as a whole, the specific tension being imitated, and the cathartic purpose of the play, he means that, like the plot and mythic structure, they are methods of imitation; that each character is best analyzed as a symbolic construct, a cluster of terms circling round a name, a mass of identifications concocted by the playwright "for producing a desired result." Dialectic, Burke says, is ideas in action; but drama is people in action: to make a play, a poet must do more than translate the tension into progressive form (plot and mythic structure); he must also translate the tension into the "equivalent terms of personality" by "dramatic dissociation into interrelated roles." The "tragic trinity of ownership," particularized in *Othello* in terms of "the disequilibrium of monogamistic love," requires at least three principal interrelated characters to symbolize the possessor (including the act of possession), what is possessed, and estrangement. The three parts of the "triune tension" or psychosis are represented in the play by the following major character recipes: Othello, Desdemona, and Iago.

Burke and the Drama of Human Relations

The minor characters also represent some "fragment of the tension" translated into the equivalent terms of personality; these Burke likes to call satellite characters because usually they tend to group around one or another of the three major characters. Aside from their function of "reflecting" some fragment of the tension, the minor characters also perform valuable and necessary plot or intrigue functions in so far as they "help the three major persons dramatically communicate with one another." Actually, then, all of the characters, no matter what their plot function, are symbolic of some part of the tension which is the generating subject of the imitation. (HR,IV, 180.)

In translating the tension into the equivalent terms of personality the playwright must invent a set of major and minor characters who can work out the perfect essence of the tension dramatically, "*in action or through action*" (HR,IV,187). What Burke means here is that in drama, anyway, the poet is intent upon "making a play, not people" (HR,IV,187); his problem as a dramatist is to "break down the psychosis" being imitated "into a usable spectrum of differentiated roles," to split it into as many "voices" as are "needed to provide a sufficient range of 'analogies' (with the over-all tension being variously represented in each of them)" (HR,IV,179). Once he has done this, the poet then translates the "roles" or "voices" into actions, for in drama, it is the agent-act ratio that must be exploited. Burke insists upon the fact that the demands of the tragic imitation control the invention and dramatic presentation of the characters, and that the sense we often have in Shakespeare's plays of "well-rounded" living characters is purely illusory. "The stupidest and crudest person who ever lived," Burke says, "is richer in motivation than all of Shakespeare's characters put together — and it would be either a stupidity or a sacrilege to say otherwise. It is as an artist, not as God, that he invents 'characters.' And to see him [or any other playwright] fully as an artist, we must not too fully adopt the Coleridgean view of art as the 'dim analogue of creation.' " (HR,IV,187–188.) Drama requires characters in action; a particular play imitating some tension requires certain specific actions; characters are invented to contribute the needed action, each one being given only those

The Dramatistic Theory of Literature

"traits that suit [him] for the action needed of [him]" (HR,IV, 179).

Someone once said that much of the play's power comes from the audience's realization that without Iago Othello and Desdemona could enjoy the continuous achieved perfection of romantic love. The power, in other words, comes from the terrible sense of what might have been. The implication, of course, is that the threat is external and that left alone they would have lived "beyond evil." Their destruction did not come from within but from without, from evil which, in the person of Iago, is always bent on destroying good. According to Burke, much of the play's power comes from the exact opposite of this, from the fact that the destruction is internally caused: with or without Iago, the continuous achieved perfection of romantic love is impossible. The tension which the play imitates is the perfect essence of the "disequilibrium of monogamistic [or romantic] love"; this disequilibrium exists with or without Iago as cause: it just is. Given the tragic protagonist's excessive engrossment in monogamistic love — in this particular case an attempt at absolute or perfect possession — the destructive motives (suspicion, threat of loss, estrangement) arise from within and are but externalized or symbolized in Iago. Iago is to be treated as one of the character recipes invented by Shakespeare to perform some of the actions needed in the tragic imitation of the tension. As such, he functions rather than is, and to treat him as a real character rather than a symbol is, Burke says, either a "stupidity or a sacrilege." One of Iago's more obvious functions is to "goad" or "torture" the plot forward, "for the audience's villainous entertainment and filthy purgation" (HR,IV,170). Another function, of course, is to act as the personal embodiment of the estrangement part of the tension. And the third function is to be one of the three principal "victims" or sacrificial agents, the other two being Desdemona and Othello. As *katharma*, he performs a major cathartic function; he is from the beginning the unclean or polluted agent to whom the audience's own pollutions can be symbolically transferred and thence carried away. As starkly as Burke intends it, Iago performs a sewer-like function: as *katharma*, he represents "that which is thrown away in cleansing . . . the offscourings, refuse"; as the play proceeds, the audience adds to the refuse pile and at the end of the play that pile, in the person of Iago, is taken away, by the proper authorities, to be disposed of in an appropriate place and way (HR,IV,166).

In general terms, Desdemona symbolizes the private property in which Othello over-invests, to the point of becoming "himself possessed by his very engrossment" in the idea of "single-mine-own-ness" (HR,IV,167). Iago symbolizes the "result" of such over-invest-ment; and Othello symbolizes the single-mine-own-ness of possession itself. The act of possession is the initiating act: it begins the tragic rhythm which, Burke says, the tragic protagonist must undergo and the play must follow. In the equivalent terms of personality used in the play, the act is the love marriage between Othello and Desde-mona. To possess in the way and for the reasons that Othello marries Desdemona is to involve oneself in the tragic tension and to set the tragic rhythm moving towards its terrible reflexive culmination. This requires of Othello an absolute commitment to Desdemona, a total spiritual and sexual investment in her, and the elimination of even the possibility of such a commitment and such an investment for either of them in anyone else. This is what Burke means when he says the play deals with an "act of spiritual enclosure" where "love, universal love" has "been made private." According to Burke, this is a form of pride (excess, *hubris*), an almost unique human motive, "natural" to man, who, following the tendency towards abstraction inherent in language, is always trying to make himself and others over in the image of his distinctive trait. Pride — Ethan Brand's un-pardonable sin — is essentially reflexive; but no tragic protagonist ever seems to realize or really believe this and must learn it — always too late — through suffering the terrible consequences of his ignorance or disbelief. Though the consequences vary, they always involve at least two and usually all three kinds of victimage, and the reduction to absolute loneliness of the tragic protagonist — the tragic irony of achieving the opposite of what is intended. In tragedy, it is always knowledge that transforms the passionate suffering into an assertion, the knowledge having been induced by the suffering and having come at the very nadir of the reductive pattern where absolute loneliness

[218]

The Dramatistic Theory of Literature

(the self confronting the guilt-ridden self) approaches paralysis and nothingness. The knowledge, which is usually factual, moral, and philosophical, transforms the self-corroding passionate suffering into an assertion because it enables the tragic protagonist to perform a new act which is in some way redemptive, both for himself and the social hierarchy of which he is a part.

Great Pride — excessive engrossment — constitutes the tragic flaw, and always involves ignorance, for pride is a kind of blindness. Tragedy translates into human terms the terrible consequences of pride by dramatizing an excessive engrossment in what all men are to varying degrees engrossed: themselves, various kinds of single-mine-own-ness. This is why all tragic protagonists move from ignorance to knowledge and why tragedies follow the mythic structure. Although not all men are capable of acts of great pride, the temptation is inherent in all social structures in the form of the hierarchic motive, and in fact is embedded in language itself. Tragedy dramatizes this motive in its pure form; it dramatizes the essence of tension itself, for all tensions result directly or indirectly from the hierarchic motive, itself simultaneously a good and a goad. Considered abstractly, great pride is little more than an idea; but translated into and dramatized in tragic terms, it becomes the basis for a powerful, moving experience, capable of arousing great pity and fear, and capable, finally, of effecting a catharsis more thorough and profound than can be brought about by any other kind of poetic symbolic action. For this reason, tragedy is one of the most vital and useful of poetic symbolic acts: tragedy presents over and over again the very essence of the drama of human relations, entertaining, edifying, and purging — all at the same time. Tragedy entertains through the beauty of its form; that form takes the spectator on a purgative journey; and the purgative journey has a number of epiphanal moments in it when, like the protagonist, who is caught in the rhythm of his own tragedy, the spectator sees into himself, the drama of his own life, and the larger drama of human relations.

Tragedy both imitates a specific tension and exploits all kinds of tensions in order to effect as complete a catharsis as possible. "To be complete," Burke says, "catharsis must involve the entire realm of privacy, along with personal and social relationships" (*Poetics*,76). What Burke means here is that through analogical imagery the tragic playwright radiates out until he has identified the specific tension with bodily, personal, familial, and religious tensions; with *other* social tensions; and with both "nature" and "supernature." Burke calls this process "cosmologizing" or "universalizing" and points out that from this process comes the hierarchic or allusive structure found in all tragedies (SeR,LX,380). Certain workings of this process are obvious and need not be discussed here at any length, for they represent standard poetic "tactics" for giving a work scope and depth; sometimes, of course, they are more than just poetic tactics for they are manifestations of a profound belief in some "underlying principle of oneness" in the universe as a whole. I refer, of course, to the use of "nature" and "supernature" as points of reference, to such things as the storm in Act III of *King Lear*, the plague and blighted crops in *Oedipus Rex*, the apotheosis of Oedipus in *Oedipus at Colonus*, the Ghost in *Hamlet*, the witches in *Macbeth*, and the many signs of supernatural displeasure in the *Oresteia* as a whole. Nature and supernature represent the two extreme limits of the hierarchy; the implication of their use, whether real or illusory, is that any disorders within the social hierarchy have "cosmological" consequences and that punishment will be visited upon the wrongdoer, not only by society and the agent himself, but by nature and the forces of supernature. Again, whether real or just poetic tactics, such cosmologizing stresses the universal consequences of individual acts of pride and, with a vengeance, man's personal responsibility for such actions. Both kinds of stress have much to do with the quantity and quality of pity, fear, and pride, which, Burke says, tragedy arouses and purges.

One of the central ideas in Burke's theory of tragedy is that the tragic play persecutes the audience in order that it may be purged; that the tragic play, through imitation, actually arouses various tensions in the audience, individually and collectively, *in order* to release them. The persecution is in part accomplished by the two forms of cosmologizing discussed above, both of which create the illusion that the vastness of nature on the one hand and the mysteries of the supernatural on the other are *actively* involved in the persecution, either because they are affected by the initiating act or because they actually administer part of the punishment. Actually, these two forms indicate the main intent of cosmologizing, which is to involve the whole in the actions of the part, to achieve what Burke calls a *"tremendous thoroughness"* (*Poetics*,284). Aside from the use of nature and supernature as points of reference, the tragic playwright also uses the bodily, personal, familial, religious, and social as points of reference; that is, he persecutes by showing how one kind of social disorder or tension spreads, like a contagious and sometimes fatal disease, until it has infected the whole person, physically as well as psychically, and affected his personal, familial, social, and religious relationships; and spreads until it has infected the other characters in the play in the same way; and spreads, finally, outward, until it has symbolically infected the whole audience and everyone is in his "very essence persecuted." There are, for example, what Burke calls the "Great Persecutional Words," the great "civic," or "social," or "moral," or "philosophic" abstractions (*Poetics*,283–284; SeR,LX,380). Among the most important of these are Law, Right, Fate, Justice, Necessity, Vengeance, and Ruin. These constitute the "civic" order of terms and belong to what Burke elsewhere calls the great moral negatives, the thou-shalt-nots which man as symbol-using animal "adds to nature." They belong to the "civic" order of terms because they are "abstractions" rather than metaphysical realities. Burke's point is that through identification with the great persecutional words the specifically human concerns with which the tragedy deals are "heroically transmogrified," the result being a kind of "terrifying thoroughness" of conviction that the moral "proprieties" will be observed: "justice" will be done, punishment will be meted out for the act of pride, vengeance will be exacted, and the law will triumph (*Poetics*, 283-284). All the great persecutional words contain this element of categorical expectancy about the inevitability of punishment and persecution for any kind of wrongdoing; they suggest that a certain kind of act will initiate the tragic rhythm which, once underway, has the irreversible finality of the formal progression in a completed poetic act.

Burke and the Drama of Human Relations

An act of great pride, the specifically human action which initiates the tragic rhythm, and the whole of the tragic rhythm itself, seems naturally to arouse what Burke calls the specifically "personal emotions as such": pity, fear, anger, and the like. That is, the tragic act, the tragic rhythm, and tragedy are "ideal" cathartics; by means of them the poet can effect the most thorough purgation; the more thorough the purge, the greater, Burke says, the healing or regenerating effect for the audience individually and collectively; the greater the regenerative effect, the better able is literature to fulfill one of its primary functions, which is to fight individual and social "illness" by means of symbolic purges. One of literature's primary purposes is to function as an instrument of individual and social "health." "Pollution," Burke says, is "the subject of catharsis"; and catharsis is the subject of poetry (HR,IV,198). In tragedy, pollution — tensions, irresolutions, psychoses, guilt, discord — is exploited for cathartic purposes. All manner of "personal" tensions are exploited in the tragic imitation to heighten the cathartic effect. The members of the audience make a direct personal identification with these tensions and react to them in the most profound personal way; their reactions are *self*-directed, even though it is Hamlet, Oedipus, and Othello whom they pity and fear. Burke's point seems to be that each of these characters is really a symbolic mirror in which each member of the audience sees some part of himself, some motive by which he has been goaded, some actual or potential action or passion. The external drama then becomes an intense internal and personal one for each member of the audience; this is what Burke means when he says that each member of the audience is in "his essence" persecuted by the tragic imitation.

Tragedy always has a double allusive or hierarchic structure and it persecutes the audience by means of outward and inward progressions: outward from the social tension to the vastness of nature and the mystery of supernature; and inward from the social tension to the familial to the personal to the private until, by means of the double progression, everything has been effected by the single cause and until, for each member of the audience, all possible relationships have been involved and he is persecuted from all sides. The last stage

[222]

of the inward persecutional progression is reached when the "entire realm of privacy" has been involved (*Poetics*,76). By "private" or "privacy" Burke means the bodily, including the cells and the biological functions. More specifically, he means the privy parts — the "three 'cloacally' interconnected" parts and their functions (KR, XXI,356). These he calls the Demonic Trinity; in the *Poetics* he discusses their "literary" function in a long chapter called "The Thinking of the Body."

As with all of the tensions or pollutions exploited by the poet in the tragic imitation, the object is to make the audience suffer the tensions. In this instance, it would be sexual, urinal, and fecal anxieties experienced as such — what Burke calls the "irresolutions of the body"— and these same anxieties as they affect and are affected by personal, familial, civic, and religious motives. By means of scatological puns (Burke calls them "body puns"), overt and covert references to the privy parts and their functions, and all kinds of natural images which are really disguised sexual, urinal, and fecal images, the poet exploits the Demonic Trinity and in this way involves the "entire realm of privacy" in the cathartic drama. "No purification is complete," Burke says, "until the fecal motive has been expressed and redeemed." By a route too devious and tedious to reconstruct here, Burke attempts to demonstrate in his chapter on "The Thinking of the Body" that the personal and specifically tragic emotions of pity, fear, and pride have their bodily or "private" counterparts in the Demonic Trinity. Pity has its counterpart in the sexual; fear in the urinal and diuretic; and pride in the fecal. The Demonic Trinity includes not only the privy parts and their functions, but also their products. This means that the Demonic Trinity can be used as a source of pollution images to express the "fecal motive" and that by shifting the emphasis to the three processes of bodily unburdening, it can also be used as one of the "primary sources of 'cathartic' imagery" (KR,XXI,356). The Demonic Trinity, then, can be used both to express and redeem the "fecal motive." When Burke argues that pity, fear, and pride have their bodily counterparts in the sexual, urinal, and fecal, he means on the one hand that excess pity tends toward sexual release, excess fear toward urinal release, and excess pride toward fecal release (in the sense of defecating upon someone below); and on the other that because of these relations, pity, fear, and pride can be expressed and hence evoked by sexual, urinal, and fecal images. Though somewhat strained because of Burke's compulsion to make the correspondence absolute — to always find the sewers from heaven to hell — and finally rather tedious in the way that all obsessions are, there is a good deal of truth in what Burke says here which it would be foolish — or, perhaps, fecal — for us to deny.

The specific civic tensions which tragedy imitates, and the various tensions which it exploits for cathartic purposes, exist outside the play as "brute realities." Given language, the "fall" is automatic and permanent: hierarchic psychoses just *are*; categorical guilt just *is* — they are "brute realities," the "stagnant miasmatic swamps" in which all symbol-users must live (*Poetics*,273). Tragedy — or any other poetic work, for that matter — cannot remove the causes of tension, but it can help to control their destructive effects. Since the general cause can never be removed — unless by total nuclear extinction — periodic symbolic purges are necessary for the health of the individual and society.

The health of the individual and society have been Burke's primary concern since the early thirties when he laid the foundations for his dramatistic system. Since 1945 he has been building that therapeutic system into a vast verbal pyramid, dedicated, somewhat ironically, to the purification of war in a century already littered, like a tragedy, with corpses and threatened with the prospect of nothing but corpses. The verbal pyramid, of course, is Burke's own therapeutic *symbolic* action — the huge verbal construct of a small man; an oversized verbal tomb and memorial for a man who, by his own admission, has been afraid of death all his life; a vast verbal dungheap, the leavings of a man who wrote his way through more than half a ruined century; and, conversely, a verbal heaven, closed and protective in the manner of all beautifully symmetrical systems. But to contemplate the personal therapeutic function of the system for Burke is only to come on the central idea of dramatism by a different route and to discover the comic center of a system which has tragedy as its representative anecdote.

Like all profound thinkers, Burke has multiple vision. Man, he has recently said, is "ROTTEN WITH PERFECTION." And, as he well knows, his own dream — that he can purify war — is rotten with irony. This capacity for comic perception is like the satyr-play which followed a group of three tragedies or a tragic trilogy and — if Euripides' *The Cyclops* is typical — mocked all the serious themes of tragedy by reducing them to the motivational level of the satyrs. In fact, Burke's most recent book — *The Rhetoric of Religion*, 1961 — is the dramatistic equivalent of a tragic trilogy followed — and mocked — by a satyr-play. The book consists of three "tragic" essays on language and the Burkean drama of human relations, followed by a "satyr-essay" entitled "Prologue in Heaven," which is a dialogue between TL (The Lord, Burke) and S (Satan, his straight man) in which Burke burlesques himself in serio-comic fashion. The dialogue concludes with this exchange between TL and S:

TL. But, to the quick summation, and the perfect symmetry: In their societies, they will seek to keep order. If order, then a need to repress the tendencies to disorder. If repression, then responsibility for imposing, accepting, or resisting the repression. If responsibility, then guilt. If guilt, then the need for redemption, which involves sacrifice, which in turn allows for substitution. At this point, the logic of perfection enters. Man can be viewed as perfectly depraved by a formative "first" offense against the foremost authority, an offense in which one man sinned for all. The cycle of life and death intrinsic to the nature of time can now be seen in terms that treat natural death as the result of this "original" sin. And the principle of perfection can be matched on the hopeful side by the idea of a perfect victim. The symmetry can be logologically rounded out by the idea of this victim as also the creative Word by which time was caused to be, the intermediary Word binding time with eternity, and the end towards which all words of the true doctrine are directed. As one of their saints will put it: "The way to heaven must be heaven, for He said: I am the way."

(TL *rises.* S *also rises immediately after.*)

TL (*continuing*). The way to heaven (the means to the end, the agency for the attainment of purpose) must be heaven (scene), for

He (agent) said (act as words): I am the way (act as The Word). Here is the ultimate of logological symmetry!

S. Formally, it is perfect. It is perfectly beautiful!

TL. It is truly culminative!

S. Words could do no more!

(*Pause.*)

S (*pensively*). In some ways they will be dismal, in some ways they will have a feeling for the grandeurs of form. But when these Word-People are gone, won't the life of words be gone?

TL. Unfortunately, yes.

S. Then, what of us, the two voices in this dialogue? When words go, won't we, too, be gone?

TL. Unfortunately, yes.

S. Then of this there will be nothing?

TL. Yes . . . nothing . . . but it's more complica——

Sudden blackness. . . . (RR,314–315.)

The concluding scene moves from tragedy to symmetry to comedy and ends with resonant dramatistic puns and the fragmentation of the term which has goaded Burke on from the beginning.

This has always been the characteristic movement in Burke; and it has been recurrent, for he has always gone on to complete the term, finish the phrase, and start through the cycle again. Burke's ideal has always been to purify war — the ineradicable brute reality. And his contribution to the health of the individual and society has been — like that of tragedy — to help purify war by means of the same verbal alchemy he has studied all his life. As Burke well knows, there are two kinds of verbal alchemists: those of hell who use words to transform gold into dross, and those of heaven who use words to transform dross into gold. The first make war and the second purify it. Like TL, Burke is one of the heavenly alchemists: he has divided his efforts between the real business of such a person — purifying war — and the comic contemplation of its ironic implications: the work of his brothers in hell who make war (sometimes on and out of him) faster than he can purify it. Yet, as his last book reminds us, the therapeutic pyramid is still abuilding. Even incomplete, it has transcended Burke and stands as a splendid monument.

Bibliography and Index

BIBLIOGRAPHY

THE BIBLIOGRAPHY is divided into three sections: works by Burke; reviews, essays, and books about Burke, including some applications of Burke's ideas and methods; and works dealing with related material. The first section, which is divided into four parts and arranged chronologically within each subdivision, is meant to be exhaustive — though I have no doubt missed some items by Burke which are in print. The second section is an annotated selection of reviews, essays, and books about Burke. Though some of my comments are critical, all are meant to be descriptive in the sense that all are intended to indicate the nature and extent of each writer's contribution to one's understanding, appreciation, and evaluation of Burke. The third section is also highly selective, for I have included only those essays and books which had — and presumably still have — a direct bearing upon the ideas and methods discussed in this study in the sense that a direct connection between something in Burke and each of the items in this section could have been established in a network of footnotes or interlaced comments in the text.

I. Works by Kenneth Burke

BOOKS

The White Oxen and Other Stories, New York: Albert and Charles Boni, 1924.

Counter-Statement, New York: Harcourt, Brace and Company, 1931; second edition, Los Altos, California: Hermes Publications, 1953; Phoenix edition, Chicago: University of Chicago Press, 1957.

Towards a Better Life, Being a Series of Epistles or Declamations, New York: Harcourt, Brace and Company, 1932.

Permanence and Change, An Anatomy of Purpose, New York: New Republic, Inc., 1935; second revised edition, Los Altos, California: Hermes Publications, 1954.

Attitudes toward History, two volumes, New York: New Republic, Inc., 1937; second edition revised, Los Altos, California: Hermes Publications, 1959; Beacon paperback edition, Boston: Beacon Press, 1961.

Burke and the Drama of Human Relations

The Philosophy of Literary Form, Studies in Symbolic Action, Baton Rouge: Louisiana State University Press, 1941; Vintage edition, New York: Vintage Books, 1957.

A Grammar of Motives, New York: Prentice-Hall, Inc., 1945; reissue, New York: George Braziller, Inc., 1955.

A Rhetoric of Motives, New York: Prentice-Hall, Inc., 1950; reissue, New York: George Braziller, Inc., 1955.

A Grammar of Motives and A Rhetoric of Motives, Meridian Books edition, Cleveland and New York: The World Publishing Company, 1962.

Book of Moments, Poems 1915–1954, Los Altos, California: Hermes Publications, 1955.

The Rhetoric of Religion: Studies in Logology, Boston: Beacon Press, 1961.

TRANSLATIONS

Thomas Mann, "Loulou," *The Dial*, LXX (1921), 428–442.

Hugo von Hofmannsthal, "Lucidor: Characters for an Unwritten Comedy," *The Dial*, LXXIII (1922), 121–132.

Richard Specht, "Arthur Schnitzler," *The Dial*, LXXIII (1922), 241–245.

Stefan Zweig, "Charles Dickens," *The Dial*, LXXIV (1923), 1–24.

Julius Meier-Graefe, "German Art after the War," *The Dial*, LXXV (1923), 1–12.

Arthur Schnitzler, "The Fate of Baron Von Leisenbohg," *The Dial*, LXXV (1923), 565–582.

Heinrich Mann, "Virgins," *The Dial*, LXXVI (1924), 123–132.

Oswald Spengler, "The Downfall of Western Civilization," *The Dial*, LXXVII (1924), 361–378; 482–504; LXXVIII (1925), 9–26.

Hugo von Hofmannsthal, "Honoré de Balzac," *The Dial*, LXXVIII (1925), 357–368.

Arthur Schnitzler, "Lieutenant Gustl," *The Dial*, LXXIX (1925), 89–117.

———, "The New Song," *The Dial*, LXXIX (1925), 355–369.

Thomas Mann, *Death in Venice*, New York: A. A. Knopf, 1925.

Emil Ludwig, *Genius and Character*, New York: Harcourt, Brace and Company, Inc., 1927.

Thomas Mann, "Humanism and Europe," *New Republic*, XC (1937), 349.

ESSAYS, REVIEWS, STORIES, AND POEMS

"Axiomatics" (review of *The Mask*, by John Cournos), *The Dial*, LXVIII (1920), 496–499.

"The Soul of Kajn Tafha" (story), *The Dial*, LXIX (1920), 29–32.

"The Modern English Novel Plus" (review of *Night and Day* and *The Voyage Out*, by Virginia Woolf), *The Dial*, LXX (1921), 572–575.

"The Editing of Oneself" (review of *The Mystic Warrior*, by James Oppenheim), *The Dial*, LXXI (1921), 232–235.

"Modifying the Eighteenth Century" (review of *Casanova's Homecoming*, by Arthur Schnitzler), *The Dial*, LXXI (1921), 707–710.

"Heroism and Books" (review of *Romain Rolland, The Man and His Work*, by Stefan Zweig), *The Dial*, LXXII (1922), 92–93.

"Heaven's First Law" (review of *Sour Grapes*, by William Carlos Williams), *The Dial*, LXXII (1922), 197–200.

Bibliography

"*Fides Quaerens Intellectum*" (review of *The Religion of Plato*, by Paul Elmer More), *The Dial*, LXXII (1922), 527–530.

"The Critic of Dostoevsky" (review of *Still Life* and *The Things We Are*, by J. Middleton Murry), *The Dial*, LXXIII (1922), 671–674.

"The Consequences of Idealism" (review of *Rahab* and *City Block*, by Waldo Frank), *The Dial*, LXXIII (1922), 449–452.

"Enlarging the Narrow House" (review of *Narcissus*, by Evelyn Scott), *The Dial*, LXXIII (1922), 346–348.

"André Gide, Bookman," *The Freeman*, V (1922), 155–157.

"Chicago and Our National Gesture," *Bookman*, LVII (1923), 497–501.

"Realism and Idealism" (review of *The Reform of Education*, by Giovanni Gentile), *The Dial*, LXXIV (1923), 97–99.

"Engineering with Words" (review of *Geography and Plays*, by Gertrude Stein), *The Dial*, LXXIV (1923), 408–412.

"Immersion" (review of *A Book*, by Djuna Barnes), *The Dial*, LXXVI (1924), 460–461.

"Deposing the Love of the Lord" (review of *Selected Religious Poems of Solomon Ibn Gabirol*), *The Dial*, LXXVII (1924), 161–162.

"Ethics of the Artist" (review of *Buddenbrooks*, by Thomas Mann), *The Dial*, LXXVII (1924), 420–422.

"Delight and Tears" (review of *The Apple of the Eye*, by Glenway Wescott), *The Dial*, LXXVII (1924), 513–515.

"After-Dinner Philosophy" (review of *The Genius of Style*, by W. C. Brownell), *The Dial*, LXXVIII (1925), 228–231.

"On Re and Dis" (review of *The Newer Spirit, A Sociological Criticism of Literature*, by V. F. Calverton), *The Dial*, LXXIX (1925), 165–169.

"Codifying Milton" (review of *Milton, Man and Thinker*, by Denis Saurat), *The Dial*, LXXIX (1925), 429–430.

"Idiom and Uniformity" (review of *The Society's Work*, by Robert Bridges; *Words and Idioms* by Logan Pearsall Smith), *The Dial*, LXXX (1926), 57–60.

"Idols of the Future" (essay-review of *Notes on the American Doctrine of Equality*, by T. V. Smith), *The Dial*, LXXXI (1926), 42–46.

"A 'Logic' of History" (review of *The Decline of the West*, by Oswald Spengler), *The Dial*, LXXXI (1926), 242–248.

"Anthology" (poem), *The Little Review*, Spring–Summer (1926), 33.

"William Carlos Williams, The Methods of," *The Dial*, LXXXII (1927), 94–98.

"Righting an Ethnologic Wrong" (review of *Primitive Man as Philosopher*, by Paul Radin), *The Dial*, LXXXIII (1927), 439–440.

"Musical Chronicle," *The Dial*, LXXXIII (1927), 535–539.

"Van Wyck Brooks in Transition?" (review of *Emerson and Others*, by Van Wyck Brooks), *The Dial*, LXXXIV (1928), 56–59.

"Musical Chronicle," *The Dial*, LXXXIV (1928), 84–88.

"Musical Chronicle," *The Dial*, LXXXIV (1928), 174–178.

"Musical Chronicle," *The Dial*, LXXXIV (1928), 265–267.

"Musical Chronicle," *The Dial*, LXXXIV (1928), 356–358.

"Musical Chronicle," *The Dial*, LXXXIV (1928), 445–447.

"Musical Chronicle," *The Dial*, LXXXIV (1928), 536–538.

"Musical Chronicle," *The Dial*, LXXXV (1928), 85–88.

"Musical Chronicle," *The Dial*, LXXXV (1928), 529–532.

Burke and the Drama of Human Relations

"Musical Chronicle," *The Dial*, LXXXVI (1929), 87–89.

"From Outside" (poems), *The Dial*, LXXXVI (1929), 91–94.

"Musical Chronicle," *The Dial*, LXXXVI (1929), 177–178.

"Musical Chronicle," *The Dial*, LXXXVI (1929), 242–243.

"Musical Chronicle," *The Dial*, LXXXVI (1929), 356–358.

"Musical Chronicle," *The Dial*, LXXXVI (1929), 447–448.

"Musical Chronicle," *The Dial*, LXXXVI (1929), 538–539.

"A Decade of American Fiction" (an omnibus review), *Bookman*, LXIX (1929), 561–567.

"Three Frenchmen's Churches," *New Republic*, LXIII (1930), 10–14.

"Waste — The Future of Prosperity," *New Republic*, LXIII (1930), 228–231.

"Boring from Within," *New Republic*, LXV (1931), 326–329.

"In Quest of the Way" (review of *A New Model of the Universe*, by P. D. Ouspensky), *New Republic*, LXVIII (1931), 104–106.

"Counterblasts on 'Counter-Statement' " (answer to Granville Hicks's review of *Counter-Statement*), *New Republic*, LXIX (1931), 101.

"The Poet and the Passwords" (an essay-review of *Fear and Trembling*, by Glenway Wescott), *New Republic*, LXXI (1932), 310–313.

"Schönberg" (review of concert), *Nation*, CXXXVII (1933), 633–634.

"In Vague Praise of Liberty" (review of *History of Europe in the Nineteenth Century*, by Benedetto Croce), *Hound and Horn*, VII (1933–1934), 704–707.

"Fraught with Freight" (review of *Past Masters*, by Thomas Mann), *New Republic*, LXXVII (1934), 257.

"The Esthetic Strain" (review of *Art as Experience*, by John Dewey), *New Republic*, LXXVIII (1934), 315–316.

"The Meaning of C. K. Ogden," *New Republic*, LXXVIII (1934), 328–331.

"The Universe Alive" (review of *Nature and Life*, by A. N. Whitehead), *New Republic*, LXXXI (1934), 26.

"While Waiting" (review of *Those Who Perish*, by Edward Dahlberg), *New Republic*, LXXXI (1934), 53.

"Orpheus in New York" (music column), *Nation*, CXXXVIII (1934), 52–54.

"Two Brands of Piety" (music column), *Nation*, CXXXVIII (1934), 256–258.

"The End and Origin of a Movement" (music column), *Nation*, CXXXVIII (1934), 422–424.

"The Art of Yielding" (review of *Stephen Foster, America's Troubadour*, by John Howard; *They All Sang; From Tony Pastor to Rudy Vallée*, by Edward B. Marks), *Nation*, CXXXVIII (1934), 484–486.

"The Most Faustian Art" (music column), *Nation*, CXXXIX (1934), 138, 140.

"Gastronomy of Letters" (review of *ABC of Reading*, by Ezra Pound), *Nation*, CXXXIX (1934), 458–459.

"Hindemith Does His Part" (music column), *Nation*, CXXXIX (1934), 487–488.

"A Most Useful Composition" (music column), *Nation*, CXXXIX (1934), 719–720.

"Rugged Portraiture" (review of *Rubicon or The Strikebreaker*, a play), *The New Masses*, April 3, 1934, p. 46.

"A Pleasant View of Decay" (review of *Music Ho! A Study of Music in Decline*, by Constant Lambert), *Nation*, CXL (1935), 200–201.

"What Shostakovich Adds" (music column), *Nation*, CXL (1935), 230–231.

"The 'Problems' of the Ballet" (dance column), *Nation*, CXL (1935), 343–344.

"The Writers' Congress," *Nation*, CXL (1935), 571.

Bibliography

"Renaming Old Directions" (review of *Redirecting Education: Vol. I, The United States*, edited by R. G. Tugwell and L. H. Keyserling), *Nation*, CXLI (1935), 166.

"Recent Records" (music column), *Nation*, CXLI (1935), 692–693.

"One Who Wrestled" (review of *Dostoevsky: A Life*, by Avrahm Yarmolinsky), *New Republic*, LXXXII (1935), 192, 194.

"Change of Identity" (review of *Judgment Day*, by James T. Farrell), *New Republic*, LXXXIII (1935), 171–172.

"Two Kinds of Against" (review of *No Thanks*, by E. E. Cummings; *Poems*, by Kenneth Fearing), *New Republic*, LXXXIII (1935), 198–199.

"The Impartial Essence" (review of *Lectures in America*, by Gertrude Stein), *New Republic*, LXXXIII (1935), 227.

"Protective Coloration" (review of *Redder Than the Rose*, by William Forsyth), *New Republic*, LXXXIII (1935), 255–256.

"Storm Omens" (review of *Pittsburgh Memoranda*, by Haniel Long), *New Republic*, LXXXIV (1935), 83.

"A Radical, But —" (review of *The Neurotic Nightingale*, by Vardis Fisher), *New Republic*, LXXXIV (1935), 221.

"Goethe and the Jews" (review of book by same name by Mark Waldman), *New Masses*, March 19, 1935, 25.

"Concern about English" (review of *Wine and Physic*, by Alexander Laing), *Poetry*, XLV (1935), 294–296.

"The Hope in Tragedy" (review of *Chorus for Survival*, by Horace Gregory), *Poetry*, XLVI (1935), 227–230.

"Coleridge Rephrased" (review of *On Imagination: Coleridge's Critical Theory*, by I. A. Richards), *Poetry*, XLVII (1935), 52–54.

"Recent Poetry" (an omnibus review), *Southern Review*, I (1935–1936), 164–177.

"A Bright Evening, With Musicians" (music column), *Nation*, CXLII (1936), 27.

"Without Benefit of Politics" (review of *Truth and Reality* and *Will Therapy*, by Otto Rank), *Nation*, CXLIII (1936), 78.

"Anatomy of the Mask" (review of *Propaganda: Its Psychology and Technique*, by Leonard W. Doob), *New Republic*, LXXXV (1936), 371–372.

"Verses for the Wrong Occasions" (2 poems), *New Republic*, LXXXVII (1936), 71.

"A Sour Note on Literary Criticism" (review of *A Note on Literary Criticism*, by James T. Farrell), *New Republic*, LXXXVII (1936), 211.

"Property as an Absolute" (review of *Who Owns America*, edited by Herbert Agar, Allen Tate), *New Republic*, LXXXVII (1936), 245–246.

"Methodology of the Scramble" (review of *Politics: Who Gets What, When, How?*, by Harold Lasswell), *New Republic*, LXXXIX (1936), 250.

"Return after Flight" (review of *Theory of Flight*, by Muriel Rukeyser), *New Masses*, February 4, 1936, 26.

"What Is Americanism? Marxism and the American Tradition" (part of a symposium), *Partisan Review and Anvil*, III (April, 1936), 9–11.

"Deft Plaintiveness" (review of *One Season Shattered*, by James Daly), *Poetry*, XLVIII (1936), 282–285.

"Cautious Enlightenment" (review of *The Double Agent*, by R. P. Blackmur), *Poetry*, XLIX (1936), 52–54.

"Symbolic War," *Southern Review*, II (1936–1937), 134–147.

Burke and the Drama of Human Relations

"A Gist of Gists of Gists" (review of *One Mighty Torrent: The Drama of Biography*, by Edgar Johnson), *Nation*, CXLIV (1937), 622–623.

"Field Work in Bohemia" (review of *This Room and This Gin and These Sandwiches*, by Edmund Wilson), *Nation*, CXLV (1937), 133–134.

"Synthetic Freedom" (review of *The Restoration of Property*, by Hilaire Belloc), *New Republic*, LXXXIX (1937), 365.

"The Esthetic Instinct" (review of *Art and Society*, by Herbert Read), *New Republic*, LXXXX (1937), 363–364.

"Spender's Left Hand" (review of *Forward from Liberalism*, by Stephen Spender), *New Republic*, LXXXXII (1937), 24–25.

"Thurber Perfects Mind Cure" (review of *Let Your Mind Alone!*, by James Thurber), *New Republic*, LXXXXII (1937), 220–221.

"A Trail Trails Off" (review of *From These Roots*, by Mary Colum), *New Republic*, LXXXXIII (1937), 205–206.

"The 'Science' of Race-Thinking" (review of *Race: A Study in Modern Superstition*, by Jacques Barzun), *New Masses*, October 5, 1937, 22.

"Tentative Proposal" (review of *The Mediterranean and Other Poems* and *Reactionary Essays*, by Allen Tate), *Poetry*, L (1937), 96–100.

"Leave the Leaf Its Springtime" (review of *New Poems*, by F. M. Clapp), *Poetry*, L (1937), 226–229.

"Responses to Pressure" (review of *Wordsworth and Milton, Poets and Prophets*, by Herbert J. C. Grierson), *Poetry*, LI (1937), 37–42.

"Intuitive or Scientific" (letter about Vivas' review of *Attitudes toward History*, in *Nation*, December 25, 1937), *Nation*, CXLVI (1938), 139–140.

"Is Mr. Hook a Socialist?" (answer to Hook's review of *Attitudes toward History*), *Partisan Review*, IV (January, 1938), 40–44.

"Weighted History" (review of *The Crisis of Civilization*, by Hilaire Belloc), *New Republic*, LXXXXIII (1938), 375–376.

"The Book of Proverbs" (review of *Racial Proverbs*, edited by S. A. Champion), *New Republic*, LXXXXIX (1939), 230.

"Why Coleridge?" (review of *Samuel Taylor Coleridge*, by E. K. Chambers; *The Life of S. T. Coleridge*, by Lawrence Hanson), *New Republic*, C (1939), 163–164.

"In the Margin," *New Republic*, CI (1939), 257.

"On Poetry and Poetics" (review of *The World's Body*, by John Crowe Ransom), *Poetry*, LV (1939), 51–54.

"The Sources of 'Christabel' " (review of *Road to Tryermaine*, by A. H. Nethercot), *New Republic*, CII (1940), 617.

"Surrealism," *New Directions in Prose and Poetry*, edited by James Laughlin, Norfolk, Connecticut: New Directions, 1940, 563–579.

"Character of Our Culture," *Southern Review*, VI (1940–1941), 675–694.

"On Motivation in Yeats," *Southern Review*, VII (1941–1942), 547–561.

"Key Words for Critics" (review of *The Intent of the Critic*, edited by Donald Stauffer; *The New Criticism*, by J. C. Ransom; *Reason in Madness*, by Allen Tate), *Kenyon Review*, IV (1942), 126–132.

"War and Cultural Life," *American Journal of Sociology*, XLVIII (1942–1943), 404–410.

"Many Moods" (review of *A Treasury of American Songs*, by Olin Downes and Elie Siegmeister), *New Republic*, CVIII (1943), 869–870.

"The Tactics of Motivation," *Chimera*, I (Spring, 1943), 21–33; I (Summer, 1943), 37–53.

Bibliography

Review of *On Native Grounds*, by Alfred Kazin, *Chimera*, II (Autumn, 1943), 45–48.

"Action As Test" (review of *The Uses of Reason*, by Arthur E. Murphy), *New Republic*, CX (1944), 220–222.

"Basic and After" (review of *The Loom of Language*, by Frederick Bodmer), *New Republic*, CX (1944), 566, 568.

"Careers without Careerism" (review of *A Century of Hero-Worship*, by Eric Bentley), *Kenyon Review*, VII (1945), 162–166.

"The Work of Regeneration" (review of *Angel in the Forest*, by Marguerite Young), *Kenyon Review*, VII (1945), 696–700.

"Kinds of Criticism," *Poetry*, LXVIII (1946), 272–282.

"Towards Objective Criticism" (review of *The Rime of the Ancient Mariner*, by S. T. Coleridge, illustrated by Calder, analyzed by R. P. Warren), *Poetry*, LXX (1947), 42–47.

"Ideology and Myth," *Accent*, VII (1947), 195–205.

"Criticism for the Next Phase" (review of *Metaphysical Imagery*, by Rosemond Tuve), *Accent*, VIII (1947–1948), 125–127.

"Vegetal Radicalism of Theodore Roethke," *Sewanee Review*, LVIII (1950), 68–108.

"American Scholar Forum: The New Criticism," *American Scholar*, XX (1950–1951), 86–104, 218–231.

"Rhetoric — Old and New," *The Journal of General Education*, V (1951), 202–209.

"Othello: An Essay to Illustrate a Method," *Hudson Review*, IV (1951), 165–203.

"Three Definitions," *Kenyon Review*, XIII (1951), 173–192.

"Thanatopsis for Critics: A Brief Thesaurus of Deaths and Dyings," *Essays in Criticism*, II (1952), 369–375.

"A 'Dramatistic' View of 'Imitation,'" *Accent*, XII (1952), 229–241.

"Form and Persecution in the *Oresteia*," *Sewanee Review*, LX, (1952), 377–396.

"Comments on Eighteen Poems by Howard Nemerov," *Sewanee Review*, LX (1952), 117–131.

"Notes on the Lit'ry Life," *Proceedings of the American Academy of Arts and Letters and the National Institute of Arts and Letters*, Second Series, Number Two, 1952, 39–50.

"Ethan Brand: A Preparatory Investigation," *The Hopkins Review*, V (Winter, 1952), 45–65.

"Mysticism as a Solution to the Poets' Dilemma," *Spiritual Problems in Contemporary Literature, A Series of Addresses and Discussions*, edited by S. R. Hopper, New York: The Institute for Religious and Social Studies, 1952, 105–116.

"Freedom and Authority in the Realm of the Poetic Imagination," *Freedom and Authority in Our Time, Twelfth Symposium of the Conference on Science, Philosophy, and Religion*, edited by Lyman Bryson, *et al.*, New York: published by the Conference and distributed by Harper and Brothers, 1953, 365–375.

"A Dramatistic View of the Origins of Language," *Quarterly Journal of Speech*, XXXVIII (1952), 251–264, 446–460; XXXIX (1953), 79–92.

"Postscripts on the Negative," *Quarterly Journal of Speech*, XXXIX (1953), 209–216.

"On Covery, Re- and Dis-" (review of *A Reading of George Herbert*, by Rosemond Tuve), *Accent*, XIII (1953), 218–226.

"The Dialectics of Imagery" (review of *Symbolism and American Literature*, by Charles Feidelson), *Kenyon Review*, XV (1953), 625–632.

"Fact, Inference, and Proof in the Analysis of Literary Symbolism," *Symbols and Values: An Initial Study, Thirteenth Symposium of the Conference on Science, Philosophy, and Religion*, edited by Lyman Bryson, *et al.*, New York: published by the Conference and distributed by Harper and Brothers, 1954, 283–306.

"The Language of Poetry 'Dramatistically' Considered," *The Chicago Review*, VIII (Fall, 1954), 88–102; IX (Spring, 1955), 40–72.

"The Criticism of Criticism" (review of *The Lion and the Honeycomb*, by R. P. Blackmur), *Accent*, XV (1955), 279–292.

"Policy Made Personal, Whitman's Verse and Prose-Salient Traits," *Leaves of Grass One Hundred Years After*, edited by Milton Hindus, Stanford: Stanford University Press, 1955, 74–108.

"Linguistic Approach to Problems of Education," *Modern Philosophies and Education, The Fifty-Fourth Year Book of the National Society for the Study of Education*, edited by Nelson B. Henry, Chicago: published by the Society and distributed by University of Chicago Press, 1955, LIV, Pt. I, 259–303.

"Likings of an Observationist" (review of *Predilections*, by Marianne Moore), *Poetry*, LXXXVII (1956), 239–247.

"Symbol and Association," *Hudson Review*, IX (1956–1957), 212–225.

"The Anaesthetic Revelation of Herone Liddell" (story), *Kenyon Review*, XIX (1957), 505–559.

"The Encyclopaedic, Two Kinds of" (review of *Literary Criticism: A Short History*, by Wimsatt and Brooks; *Anatomy of Criticism: Four Essays*, by Northrop Frye), *Poetry*, XCI (1957–1958), 320–328.

"The Carrot and the Stick, or . . ." (review of *Battle for the Mind*, by William Sargant; *The Hidden Persuaders*, by Vance Packard; *The Organization Man*, by William H. Whyte), *Hudson Review*, X (1957–1958), 627–633.

"Towards a Total Conformity: A Metaphysical Fantasy," *The Literary Review*, II (1957–1958), 203–207.

"The Poetic Motive," *Hudson Review*, XI (1958), 54–63.

"Towards a Post-Kantian Verbal Music" (essay-review of *The Art of Poetry*, by Paul Valéry), *Kenyon Review*, XX (1958), 529–546.

"On Catharsis, or Resolution," *Kenyon Review*, XXI (1959), 337–375.

"Democracy of the Sick" (review of *Freud: The Mind of the Moralist*, by Philip Rieff), *Kenyon Review*, XXI (1959), 639–643.

"The Independent Radical" (review of *The Tradition of the New*, by Harold Rosenberg), *Hudson Review*, XII (1959), 465–472.

"He Was a Sincere, etc." (poem), *Nation*, CLXXXIX (September 12, 1959), 140.

"Myth, Poetry and Philosophy," *Journal of American Folklore*, LXXII (1959), 283–306.

"Civil Defense" (poem), *Nation*, CXCI (September 24, 1960), 188.

"Motion, Action, Words," *Teachers College Record*, LXII (1960), 244–249.

"The Brain Beautiful," *Bennington College Bulletin*, XXIX (November, 1960), 4–7.

"Catharsis — Second View," *Centennial Review*, V (1961), 107–132.

Bibliography

"What Are the Signs of What? A Theory of 'Entitlement,'" *Anthropological Linguistics*, IV (June, 1962), 1–23.

"Invective against the Father" (review of *Milton's God*, by William Empson), *Nation*, CXCIV (June 16, 1962), 540–541.

UNPUBLISHED MATERIAL

"Poetics, Dramatistically Considered," 1–391 (an incomplete manuscript version of "A Symbolic of Motives").

II. Works about Kenneth Burke

Auden, W. H., "A Grammar of Assent," *New Republic*, CV (July 14, 1941), 59.

A useful review because Auden places Burke — correctly — in the Richards, Empson line, accurately locates one center of Burke (the concentration on symbolic meaning), and sanely points out the foolishness of throwing out all of Burke because some parts of him are suspect.

Bewley, Marius, "Kenneth Burke as Literary Critic," *The Complex Fate*, London: Chatto & Windus, 1952, 211–243.

Mr. Bewley's attack on Burke is violent and polemical. However, the analysis of Burke's literary theory and critical practice is very perceptive, and the attack is persuasive if one happens to agree with Mr. Bewley's critical position, which I find rather limited. The essay does not lend itself to synoptic quotation without unfair distortion: it must be read whole to get the tone as well as the argument of it.

Black, Max, *The Philosophical Review*, LV (1946), 487–490.

Another attack on Burke which is most useful as a representative example of how most systematic philosophers have reacted to Burke. Mr. Black calls *A Grammar of Motives* a "vast rambling edifice of quasi-sociological and quasi-psychoanalytical speculation" which "seems to rest on nothing more solid than a set of unexamined and uncriticized metaphysical assumptions."

Chase, Richard, "Rhetoric of Rhetoric," *The New Partisan Reader, 1945–1953*, edited by William Phillips and Philip Rahv, New York: Harcourt, Brace and Company, 1953, 590–593.

Like Mr. Bewley's essay, a violent and polemical anti-Burke review which attempts to reduce to absurdity two of Burke's central tenets: the theory of symbolic action and language as reality. To get the full force of Mr. Chase's objections one should also read *The Democratic Vista*, especially pp. 70–87, where he attempts to demonstrate that, contrary to what Burke says, the modern emphasis on the death and rebirth myth — he says it is almost the archetype of the modern mind — indicates a buried death wish, a weariness with the idea of the self and the problems of the self in the world.

Cowley, Malcolm, "Prolegomena to Kenneth Burke," *New Republic*, CXXII (June 5, 1950), 18–19.

Nearly everything Mr. Cowley has written about Burke is sound and useful. Here he points out that Burke is "one of the few truly speculative thinkers of our time," that it is a mistake to approach Burke as primarily a literary critic, and that the *Grammar* and *Rhetoric* are the beginnings of a "philosophical system on the grand scale."

————, "A Critic's First Principle," *New Republic*, CXXIX (September 14, 1953), 16–17.

An excellent brief discussion of the coherence of Burke's development from *Counter-Statement*.

Duffey, Bernard, "Reality as Language: Kenneth Burke's Theory of Poetry," *Western Review*, XII (1948), 132–145.

The title states one of the central points which Mr. Duffey makes about Burke, and he is certainly correct enough. Beyond that, the essay is good on Burke's organic development and is useful as an attempt to place Burke in relation to other contemporary critics — notably Richards and Ransom — and the "new critics" generally.

Duncan, Hugh Dalziel, *Language and Literature*, Chicago: University of Chicago Press, 1953.

————, *Communication and Social Order*, New York: The Bedminster Press, 1962.

Mr. Duncan is one of Burke's most enthusiastic apologists. Both of these books have long sections on Burke, both are applications of Burke's theories and methods by a sociologist, and both are useful as examples of how Burke has been used by non-literary critics.

Feidelson, Charles, Jr., *Symbolism and American Literature*, Phoenix edition, Chicago: University of Chicago Press, 1959.

Though Mr. Feidelson's book is not directly about Burke and more properly belongs in section III of this bibliography, he made one of those brilliant single comments on Burke which one never forgets: "Burke, indeed, might be said to have reduced logic to literature." Certainly this is one of the keys to *A Grammar of Motives*, which in turn provides Burke with the logic for his whole system.

Fergusson, Francis, "Kenneth Burke's Grammar of Motives," *The Human Image in Dramatic Literature*, Garden City, New York: Doubleday Anchor Books, 1957, 193–204.

Though only a review, this is one of the best essays ever written on Burke, by a critic who has absorbed and used him in his own work with great resourcefulness. In fact, all of Mr. Fergusson's work is relevant here, for he is centrally concerned with and has written brilliantly about many of the same things Burke has investigated all of his life.

Fogarty, Daniel, S.J., "Kenneth Burke's Theory," *Roots for a New Rhetoric*, New York: Bureau of Publications, Teachers College, Columbia University, 1959, 56–87.

Lately, Burke's influence has spread to the educationists. (See, for example, *Modern Philosophies and Education* (1955), in which Burke has a long and important essay.) This essay is not only useful for what it says of Burke's theory of rhetoric and its relationship to other modern theories but, like Mr. Duncan's books, for what it shows of Burke's influence outside of literary circles.

Ford, Newell F., "Kenneth Burke and Robert Penn Warren: Criticism by

Bibliography

Obsessive Metaphor," *Journal of English and Germanic Philology*, LIII (1954), 172–177.

The central idea of the essay is contained in the second half of the title, which is very apt. Mr. Ford's analysis and evaluation of the method are skillful and very witty. He also characterizes Burke in a witty — but again very accurate — way when he says "Mr. Burke is always stimulating even when he is absurd; he has a lively and agile mind, and a touch of the circus-rider in him."

Fraiberg, Louis, "Kenneth Burke's Terminological Medium of Exchange," *Psychoanalysis and American Literary Criticism*, Detroit: Wayne State University Press, 1960, 183–201.

The title promises more than the essay ever delivers. Mr. Fraiberg attempts to study one of the really important influences on Burke and other American literary critics; but his view of psycho-analysis is so limited he actually says very little about the profound way in which Burke was influenced by Freud. Mr. Bewley, for example, really says a good deal more in his discussion of the way in which Burke psycho-analyzes a poet through his image-clusters.

Glicksberg, C. I., "Kenneth Burke: The Critic's Critic," *South Atlantic Quarterly*, XXXVI (1937), 74–84.

An early and still good essay on some of Burke's central ideas and critical methods.

———, *American Literary Criticism, 1900–1950*, New York: Hendricks House, Inc., 1951, 307–309.

Like the essay cited above, the three pages of comment here are a very compact and accurate summary of Burke.

Hayakawa, S. I., "The Linguistic Approach to Poetry," *Poetry*, LX (1942), 86–94.

Burke was influenced by the semanticists — notably Korzybski — is himself a verbal analyst, and in turn had an influence on some other semanticists, among them Mr. Hayakawa. This review, as well as Mr. Hayakawa's other work, is useful in showing that influence.

Hochmuth, Marie, "Kenneth Burke and the New Rhetoric," *Quarterly Journal of Speech*, XXXVIII (1952), 133–143.

Partly because of the articles on the "negative" which he published in this journal, and partly because of *A Rhetoric of Motives*, Burke's influence has spread to the people in speech. Miss Hochmuth's essay is not only a good summary of Burke's "new rhetoric," but a good example of how and why he has influenced the speech people. Miss Hochmuth, like Mr. Duncan, Miss Holland, and Mr. Knox, is an ardent and enthusiastic apologist.

Holland, L. Virginia, *Counterpoint: Kenneth Burke and Aristotle's Theories of Rhetoric*, New York: The Philosophical Library, Inc., 1959.

The second (in order of publication) of the two books which have now been written about Burke, and like Mr. Knox's, very difficult for me to comment on. Though the title is specific and the book does make some contribution to our knowledge of the similarities and differences between Aristotle and Burke, Miss Holland really only touches upon this enormously complex problem. The book is best read, I think, as a general essay on Burke, remembering that it is the work of an ardent apologist. Like Mr. Knox, Miss Holland succumbed to the editorial we which is so annoying in Burke, and her book, like Mr. Knox's, has a proprietary tone which is disconcerting.

Hook, Sidney, "The Technique of Mystification," *Partisan Review*, IV (1937), 57–64.

Usually, the *Partisan Review* has simply ignored Burke, but the two reviews (that I know of) which it has permitted have both been vituperative blasts. Like Mr. Chase's, Mr. Hook's attempt is at demolition; and like Mr. Black's, it is the work of a systematic philosopher. Just why Burke should so enrage the systematic philosophers is not really clear to me.

Hubler, Edward, "The Sunken Aesthete," *English Institute Essays, 1950*, edited by Alan Downer, New York: Columbia University Press, 1951, 32–56.

Only a small portion of this essay is about Burke, but it consists of a first-hand report on Burke in action and contains an excellent example of Burke's tendency — and, Mr. Hubler argues, the tendency of modern criticism in general — to blast off from an aesthetic object and never return to it. Mr. Bewley and Mr. Ford also make this same point.

Hyman, Stanley Edgar, "Kenneth Burke and the Criticism of Symbolic Action," *The Armed Vision: A Study in the Methods of Modern Literary Criticism*, New York: Alfred A. Knopf, 1948, 347–394.

The most extensive attempt at placing and evaluating Burke which has yet been undertaken. Actually, there is a little bit of everything in this long and enthusiastic essay: two sections are devoted to synopsis, exposition, and development; one section is devoted to sources, influences on Burke, and the influence of Burke on others; and a final section is devoted to an evaluation in which Burke is set up as the ideal (because he is the most inclusive) critic.

Jarrell, Randall, "Changes of Attitude and Rhetoric in Auden's Poetry," *Southern Review*, VII (1941), 326–349.

The application, as Jarrell points out, of certain ideas and methods from *Attitudes toward History*, in the analysis of Auden's poetry. This essay is a good example of how Burke's influence has worked: a great many individual critics have taken particular ideas or methods from Burke and used them in their own way.

Kaplan, Abraham, *Journal of Aesthetics and Art Criticism*, V (1947), 233–234.

Though only a review and very brief, this is one of the best things ever written on Burke. Mr. Kaplan goes directly to the central problem of *A Grammar of Motives*, which is that "Burke explicitly declares his concern to be with the analysis of language, not 'reality.' But it remains doubtful whether he has in fact clearly distinguished the two and successfully limited himself to the linguistic level." The central point of Mr. Kaplan's review is that Burke has mistaken language for reality, with disastrous results.

Knickerbocker, William, "Wam for Maw, Dogma versus Discursiveness in Criticism," *Sewanee Review*, XLIX (1941), 520–536.

Again, though only a review, this is probably one of the best pieces ever written on what Burke is attempting to do in his literary criticism. Mr. Knickerbocker did what almost no one else has ever done: he turned Burke on Burke, using the theory of symbolic action as his own instrument to find out what Burke was really about. After joycing Kenneth to mean "know what lies under," and Burke to "burg," Mr. Knickerbocker says that the "meaning of

Bibliography

Kenneth Burke's critical effort is the reconstruction of the burg (or present society) by resorting to grubbing, or delving for roots, motivated by the desire for physical food ('grub') and, at times, he transcends this by his sense of grub as larva with the hope of biological metamorphosis of larva into winged, aërial creatures."

Knox, George, *Critical Moments: Kenneth Burke's Categories and Critiques*, Seattle: University of Washington Press, 1957. Representative reviews: Bernard Duffey, *American Literature*, XXI (1959), 93–95; William H. Rueckert, *Journal of English and Germanic Philology*, LVII (1958), 849–852; Richard Williams, *Criticism*, I (1959), 80–82; Margarita Worth, *Prairie Schooner*, XXXIII (1959), 2–3.

I have already stated my opinion of Mr. Knox's book in print and see no reason to repeat it here. I would like to add, however, that in retrospect I think I was somewhat unjust in my review, for Mr. Knox does say useful things about the problem of the "intrinsic" in Burke and he does suggest some of the ways in which the central problem of *A Grammar of Motives* (the perpetual motion of dialectics) is solved in *A Rhetoric of Motives* by means of the theory of hierarchy.

Lansner, Kermit, "Burke, Burke, the Lurk," *Kenyon Review*, XIII (1951), 324–335.

Another one of the brilliant essay-reviews which combines sound evaluation with exposition and appreciation. Mr. Lansner is especially good on the place of literature in dramatism as a whole. As he correctly points out, "the order of literature sometimes seems to be taken as one among many by Burke, but fundamentally . . . he takes it as the prototype of all order and certainly the most precious of all orders of discourse — what would be called an ultimate order."

Morris, Charles, "The Strategy of Kenneth Burke," *Nation*, CLXIII (1946), 106.

An excellent brief review, which opens with the following high praise: "It is the same Burke with the same quest ["after a way of life for himself and modern man"] and the same strategy, as baffling, as inconclusive, as penetrating, as rewarding as ever, working on the largest and most important job of criticism that is being done among us."

Munson, Gorham B., "In and About the Workshop of Kenneth Burke," *Destinations, A Canvas of American Literature*, New York: J. H. Sears and Company, Inc., 1928, 136–159.

This essay is most useful as an early portrait of Burke when he was still treated as a writer of fiction and just emerging as a critic.

Nemerov, Howard, "The Agon of Will as Idea, A Note on the Terms of Kenneth Burke," *Furioso*, II (Spring, 1947), 29–42.

An obscure but very perceptive essay on Burke, especially upon language as reality and the relations between language and morality.

Parkes, Henry Bamford, "Kenneth Burke," *The Pragmatic Test, Essays on the History of Ideas*, San Francisco: The Colt Press, 1941, 202–220.

An excellent general essay on Burke's work of the thirties and, from a later vantage point, a valuable contribution to our understanding of Burke's steady movement toward a permanent set of values. Mr. Parkes also points out correctly that Burke was a Marxist but never a communist. The influence of Marx — or perhaps "theoretical communism"— on Burke has been profound, and Mr. Parkes is one of the few critics of Burke who has ever even attempted to show how, as has always been the case, Burke took only such ideas from Marx as suited his needs and absorbed them into his own system. Burke is not a Marxist (or a Freudian, for that matter), though he has used — and continues to use — some of Marx's ideas. The emphasis upon the reality of economic motivation that first appeared in Burke's work during the thirties has stayed with him right up to the present.

Ransom, John Crowe, "Mr. Burke's Dialectic," *New Republic*, CXIV (1946), 257–258.

Mr. Ransom makes many good points in this short review, among them that Burke is a modern humanist, that *A Grammar of Motives* is "like an end-work which assimilates to a new perspective the fragments of one's earlier writings," that Burke always assumes the "rational or purposive agent," and that "Hegel's logic, more than drama, is the classical locus" for Burke's dialectic.

Rosenfeld, Isaac, "Dry Watershed," *Kenyon Review*, VIII (1946), 310–317.

The central point of Mr. Rosenfeld's blast is suggested by the title of his essay-review. Like almost all of the attacks after *A Grammar of Motives*, this one centers on Burke's theory of language, which, Mr. Rosenfeld says, is a kind of "linguistic solipsism," a vast oversimplification of reality for which Burke makes fantastic claims, and finally little more than the "dry watershed" of the title.

Rueckert, William H., "Burke's Verbal Drama," *Nation*, CXCIV (1962), 150.

A review of *The Rhetoric of Religion* (which, shockingly and inexplicably, was hardly reviewed at all) in which the central tenets of dramatism are summarized in a highly condensed way.

Stauffer, Donald, "Salvation Through Semantics," *Virginia Quarterly Review*, XXII (1946), 454–460.

———, "The Key Is 'Substance,'" *New York Times Book Review*, June 11, 1950, 30.

Both of Mr. Stauffer's reviews are generally sound in their criticism of Burke, as well as clear and concise in their exposition of what Burke is saying and trying to do. Three of his remarks are good enough to quote: he speaks of Burke's "quixotic attempt to encompass the world," of Burke as a "Thomas Wolfe in criticism," and says that *A Grammar of Motives* is "useful for anyone with a strenuous brain who wishes to go pioneering."

Warren, Austin, "Kenneth Burke: His Mind and Art," *Sewanee Review*, XLI (1933), 225–236, 344–364.

———, "Sceptic's Progress," *American Review*, VI (1936–1937), 193–213.

The first of Mr. Warren's two excellent essays on Burke is one of the real pioneering works and one of the few essays which deals seriously and at length with Burke's fiction. The second, an essay-review of *Permanence and Change*, ranks with the very best that has been written about Burke. Mr. Warren's title very aptly describes Burke's development through the thirties and early forties.

Bibliography

III. Related Material

Abrams, M. H., *The Mirror and the Lamp: Romantic Theory and the Critical Tradition*, New York: W. W. Norton & Company, Inc., 1958.

Alain, *Système des beaux arts*, 5éd., Paris: Gallimard, 1926.

Aristotle, selected and translated by Philip Wheelwright, enlarged edition, New York: Odyssey Press, 1951.

Arnold, Matthew, *The Portable Matthew Arnold*, edited by Lionel Trilling, New York: Viking Press, 1949.

Arrowsmith, William, introductions to "Cyclops," "Heracles," "Hecuba," "Orestes," and "The Bacchae," *The Complete Greek Tragedies*, edited by David Grene and Richmond Lattimore, Chicago: University of Chicago Press, 1959, III, 224–230, 266–281, 488–493; IV, 186–191, 530–541.

Auerbach, Erich, *Mimesis*, Anchor edition, Garden City, New York: Doubleday & Company, Inc., 1957.

Bachelard, Gaston, *La Psychoanalyse de feu*, Paris: Gallimard, 1949.

Bezzola, Reto, *Le Sens de l'aventure et de l'amour (Chrétien de Troyes)*, Paris: La Jeune Parque, 1947.

Bodkin, Maud, *Archetypal Patterns in Poetry*, New York: Vintage Books, 1958.

Brooks, Cleanth, *Modern Poetry and the Tradition*, Chapel Hill: University of North Carolina Press, 1939.

———, *The Well-Wrought Urn*, Harvest edition, New York: Harcourt, Brace and Company, n.d.

Brown, Norman O., *Life against Death: The Psychoanalytical Meaning of History*, Modern Library paperback edition, New York: Random House, Inc., 1959.

Campbell, Joseph, *The Hero with a Thousand Faces*, New York: Meridian Books, 1956.

Coleridge, S. T., *Selected Poetry and Prose of Coleridge*, edited by Donald Stauffer, Modern Library edition, New York: Random House, Inc., 1951.

Crane, R. S., *The Languages of Criticism and the Structure of Poetry*, Toronto: University of Toronto Press, 1953.

Criticism, The Foundations of Modern Literary Judgment, edited by Mark Schorer, *et al.*, New York: Harcourt, Brace and Company, 1948.

Critics and Criticism, Ancient and Modern, edited by R. S. Crane, Chicago: University of Chicago Press, 1952.

Critiques and Essays in Criticism, 1920–1948, selected by Robert Wooster Stallman, New York: The Ronald Press, 1949.

Eliot, T. S., *Selected Essays*, new edition, New York: Harcourt, Brace and Company, 1950.

Empson, William, *Some Versions of Pastoral*, London: Chatto & Windus, 1935.

———, *Seven Types of Ambiguity*, New York: Meridian Books, 1955.

Fergusson, Francis, *The Idea of a Theater*, Anchor edition, Garden City, New York: Doubleday & Company, Inc., 1953.

———, *Dante's Drama of the Mind: A Modern Reading of the "Purgatorio,"* Princeton: Princeton University Press, 1953.

Freud, Sigmund, *A General Introduction to Psycho-analysis*, Permabook edition, Garden City, New York: Doubleday & Company, Inc., 1953.

———, *Civilization and Its Discontents*, Anchor edition, Garden City, New York: Doubleday & Company, Inc., 1958.

Fromm, Erich, *The Art of Loving*, New York: Harper and Brothers, 1956.

Burke and the Drama of Human Relations

Frye, Northrop, *Anatomy of Criticism*, Princeton: Princeton University Press, 1957.

Grene, David, "Introduction to 'Prometheus Bound,'" *The Complete Greek Tragedies*, edited by David Grene and Richmond Lattimore, Chicago: University of Chicago Press, 1959, I, 304–308.

Heller, Erich, *The Disinherited Mind*, New York: Meridian Books, 1959.

James, William, *The Varieties of Religious Experience*, Modern Library edition, New York: Random House, n.d.

Jarrell, Randall, *Poetry and the Age*, New York: Alfred A. Knopf, 1953.

Jung, C. G., *Psychology and Religion*, New Haven: Yale University Press, 1938.

———, *The Integration of the Personality*, New York: Farrar & Rinehart, Inc., 1939.

———, *Psyche and Symbol*, edited by Violet S. de Laszlo, Garden City, New York: Doubleday Anchor Books, 1958.

———, *The Undiscovered Self*, Mentor edition, New York: New American Library, 1959.

Kitto, H. D. F., *Greek Tragedy*, Anchor edition, Garden City, New York: Doubleday & Company, Inc., 1955.

Knight, G. Wilson, *The Wheel of Fire*, New York: Meridian Books, 1957.

La Drière, Craig, "Structure, Sound, and Meaning," *Sound and Poetry*, edited by Northrop Frye, New York: Columbia University Press, 1957, 85–108.

Langbaum, Robert, *The Poetry of Experience: The Dramatic Monologue in Modern Literary Tradition*, New York: Random House, 1957.

Langer, Susanne K., *Feeling and Form*, New York: Charles Scribner's Sons, 1953.

Lattimore, Richmond, "Introduction to the 'Oresteia,'" *The Complete Greek Tragedies*, edited by David Grene and Richmond Lattimore, Chicago: University of Chicago Press, 1959, I, 1–31.

Lawrence, D. H., *Studies in Classic American Literature*, Anchor edition, Garden City, New York: Doubleday & Company, Inc., 1953.

Lewis, R. W. B., *The American Adam*, Phoenix edition, Chicago: University of Chicago Press, 1959.

———, *The Picaresque Saint*, New York: J. B. Lippincott Co., 1959.

Maritain, Jacques, *Creative Intuition in Art and Poetry*, New York: Meridian Books, 1955.

Nelson, Norman E., "Science and the Irresponsible Imagination," *Yale Review*, XLIII (1953), 71–88.

O'Connor, William Van, *Sense and Sensibility in Modern Poetry*, Chicago: University of Chicago Press, 1948.

Ortega y Gasset, José, *The Dehumanization of Art and Other Writings on Art and Culture*, Anchor edition, Garden City, New York: Doubleday & Company, Inc., 1956.

———, *On Love: Aspects of a Single Theme*, New York: Meridian Books, 1960.

Paul, Sherman, *The Shores of America: Thoreau's Inward Exploration*, Urbana: University of Illinois Press, 1958.

Ransom, John Crowe, *The World's Body*, New York: Charles Scribner's Sons, 1938.

Richards, I. A., *Principles of Literary Criticism*, New York: Harcourt, Brace and Company, 1949.

Bibliography

Riesman, David, *et al.*, *The Lonely Crowd*, abridged Anchor edition, Garden City, New York: Doubleday & Company, Inc., 1953.

Shapiro, Karl, *Beyond Criticism*, Lincoln: University of Nebraska Press, 1953.

Spurgeon, Caroline, *Shakespeare's Imagery and What It Tells Us*, London: Cambridge University Press, 1935.

Trilling, Lionel, *Matthew Arnold*, New York: Meridian Books, 1955.

——, *The Liberal Imagination*, Anchor edition, Garden City, New York: Doubleday & Company, Inc., 1953.

——, *Freud and the Crisis of Our Culture*, Boston: Beacon Press, 1955.

——, *The Opposing Self*, Compass edition, New York: Viking Press, 1959.

Underhill, Evelyn, *Mysticism*, New York: Meridian Books, 1955.

Wasserman, Earl R., *The Finer Tone, Keats' Major Poems*, Baltimore: The Johns Hopkins Press, 1953.

Wellek, René, and Austin Warren, *Theory of Literature*, New York: Harcourt, Brace and Company, 1949.

Wheelwright, Philip, *The Burning Fountain, A Study in the Language of Symbolism*, Bloomington: Indiana University Press, 1954.

Whyte, William H., Jr., *The Organization Man*, New York: Simon and Schuster, 1956.

Wilson, Edmund, *Axel's Castle*, New York: Charles Scribner's Sons, 1950.

Wimsatt, William K., Jr., *The Verbal Icon: Studies in the Meaning of Poetry*, New York: Noonday Press, 1958.

——, and Cleanth Brooks, *Literary Criticism: A Short History*, New York: Alfred A. Knopf, 1957.

INDEX

Abrams, M. H.: *The Mirror and the Lamp*, 4
Abstraction: as verbal resource, 133, 135–145 *passim*; effect on man, 135–145 *passim*; in poetic imitation, 166, 167–178 *passim*
Aeschylus: *Oresteia*, 97, 163, 169, 209, 220
Agon: analysis of in poetry, 86–90, 126–127
Alain-Fournier, Henri: *Le Grand Meaulnes*, mentioned, 20, 107, 197
Alienation in modern society, 36
Anderson, Maxwell: *Winterset*, mentioned, 26
Archetypes: analysis of in poetry, 90–111 *passim*; of the self, 96; of the rhetoric of rebirth, 96–111 *passim*. *See also* Order-cluster; Socioanagogic criticism; Substance-clusters
Aristotle, 130, 140, 167, 196, 239
Arnold, Matthew: *Sohrab and Rustum* as symbolic action, 99–102; mentioned, 151, 163, 177
Auden, W. H.: mentioned, 30, 81
Austen, Jane: mentioned, 17, 107

Bodkin, Maud, 15
Browning, Robert: mentioned, 17
Burke, Kenneth: as music critic, 3; in relation to times, 3, 7, 8, 34–36, 160–

162, 224–226; as poet, 3, 8, 9, 10, 28, 34; as reviewer, 3, 34; influence of, 3, 237, 238, 239, 240; reputation of, 3, 237–242; life of, 4; critics of, 4–5, 6, 237–242; influences on, 4, 34, 237–242; style of, 5; development of, 5, 8–9, 10–11, 33, 34–35, 41–42, 51, 56, 61, 128–130, 139–141, 153, 157–158, 161, 208–210, 224–226, 237–242; qualities of his mind, 6; use of religious terms, 31–32, 46–48, 103–104, 126–127, 133–134, 145, 209, 224–226; as a romantic, 50–51; as cryptologist, 71–72, 92–93; nature of his achievement, 160–162, 224–226; comic center of, 224–226; personal function of dramatism for, 224–226
Byron, Lord: *Childe Harold's Pilgrimage*, 16, 17; *Manfred*, 17, 106–107, 194, 212; *Don Juan*, 22, 106–107

Castiglioni, Baldassare: *The Courtier*, 144
Catharsis: as rhetorical function of poetry, 25–28; as grace, 32; as central term in poetic realism, 46–49; as central term in theory of symbolic action, 56–63, 66–68; in all verbal action, 76; as central term in dramatism, 131–134 *passim*; poetry as vehicle for, 166–167; as central term in

Index

poetic theory, 169; in the lyric, 196; and poetry, 208–224 *passim*; in tragedy, 208–224 *passim*; paradigm of, 209. *See also* Mortification; Redemption; Rhetoric of rebirth; Victimage

Cervantes, Miguel de: *Don Quixote*, 16, 17, 20

Chrétien de Troyes: *Percival*, 170–171; *Yvain*, mentioned, 170–171; mentioned, 20, 108

Clusters: nature of, 84–86; analysis of, 84–90 *passim*, 126–127; dramatistic theory of, 173–191 *passim*; as poetic resources, 176–178

Coleridge, S. T.: 82, 193, 194, 216; symbolic action in the poetry of, 111–125

Comedy: uses of in poetic realism, 55–56

Conrad, Joseph: *Heart of Darkness*, mentioned, 20

Counter-statements to scientism: in poetic realism, 38–42, 49–56; in magical orientation, 47–48; in religious orientation, 47–48; in dramatism, 160–162

Crane, Hart: poetry of as rhetoric of rebirth, 28–29; mentioned, 22, 30

Creative process: differentiated from dreaming, 15–16, 69–70; in *Counter-Statement*, 15–24 *passim*; in theory of symbolic action, 68–71; in dramatism, 168–178

Croce, Benedetto, 196

Cummings, E. E.: clusters in the poetry of, 84–85; mentioned, 80

Dante Alighieri: *Divine Comedy*, purgative structure of, 97, 110, 209; *Divine Comedy* and Burke's psychological equivalents of Hell, Purgatory, and Heaven, 103–104; *Divine Comedy* and Burke's comedy of language, 138–140; mentioned, 20, 25

Demonic Trinity: nature of, 93–96; as source of pollution archetypes, 102–107 *passim*, 127; and guilt, 149; and mortification, 149; and the negative, 149; in tragedy, 222–224

Depression, the: effect on Burke, 34–36

Dial, The: Burke's associations with, 34

Dialectics: as verbal resource, 137–140; as purgatorial, 139; in relation to hierarchy, 139–140

Donne, John: *The Ecstasy*, 109; mentioned, 93

Dostoevsky, Feodor: purification in *Crime and Punishment*, 105–107

Dramatism: as secular variant of Christianity, 133–134; as counter-statement to scientism, 160–162; main goals of, 160–162; and the analysis of poetry, 203–208; as a rhetoric of rebirth for Burke, 224–226

Dream of the Rood, 109

Dryden, John: mentioned, 20

Elegy: uses of in poetic realism, 54–55

Eliot, T. S.: *The Waste Land*, 74; *The Love Song of J. Alfred Prufrock*, 94; mentioned, 22, 30, 84, 163

Eloquence: in poetry, 18–25 *passim*

Empson, William: *Seven Types of Ambiguity*, 90–91; and Burke, 237

Epic: uses of in poetic realism, 52–53

Euripides: *The Cyclops*, 225

Exaltation: in poetry, 18–25 *passim*

Faulkner, William: *Absalom, Absalom!*, 19; mentioned, 20, 30

Fergusson, Francis: *The Idea of a Theatre*, 108

Fitzgerald, F. Scott: mentioned, 143

Flaubert, Gustave: on pure art, 9, 10; *Madame Bovary*, 16–17, 17–18, 20, 88, 93

Form: as norm, 12–13, 21; as essence, 13; as logical formula, 13; as structure, 13; progressive, 13, 21–22, 83–84, 96–97; as structure and formula, 13, 31, 33; as basic material of poetry, 14; repetitive, 22–23; minor or incidental, 23; conventional, 23, 78–81; as purgative journey, 25–27, 62, 96–111 *passim*; 208–224 *passim*; hierarchic, 132; in creative process, 169–173; dramatistic theory of, 173–191 *passim*; as persecutional in tragedy, 220–224. *See also* Mystic Way; Rhetoric of rebirth; Structure; Upward Way

Forster, E. M.: dialectical structure of

A Passage to India, 110–111; cluster analysis of *Howards End,* 179–190; mentioned, 30

Frank, Waldo: *The Death and Birth of David Markand,* 197–198

Freud, Sigmund: and Burke, 31, 95, 143, 204, 239, 242

Genesis: Burke's treatment of the creation and fall, 46, 133–134, 156–157, 225–226

Gide, André: as counter-agent, 29–30

Goethe, Wolfgang: *Faust,* Part I, 93, 167, 174, 177; *Faust,* Part I, as hierarchic allegory, 202, 206–207; mentioned, 20, 163, 212

Grace: as poet's moral contribution, 31–32

Guilt: as norm denied by scientism, 40–41; as norm in poetic realism, 46–48; as major motive in poetry, 66–68; as central problem for self, 97–98; as key term in dramatism, 131–134 *passim*; main causes of, 131–134 *passim*; role of in dramatism, 134–153 *passim*; in the analysis of poetry, 203–208; in tragedy, 208–224 *passim. See also* Rhetoric of rebirth

Hawthorne, Nathaniel: *Ethan Brand,* 102–103, 163, 218

Hegel, Friedrich: and Burke, 242

Herbert, George: *The Collar,* mentioned, 195

Hermes: as Burke's figure for himself, 139–140

Hierarchy: and guilt, 131–133; as key term in dramatism, 131–134 *passim*; progressive form of, 132; idea and principle of in dramatism, 139–145; in literary analysis, 141, 202–208; in creative process, 168–178 *passim*; in poetic form, 169–170; as poetic resource, 177–178, 190–191; and literary symbolism, 203–208; in tragedy, 208–224 *passim*

hierarchic motives, 132, 142; hierarchic modes of thought and action, 135–145 *passim*; hierarchic psychosis, 131–134 *passim*; hierarchic structure in tragedy, 220–224

History: idea of in Burke, 37–38

Hitler, Adolf: *Mein Kampf,* 151

Homer: *The Odyssey,* mentioned, 20, 25

Hopkins, G. M.: lyric imitation in *God's Grandeur,* 194–196; mentioned, 81, 163

Huxley, Aldous: mentioned, 30

Ibsen, Henrik: *Ghosts,* 19–20, 21

Identification: process of in orientations, 39; rational vs. emotional in scientism, 39–41; process of in relation to the self, 43–46; in victimage, 151–152; in creative process, 173–191 *passim*

Identity: as central problem for the self, 97–98. *See also* Self

Imagery: dramatistic theory of, 171–178. *See also* Clusters

Imitation: in the lyric, 192–196; in the lyric novel, 197–200; multiple uses of poetic imitations in dramatism, 200–208; in tragedy, 210–224 *passim*

James, Henry: mentioned, 20, 163, 212

Joyce, James: *Finnegans Wake,* 81; *A Portrait of the Artist as a Young Man,* 108, 163, 169; *The Dead,* mentioned, 163; imitation in *A Portrait,* 171–172; *A Portrait* as lyric novel, 197–200.

Joycing: as variant of pun analysis, 90, 93–96, 126–127

Jung, C. G.: mentioned, 95, 99

Kafka, Franz: *The Castle* as hierarchic allegory, 144, 163, 202, 204

Kant, Immanuel: cited by Burke, 11

Keats, John: *Ode to a Nightingale,* 22, 109, 193; *Ode on a Grecian Urn,* 94; puns in *Ode on a Grecian Urn,* 169

Knickerbocker, William: on Burke, 10

Lawrence, D. H.: *Lady Chatterley's Lover,* 171; mentioned, 30, 136

Lyric, the: defined and discussed, 191–196

Lyric novel, the: defined and discussed, 197–200

Index

Malory, Thomas: *Quest of the Holy Grail,* mentioned, 20

Mann, Thomas: as counter-agent, 29–30

Marlowe, Christopher: *The Jew of Malta,* mentioned, 212

Marvell, Andrew: *The Garden,* mentioned, 109

Marx, Karl: and Burke, 242; mentioned, 95, 99

Melville, Herman: *Moby Dick,* 102–103

Meredith, George: *Modern Love,* 80; clusters and agon in *The Ordeal of Richard Feverel,* 88–89, 92; puns in *The Ordeal of Richard Feverel,* 107

Miller, Arthur: *The Crucible,* 19–20, 26; *Death of a Salesman,* 26

Milton, John: symbolic action in *Lycidas,* 77–78; mentioned, 80, 163

Monroe, Harriet: mentioned, 28

Moore, Merrill: mentioned, 80

Mortification: as key term in dramatism, 131–134 *passim;* as mode of purification, 146–153 *passim;* distinguished from victimage, 146–153; in the analysis of poetry, 203–208; in tragedy, 208–224 *passim*

Mystic Way: dialectic of, 96; dialectic of as purgative structure, 96, 107, 109, 110, 111

Nation, The: Burke's associations with, 34

Negative, the: as essence of language, 130–134 *passim;* Burke's theory of, 130–153 *passim;* and guilt, 131–133; as key term in dramatism, 131–134 *passim;* and moral action, 145–153 *passim;* in mortification, 146–153 *passim;* in victimage, 146–153 *passim;* in the analysis of poetry, 203–208; in tragedy, 208–224 *passim*

Nemerov, Howard: *The Scales of the Eyes,* mentioned, 163

New Republic, The: Burke's associations with, 34

Norms: of psycho-physical experience, 11–14; as forms, 13; as basic materials of art, 14–33 *passim;* denied by scientism, 34–35; loss of in historical process, 37–38; in poetic realism, 41–43; poetry as embodiment of, 48–50; in dramatism, 153–162 *passim;* in poetic imitation, 168–169, 200

O'Connor, Frank: mentioned, 81

Odets, Clifford: *Golden Boy,* mentioned, 26

Order-cluster: as central to dramatism, 131–134 *passim;* as substance-cluster, 156–157, 159–160; as substance of human drama, 160; in the analysis of poetry, 202–208; in tragedy, 208–224 *passim*

Orientation: concept of, 35–42 *passim;* national-social, 36–38; magical, 37; religious, 37; scientific, 37; in relation to norms, 37–38; religious as counter-balance to scientism, 41, 47–48; magical as counter-balance to scientism, 41, 47–48. *See also* Poetic realism

Orwell, George: *1984,* mentioned, 202, 212

Partridge, Eric: *Shakespeare's Bawdy,* mentioned, 90

Pearl, The: mentioned, 109

Pentad and ratios: in literary analysis, 73–83; defined and discussed, 73–83, 134–135, 152; scene-act ratio, 74–75; agent-act ratio, 75; agency-act ratio, 75–76; act-purpose ratio, 76–78; act-act ratio, 78–81; paradigmatic ratio in Burke, 79; as logo-logic, 153–156

Perseus: as Burke's figure of the poet, 62–63

Plato: cited by Burke, 11, 214; *Phaedrus,* 76, 97, 110, 137; *Symposium,* 144

Poet, the: nature of, 14–15, 49–50, 62–63, 68–71; as Perseus, 62–63

Poetic language: dramatistic theory of, 173–191 *passim*

Poetic realism: 34–63 *passim;* as development from *Counter-Statement,* 34; as counter-statement to scientism, 38–42, 49–56 *passim,* 63; main co-ordinates of, 46–56; as a philosophy of living, 50–56 *passim*; culmination in theory of symbolic action, 56–63; developed into dramatism, 128–130

Poetry: as revelation (in *Counter-Statement*), 10, 15–18, 27–32; as rhetoric of catharsis (in *Counter-Statement*), 10, 25–27; as ritual (in *Counter-Statement*), 15, 18–25; as distinguished from life, 24–25; as rhetoric of statement (in *Counter-Statement*), 27–32; as counter-statement, 31; social function of, 31; as grace, 32; as symbolic autobiography (self-portraiture), 32, 68–69, 126, 177, 190–191, 200–201, 207–208; as counterforce to scientism, 37; as paradigm of human drama, 48–56; role of in poetic realism, 48–56; nature of, 49–50, 60–63, 165–167; and the self, 50, 61–62, 68–70, 75; uses of in poetic realism, 51–56; approaches to, 64–68, 71, 81–83, 126–127, 163–165, 199–208; as rhetoric of rebirth, 97–107 *passim*; as the essence of verbal action, 128–129; distinguished from other verbal acts, 158–159, 164–167, 180, 201–202; place of in dramatism, 164–165, 207; as knowledge, 199–208 *passim*; as purgative-redemptive, 200–201, 207–208; as social portraiture, 201–208; as hierarchic allegory, 202–208; and the drama of human relations, 208; and tragedy, 208–210

Pope, Alexander: mentioned, 20

Porter, Katherine Anne: *He*, 27; mentioned, 7

Puns: analysis of, 90–96, 126–127, 176–177; in tragedy, 222–224. *See also* Demonic Trinity

Quest: as norm, 20. *See also* Self

Ransom, John: in relation to Burke, 10, 238

Redemption: as key term in dramatism, 131–134 *passim*; by means of language, 137–153 *passim*; in the analysis of poetry, 203–208; in tragedy, 208–224 *passim*

Religious terms: use of in Burke, 31–32, 46–48, 103–104, 126–127, 133–134, 145, 209, 224–226

Rhetoric of rebirth: in Hart Crane's poetry, 28–29; poetry as, 32, 96–117 *passim*; symbolic action as, 46–47; as central idea in poetic realism, 49; archetypes of, 96–107, 126–127; archetypal structure of, 96–97, 98–99, 107–111, 126–127; as central idea in theory of symbolic action, 97; in Matthew Arnold's poetry, 99–102; pollution as archetype of, 102–104, 133; psychological vs. metaphysical reality of, 103–104; purification as archetype of, 104–106; in Dostoevsky's *Crime and Punishment*, 105–106; redemption as archetype of, 106–107; in S. T. Coleridge's poetry, 111–125; in relation to Christianity, 127, 134; Burke's obsession with, 133; dramatism as Burke's own, 224–226

Richards, I. A.: in relation to Burke, 237, 238

Roethke, Theodore: mentioned, 30, 81, 163

Saint Augustine: puns in *Confessions*, 177

Salinger, J. D.: *The Catcher in the Rye*, mentioned, 197

Satire: uses of in poetic realism, 54

Scientism: as dominant modern orientation, 35–42 *passim*; inadequacies of, 35–42, 47–48

Self, the: poet's knowledge of, 15; nature of, 43; Burke's idea of, 44–46; in poetry, 61–62, 68, 71; in lyric poetry, 87, 193; poetry as a drama of, 90; archetypes of, 96–99; in relation to hierarchy, 132–133; as a source of poetic unity, 178, 190–191; in lyric novel, 198; as basis of poetic symbolism, 203

    search for: as norm, 20, 43–46; as moral drama, 44–45; in relation to symbolic action, 45–46, 61–62; in relation to poetry, 48–49; as purgative journey, 108–109, 111; as progressive form, 170–171; in creative proc-

Index

ess, 170–171. *See also* Poetic realism; Rhetoric of rebirth; Symbolic action
Shakespeare, William: *Othello*, 19, 89, 97, 107, 108, 146, 154, 163, 167, 169, 202, 222; *Venus and Adonis*, 20; *Hamlet*, 22, 146, 220, 222; *King Lear*, 25, 97, 107, 146, 220; clusters and agon in *Othello*, 87–89; puns in *Othello*, 93; *Rape of Lucrece*, mentioned, 107; hierarchic allegory in *Venus and Adonis*, 202, 204–205, 206; tragic imitation in *Othello*, 212–219; *Macbeth*, 212, 220
Shaw, G. B.: *Mrs. Warren's Profession*, 19–20
Shelley, P. B.: mentioned, 17
Shuttle terms: nature of in Burke, 33, 96
Socioanagogic criticism: defined and discussed, 141–145, 202–208
Sonnet, the: as a symbolic form, 80–81
Sophocles: *Oedipus Rex*, 21, 123, 146, 169, 220, 222; *Oedipus Rex*, mentioned, 20, 25; *Oedipus at Colonus*, 97, 220; *Antigone*, 146, 212
Spenser, Edmund: *The Faerie Queene*, mentioned, 20, 108; mentioned, 80
Structure: analysis of, 83–90, 126–127; as purgative journey, 107–111; analysis of in *The Rime of the Ancient Mariner*, 111–116; in creative process, 169–175; analysis of in tragedy, 211–215; hierarchic or allusive in tragedy, 220–224. *See also* Form
Substance: Burke's theory of, 153–157
Substance-clusters: nature of, 154–160; and poetic imitation, 167–178 *passim*
Swift, Jonathan: mentioned, 17, 20
Symbolic action, theory of: as core of poetic realism, 56; in relation to dramatism, 56; defined and discussed, 56–63; application of to study of poetry, 64–68; basic assumptions of, 64–71; central tenet of, 67, 97–98
Symbolic autobiography: poetry as, 32, 59–60, 99–100, 121–125

Symbolism: dramatistic analysis of in *Howards End*, 180–191; techniques of, 190–191; socioanagogic theory of, 205–208
Symbols: nature of, 16–17; use in poetry, 16–21; as Janus devices, 19, 33; of authority, 36; theory of, 70–71, 173–179; man as symbol-using animal, 130–153 *passim*

Technological psychosis: as characteristic of scientism, 35, 63
Tennyson, Alfred Lord: *In Memoriam*, mentioned, 74
Tolstoy, Leo: *War and Peace*, mentioned, 25
Tragedy: uses of in poetic realism, 53–54; defined and discussed, 208–224
Tragic rhythm, 21, 108–109, 111, 169, 170, 210–224 *passim*
Twain, Mark: mentioned, 20

Unity: kinds of in poetry, 174–178
Universals. *See* Norms
Upward Way, dialectic of: 96, 126–127; as purgative structure, 107, 110–111; in *A Passage to India*, 110–111; as verbal resource, 138–139; in poetic imitation, 168–173

Victimage: as key term in dramatism, 131–134 *passim*; as mode of purification, 146–153 *passim*; distinguished from mortification, 146–153; in symbolic action, 152; in poetry, 152, 203–208; in tragedy, 208–224 *passim*
Virgil: mentioned, 20

Warren, Austin: on Burke, 140
Warren, R. P.: *All the King's Men*, mentioned, 212
Wescott, Glenway: *The Grandmothers*, 197–198
White, E. B.: mentioned, 30; *The Door*, 138

Whitman, Walt: mentioned, 81; *Democratic Vistas*, 163; *Leaves of Grass*, 163, 176

Wilder, Thornton: *Our Town*, mentioned, 81; *The Skin of Our Teeth*, mentioned, 81

Wordsworth, William: idea of the poet as similar to Burke's, 68; *Tintern Abbey*, clusters and agon in, 85–87

Yeats, W. B.: 69, 163; *A Dialogue of Self and Soul*, 194; "Crazy Jane" poems, 194; *Sailing to Byzantium*, 194

Zola, Émile: mentioned, 167